The
Design
of
Discord

Studies of Anomie

Second Edition

ELWIN H. POWELL

THE DESIGN OF DISCORD

THE DESIGN OF DISCORD

Studies of Anomie

ELWIN H. POWELL

Transaction Books
New Brunswick (U.S.A.) and Oxford (U.K.)

AAW5967

Library of Congress Catalog Number: 87-10751
ISBN 0-88738-704-7
Printed in the United States of America

Library of Congress Cataloging-in-Publication Data

Powell, Elwin H. (Elwin Humphreys), 1925–
    The design of discord.

    Bibliography: p.
    Includes index.
    1. Anomy. I. Title.
HM291.P68 1987   302.5   87-10751
ISBN 0-88738-704-7

"This discord in the pact of things,
Eternal war twixt truth and truth"

BOETHIUS, *Consolations of Philosophy*

For Nita

Preface to the Transaction Edition: notes for a narrative sociology

> Process is abstract narration, just as narration is concrete process. A narrative is about a particular person and happens once; a process is about a class of persons and recurs.
>
> LEO ROCKAS, *Modes of Rhetoric* (1964, p. 113)

A book once printed cannot be unprinted; it's now too late to correct the inherent flaws of *Design of Discord: Studies of Anomie* (1970). But perhaps this preface can provide a new context for reading the old text.

Design of Discord is more a meditation than a treatise on anomie. N.C.A. Parry called it

> a stimulating book, full of unusual and striking factual information and dedicated to nothing less than a general sociological explanation of suicide, crime and war. . . . It is unique in the American sociological literature (Review in *Urban Studies*, July 1972).

But James Conlin found the book frustrating, contradictory:

> Suicide is viewed as caused by anomie; anomie is manifested by suicide. Which comes first, the chicken or the egg? Indeed there is a constant confusion of the dependent and independent variables . . . and a balloon concept of anomie, which is what you make it. . . . The book needs an editing if not a rewriting. . . . Too much is attempted, too little accomplished (Review in *Best Sellers*, March 1, 1971).

Readers who can play with paradox may go with Parry; those who want certainty will agree with Conlin. *Design of Discord* poses questions, but seldom offers answers; it should be read from the inside out, not cover-to-cover.

An empirical book, *Design of Discord* emerged by trial and error, guided by my personal need to know; the book grew out of life as I lived it; it grew out of a sloshing process (to slosh is to "flounder or splash through water, mud, or slush"—*Webster's* definition).

In fall 1956 I was a comfortable, new Ph.D. at the University of Tulsa when a graduate student brought me a body count of local suicides. As if studying rocks, we made the numbers into rates and drew charts and graphs. Then one Sunday afternoon I read a scribbled suicide note in the files of the Tulsa Police Department and inert statistics turned into suffering flesh. Entangled in the appalling mystery of suicide I scanned a thousand issues of the *Tulsa World* and *Tulsa Tribune* (1936–56), inspected ecological areas, and talked with people who knew the victims. Nothing made sociological sense; the suicides seemed so very normal. Thus I floundered.

In August 1957 I packed my index cards, went to England, and read everything on suicide in the library of the London School of Economics. After 14 months and 5,000 hours of work I had a 20-page manuscript. This manuscript, "Occupation, Status and Suicide: Toward a Redefinition of Anomie" (*American Sociological Review*, April 1958) changed my life: it dramatized for me the energizing dilemma of human existence, the problem of order-in-freedom; it taught me sociological method; and it brought me to Buffalo.

So in autumn 1958 I was sloshing through Buffalo looking for anomie. Driven indoors by the cold I started tinkering with the card file in the public library and found myself lost in the 1830s; before my very eyes I could see *Gemeinschaft* vanishing in the 19th century. Papers on anomie and urban history eventually appeared and my gracious chairman Llewellen Gross got me tenure at the University of Buffalo. Now I could splash.

Leaving the library one Saturday in 1960 I stopped to gawk at a scraggly clump of about 20 people in the parking lot. As the clump moved into the street I followed, marching behind banners calling for a ban on atmospheric nuclear testing. Never before had I been in a peace march, and I was so embarrassed by my unprofessional conduct that I joined the Committee for a Sane Nuclear Policy to restore my respectability. Later I created a course on the sociology of war, and thereafter I could demonstrate and call it research. I wrote papers on anomie and war.

In May 1965 I assembled my papers, named them *Design of Discord: Studies of Anomie*, and mailed them to my friend Irving Louis Horowitz. Back came a contract from Oxford University Press, and what should have taken five weeks required five years: in rewriting the manuscript I caught the disease I sought to diagnose. When the book was finally in the hands of the printer I never wanted to hear the word "anomie" again.

Both friends and enemies seemed to ignore the book when it started circulating in 1971. Reviews were mixed—and mixed up; I stored them in a manila folder for later scrutiny. Now I find that the critics' negation of the book has given me a new way of seeing *Design of Discord*.

From Paul Dawson I learned I used anomie as a metaphor: this he deplores and I delight in:

> *Design of Discord* does deepen and amplify the concept of anomie, but this is a mixed blessing. . . . Powell's metaphoric images may create satisfying insights . . . but they are not sufficiently clear to permit *systematic inquiry* [my italics]. Here "anomie" does not exist as a discrete variable since it is not viewed, either conceptually or operationally, as independent of the behaviors it purports to explain ("Review" in the *American Political Science Review*, May 1972).

Systematic inquiry is like dry water—possible to imagine, impossible to drink. In the social sciences "systems of inquiry" only work by leaving out life, excluding narrative. In any case, *Design of Discord* never aspired to system-hood; it is only a record of the truths I myself have witnessed. I have never been able to abstract anomie from conduct; I cannot "distinguish the dancer from the dance" (to quote Yeats). My idea of anomie is unambiguous—and it has served me well (see the Appendix, "On Durkheim, Suicide and Anomie: Correspondence Between Isabel Cary-Lundberg and Elwin H. Powell," *American Sociological Review*, April 1959).

Leon de Sousberghe called *Design of Discord* the work of an amateur and he found naive my speculation that suicide may have emerged out of war. On p. 137 I asked: "Did the institution of suicide, which seems so antithetical to the biological law of self preservation, have its origins in the institution of war?" And Sousberghe replied, "How can one speak of suicide, defined elsewhere as anomie, as an institution?"(Review in *Anthropos*, 1976).

Of course suicide itself is *not* anomie but rather a "meaningful response to meaninglessness" (*Design of Discord*, p. 21). And it *is* an institution, i.e., a culture pattern passed on over generations. Under the influence of Maurice Davie's *Evolution of War* (1929), I tried to ask if the socialization for sacrifice, necessitated by the war system, became secularized into suicide (details are given in an explanatory footnote on p. 231). Since then I have learned that the first recorded suicides in Western history (*circa* 1500 B.C.) are of warriors after defeat in battle; I have reexamined 200 years of statistics which invariably show a leap in the suicide rate after wars, and I have read the paper by Hearst et al. which states:

> Between 1974 and 1983, there were 14,145 deaths among California and Pennsylvania men whose dates of birth were in the years for which the draft lottery was held. The group of men with birthdates that made them eligible for the draft had a higher mortality rate than the group with birthdates that exempted them from the draft: suicide was increased by 13 percent . . . death by motor vehicle accidents by 8 percent. . . . A separate analysis that compared the causes of death in veterans and non-veterans yield similar estimates: veterans were 65 percent and 49 percent more likely to die from suicide and motor vehicle accidents, respectively. (Norman Hearst, Thomas B. Newman, and Stephen B. Hulley, "Delayed Effects of the Military Draft on Mortality: A Randomized Natural Experiment," *New England Journal of Medicine* 314 (1986), 620–23. The quote appears on 620.)

Between 1963 and 1983 the suicide rate for people under 25 increased by 300 percent: could this be a product of the depreciation of life which has come with the establishment of a permanent warfare state in America? That violent crime may also be a function of war-induced anomie is shown in chapter 8 of *Design of Discord*, which grapples with arrest data in Buffalo between 1830 and 1970.

In reviewing *Design of Discord*, Warren Breed found that

> Powell's biggest punch is his linkage between war and domestic dis-

turbance. Not satisfied with the well-known hypothesis that war is used to dissipate dissent at home, he asserts that during periods of internal unrest (e.g. class conflict) the military grows, unintentionally creating conditions for war. Society becomes militarized, so that the rulers more readily turn to coercion instead of peaceable exchange and negotiation. This in turn reinforces the class system, so that the need to preserve internal solidarity—via war abroad and repression at home—is exacerbated. Bismarck is quoted: "Troops are the only answer to democracy" (Review in *Southwestern Social Science Quarterly*, Spring 1972).

Is force the order which gives rise to disorder? War begins as lawful action and ends in the lawlessness of collective self-destruction. Normally we think of suicide as an individual act but organizations also engage in self-defeating conduct. In 1886 John Ruskin wrote of the Peloponnesian war as "the suicide of Greece, the greatest tragedy the world has known." The Ruskin quote is listed in the *Oxford English Dictionary* under suicide. Even though the warring city-states of Greece did not intend to kill themselves, such was the consequence of their military policy. Rome too brought about her own demise through militarization—beginning as a sanctuary for the oppressed she ended as the seat of the oppressor (see chapter 14, "Anomie and Force: The Case of Rome"). And what of the suicidalness of American war policy? In 1966 Martin Luther King said, "The bombs we drop abroad explode at home."

In 1987 the bombs are still exploding. The $300 billion a year we give to the Pentagon buys us new insecurity. The social fabric continues to unravel and with the deepening malaise the word "anomie" enters our living language. While the *Oxford English Dictionary* (1971) lists anomie as an obsolete word from 17th century theological discourse, *Webster's* (1974) says

> **an·o·mie** *or* **an·o·my** . . . *n* [F *anomie*, fr. Gk *anomia* lawlessness . . . fr. *a* + *nomos* law, fr. *nemein* to distribute—more at NIMBLE]: a state of society in which normative standards of conduct and belief are weak or lacking; *also*: a similar condition in an individual commonly characterized by *disorientation, anxiety*, and *isolation* [My italics].

But when you read the "more at NIMBLE," the cloud of anomie takes on a silver lining, for nimble means alert, agile, resourceful. The disorientation of anomie may sharpen the wits for survival. Recognition of anomie is the beginning of wisdom—confusion and consciousness are twin-born.

Can *Design of Discord* be used to negotiate the wilderness of contemporary life? I circulate the book to my students, saying to them "see if you can find in it *analogues* for writing your own autobiography; don't worry about exact definitions and independent variables—take what you can use and forget the rest." My students spend a semester creating their own narrative—*their* "book," as we call it. Excerpts from the better "books" collected over a five-year period were published in *Catalyst 16*, 1985. Let me cite a few samples of this narrative sociology: Not a bookworm but a jock ran down the literature cited in my Rome piece and wrote "The Football Player as Gladiator: My Story" (*Catalyst 16*, pp. 86–89). And a young woman from the South Bronx wrote "Growing Up Around Drugs Gave Me a Knowledge of Right and Wrong" (Ibid., pp. 95–97), saying

> it was sad to see them stoned or as we called it fucked up out of their minds . . . my friend Fabio held up a bar because he didn't have money to buy speed. He shot a man and walked away as if only stepping on a roach. . . . *Anomie is a condition of misunderstanding the rules*. Fabio misunderstood the self-fulfilling prophesy rule. . . . The role (script) is the product of a body of rules which prescribes certain action. An example in a drug addicting environment is the tough guy who has to portray the image of cool drug dealer. A friend named Jesus was the cool guy on my block . . . no one dared bother him because he had the dope to get them stoned and the weapons to protect himself and his drugs. What happened to Jesus the tough guy? Well he is in jail now playing a different role. Now he is following jail rules instead of giving rules as he did before. . . . *Anomie is the source of drugs on campus*. It seems everyone walks around lonely and not so sociable. My floormates say "Come on Evelyn, smoke some pot," but it won't work on me. . . . I hate to see them stoned because I know what too much drugs can do. . . . My engineer friend thinks being bored with his studies is natural but I think life itself should be a good time . . . should be lived as art and as play.

Another young woman "My Attempted Suicide: A Function of Anomie?" (Ibid., p. 107):

> Taken from my hospital room and wheeled to a psychiatrist chair the first words I can recall were "deviant behavior". . . . Everything around me was falling apart. . . . I was existing in a space I had created for myself, and I did not feel alive at all. I remember the warm feeling of peace and comfort I got from just curling up in a ball and staring into utter darkness. I could not see a thing or think a thing. I was content inside a body feeling nothing. It came to the point where I did not want to exist . . . in essence my social life just wasn't . . . I was not participating in society. I would go to school, mind my own business and go home. All there was was me. . . . I felt no love and friendship and the pursuit of an unattainable goal was futile. There was weariness, despair and atrophy. I attempted suicide on December 17, 1983.

Finally a young man wrote of his evolution, "From Football Hero to Supermarket Clerk: New Project, New Purpose" (Ibid., 58–59), saying

> My father considered sports as the ultimate success. . . . There were times when he would call me by my last name, or the number I was wearing at the time. . . . "Come on 34; time for dinner" and this I despised.
>
> The ultimate destruction of my predetermined social role came during my junior year in high school. [An injury forced me to give up the game for good] and my parents' dreams of football heroes would now rest with my younger brother.
>
> With football out of my life I began to get a feeling of anomie; that is I felt I no longer had any real purpose. . . . After about a year of wasting away, I began to fight back. I . . . got a job at the local supermarket. Soon my feeling of anomie disappeared as I was making friends at work and being appreciated by my peers and management. I began the job as stockboy and soon was given more responsibility . . . all the energy I once put into sports now went into work. . . . I was continually called in to work, even on my off days. I felt needed — needed not just because I could run fast or throw a football but because I was a good and conscientious worker. The

people at work also called me by my first name—something really new to me. . . . My life was exciting. There was no room for living as a robot with society holding control. My job was my new institution.

But as I write this report I also see that it was not only the job that changed my direction. It was my *looking for the job* that counted. This was a positive direction I had chosen for myself. Even before I found a job I had achieved an inner purpose—to change my life and begin to interact with people around me. I feel I can deal with my social self because I shaped it and not my parents or my peers.

George Bernard Shaw said, "normal people adapt to the world, abnormal people try to change it. Therefore all change is accomplished by abnormal people."

I want to be one of those "abnormal" people.

Thus the metaphor of anomie illuminates the inner life while simultaneously connecting the person to the larger objective world. As Miester Eckhardt said, "Our work does not make us holy; we make it holy."

Writing in the *Annals*, Daniel Robinson found *Design of Discord*

fascinating, disturbing . . . informative and perceptive. Even the routine statistical accounts move fluidly and with style . . . Powell is devoted to his topic and his enthusiasm rebounds from every sentence. Thus the book is to be recommended far more as rhetorical than as social science scholarship (Review in *Annals of the American Academy of Political and Social Science*, May 1972).

Rhetorical scholarship? An appealing idea: rhetoric is language designed to move people to act. Hopefully *Design of Discord* will draw people into the act of self-examination; I want people to use the book to locate themselves in society and in history.

Yes, the book needs a rewriting but that task I will leave to others. The intellectual life is nothing but the writing and rewriting of books. So I would say to people, plagiarize *Design of Discord*: slash it up, cut and paste, turn it in as a term paper, make it yours. As T.S. Eliot said, "Good writers borrow; great writers steal."

Buffalo, N.Y.
March 1987

Preface

Every entry in the catalogue of human aberration can be linked to anomie. Out of the soil of nihilism has grown both the personal anxiety and the public turmoil of our time. Denoting a condition of normlessness, anomie carries the connotation of alienation, isolation, and desocialization. Anomie is the discord in the rhythm of social life.

Sociology itself was born of anomie. Behind the positive philosophy of Auguste Comte was the search for a new consensus to replace the institutions eroded by the Enlightenment and finally shattered by the French Revolution. The nineteenth century witnessed the unraveling of the very fabric of daily life. Society, in Durkheim's words, became a disorganized dust of individuals. The rules which once gave form to social action lost their binding power. This phenomenon of de-regulation, Durkheim labeled anomie—lawlessness.

Durkheim first sketched the idea of anomie in his *Division of Labor*. Industrial relations in the nineteenth century deteriorated into a war of each against all. Manager and worker, no longer inhabiting the same world, were stripped of all sense of mutual obligation, with "each regarded as the permanent enemy of the other." With the growth of the division of labor, the sense of communality was undermined, the collective conscience fragmented. Here was "the differentiation which disintegrates" like a cancer where the process of cell division goes wild. Anomie is in fact the cancer of the body-social.

The present work attempts to deepen and amplify the meaning of anomie through studies of suicide, the city, and war. Part One focuses on the social psychology of self-destruction. Chapter 2 examines the statistical relationship between occupation and the suicide rate. Chapter 3 seeks to penetrate the subjective dimension of the problem using suicide notes and newspaper biographies as data. Chapter 4 deals with suicide in the black and white population.

The city has become a place of anomie, of institutional dislocation. But the roots of present urban chaos lie in the past, in the process of individuation which dissolved communal bonds and left men isolated from each other—this is the theme of Part Two. Chapter 5 sketches the relationship between social disorganization and urbanization, an idea elaborated in a series of case studies of one American city, Buffalo, New York. Chapter 6 delineates the evolution of Buffalo and the growth of anomie between 1810 and 1910. Chapter 7 analyzes reform, revolution, and repression during the crucial decade 1910-20. Chapter 8 investigates crime and police activity in Buffalo over the years 1830-1970.

Part Three explores the complex connection between anomie and war. Chapter 9 discusses the self-perpetuating and self-destructive character of the war system. Chapter 10 traces the interplay between war and revolution as background for understanding World War I as a kind of collective suicide, the theme of Chapter 11. Chapter 12 diagnoses the Nazi movement as an extension of the suicidal war cult generated by World War I. Chapter 13 generalizes on the cohesive and divisive nature of war.

Acknowledgments

This book is a labor of love, and anguish. Perhaps the two always go together. It is part of me, and I am part of all those who have touched my life.

I owe much to my teachers: to Glen Harrison, who set me on this course thirty years ago; to Stanley Taylor, who sustained me through painfully joyous years of intellectual adventure at the University of Texas.

For the dialogue opened in friendship which has resonated years after in silence, I am especially indebted to Weldon Ebeling, Julius Walker, Val Whitacre, Jim Maloney, Ken Bowden. For protracted communication on the sociological content of this work I am indebted to Martin and Carol Needleman, Mark Kennedy, Jesse Nash, Bob Reinders, Rich Salter, Sid Willhelm.

I am indebted to Bill Kolb, who nursed me through the long illness of a doctor's dissertation at Tulane; to Llewellyn Gross, my department chairman at the University of Buffalo, who kept me from perishing while I was striving to publish; to Irving Horowitz for his initial interest in this manuscript; to Sheldon Meyer for patiently ignoring five years of missed deadlines; to Edna Paine, my typist, for correcting a hundred misspelled words; to Janet Hobhouse for the hard task of copy editing.

I owe much to my family—to my father, to Jane and Harold La Font, to my two children, Jim and Steve.

The debt to my wife, to whom this book is dedicated, is beyond measure.

Buffalo, New York   E.H.P.
March 1970

Grateful acknowledgment for permission to quote is extended to the following publishers:

G. P. Putnam's Sons for "In Flanders Fields" by John McCrae. Copyright © 1919, renewed 1946 by G. P. Putnam's Sons.

The Viking Press for *The World of Yesterday: An Autobiography* by Stephen Zweig. Copyright 1943 by the Viking Press, Inc.

Yale University Press for *The Evolution of War: A Study of Its Role in Early Societies* by Maurice R. Davie. Copyright 1929 by the Yale University Press.

Houghton Mifflin and H. Pordes for *Der Fuehrer: Hitler's Rise to Power* by Konrad Heiden, translated by Ralph Manheim. Copyright 1944 by Houghton Mifflin.

Houghton Mifflin for *Mein Kampf* by Adolf Hitler, translated by Ralph Manheim. Copyright 1944 by Houghton Mifflin.

Contents

Illustrations

PART ONE

SUICIDE

Certain it is that *work, worry, labour* and *trouble,* form the lot of almost all men their whole life long. But if all wishes were fulfilled as soon as they arose, how would men occupy their lives? what would they do with their time? If the world were a paradise of luxury and ease, a land flowing with milk and honey, where every Jack obtained his Jill at once and without any difficulty, men would either die of boredom or hang themselves; or there would be wars, massacres, and murders; so that in the end mankind would inflict more suffering on itself than it has now to accept at the hands of Nature.

ARTHUR SCHOPENHAUER, *Studies in Pessimism* (1841)

1

The question of suicide

Our will requires an aim. It would sooner have the void for
its purpose than be void of purpose.

FRIEDRICH NIETZSCHE, *Genealogy of Morals*

Man is distinguished by his capacity for self-torture. All organisms
search for pleasure; man alone seeks pain. Through ages of evolution he has learned not only to endure but to cherish suffering. History is a refutation of hedonism.

Through his genius for self-denial man overrules the rule of nature: no other creature is capable of conscious suicide, of nullifica-
tion of the will to live. And unconscious suicide comes in countless
varieties. All mental disorder is a variation on the single theme of
self-destruction, and not only alcoholism and psychoses but even
asceticism and martyrdom have been classified as forms of chronic
suicide.[1]

Sacrifice shades into suicide. Western civilization, perhaps all civilization, has a deep sacrificial-suicidal undercurrent. Both Socrates
and Christ chose death rather than alter their conduct and thus be-
tray their principles. Thousands of early Christian subversives preferred slaughter by the Romans to a renunciation of their faith. Millions of men have laid down their lives on the altar of war; millions
more have killed themselves in pursuit of some grand or trivial adventure. Not longevity but meaning is the aim of human existence.

When existence is stripped of meaning, men prefer death to mere

3

continuation as a biological organism. Paradoxically, suicide itself is a quest for meaning. Suicide is a kind of experiment, says Schopenhauer, "a question which man puts to Nature, trying to force her to an answer. The question is this: What change will death produce in man's existence and in this insight into the nature of things?"[2] Of course it is a clumsy experiment if successful, Schopenhauer adds, since it destroys the consciousness which puts the question and awaits the answer. But recent clinical studies give some validity to Schopenhauer's curious observation: the attempted suicide is often a "gamble with death," an effort to discover whether "fate" wants us to live or die.[3] Yet even to raise the question of the possible preference of death to living bespeaks a kind of torment which only man can know.

What is the source of the melancholy which gives rise to the wish to die? Writing in 1625 Robert Burton describes a kind of agitated depression where men entertain "feral thoughts to offer violence to their persons."[4] Solitariness and idleness are the chief causes of the disease. The melancholiacs "avoid and hate men without reason." Is it for pleasure they are so solitary, Burton asks, or for pain? For both, he says, "yet I rather think for fear and sorrow."[5] For therapy, Burton prescribes exercise of body and mind because "the heavens themselves run continually round, the sun riseth and sets . . . the waters ebb and flow . . . to teach us we should ever be in action." The patient should never be left alone or idle; should have "honest sports, companies and recreations," should even be "incited to Venus by seeing and touching beautiful women . . . to be drawn to such consorts whether he will or no, and should not be an auditor only or a spectator but sometimes an actor himself."[6]

Burton correctly detected the social roots of melancholia. The condition is not a physical disease but a disorder of interpersonal relations. And behind the interpersonal is the institutional. Burton thought the disorder most pronounced among the upper classes, "where the badge of gentry is idleness." Prosperity may be more lethal than poverty—the former "deceives," the latter "instructs."[7]

Social role is also a variable. Scholars, for instance, "come to this malady [melancholia] by continual study" and because they live a "sedentary, solitary life."[8]

Regrettably, although Burton's work was widely read it was seldom utilized. For two and a half centuries philosophers speculated on the meaning of suicide, but no one systematically studied the phenomenon. Hume, Rousseau, Goethe, Montesquieu—all with at least one essay on suicide, addressed to such questions as whether suicide was a crime, a sin, an inalienable right, a form of self-liberation.[9] Not until statistics of suicide accumulated in the nineteenth century was it possible to get an empirical assessment of the phenomenon. Then came the work of Boismont (1856), Morselli (1882), and Durkheim (1899).

Durkheim combined the imagination of the artist with the discipline of the scientist. Contemporary theorists, apt to ridicule quantitative sociology, fail to appreciate the objective validity which statistics give to Durkheim's work.[10] Without statistics, Durkheim's work would be only one more philosophic treatise. With the statistics, Durkheim achieved a fundamental breakthrough in the understanding of man.

Durkheim differentiated three types of suicide: the egoistic, the altruistic, and the anomic. Egoism denotes psycho-social isolation, aloneness; altruism is its opposite, the submergence of the ego in the collectivity. But both conditions are suicidogenic only when they eventuate in anomie, the loss of purpose. If their values remain intact, "egoists" can live with a minimum of social interaction—there are serene isolates, for example Spinoza, Kant, Santayana. And "altruists" resort to suicide only when catastrophe precludes continuation of their accustomed life: Socrates rejected the option of physical survival in exile because existence had no meaning for him apart from Athens. He chose a meaningful death to a meaningless life. Egoism and anomie are used interchangeably; Durkheim himself notes they are "usually merely two different aspects of one social state."[11]

How then is anomie translated into self-destruction? Man derives his identity from his action. Action is more than motion, a mere doing things; it implies purpose, the pursuit of a goal. Without some aim beyond the moment, life becomes intolerable, meaningless. "All man's pleasure in acting, moving and exerting himself," Durkheim writes, "implies the sense that his efforts are not in vain and that by walking he has advanced. However, one does not advance when one walks toward no goal, or—which is the same thing—when his goal is infinity. . . . To pursue a goal which is by definition unattainable is to condemn oneself to a state of perpetual unhappiness."[12] Weariness follows, then despair—the logical end of an endless pursuit. Suicide is the supreme manifestation of despair.

2

Anomie as meaninglessness: work and the suicide rate

> For work, and work alone, gives man the only concrete
> footing he is destined to know . . . Work is the process by
> which man refuses to acknowledge that life is vanity.
>
> AARON LEVENSTEIN, *Why People Work*

Suicide presupposes self. Because the self has its being in the social process, suicide rates vary with the character of society: rural suicide rates are lower than urban rates; the deteriorated inner city is highly "suicidal," but, when stable residential areas are compared the wealthier sections appear to have more suicide than low-income neighborhoods.[1] While religious affiliation is not a decisive variable in American suicide statistics, there is a rate differential by age, sex, marital status, ethnicity, and socio-economic level.[2]

Suicide rates correlate with social status, defined here not as rank but as position in any social system. Role is the function or behavior called forth by status. The roles a person plays, first as a child in the family, later in the peer group, finally as an adult in the community, become incorporated into the structure of the self. Loss, contradiction, and ambiguity of role disintegrates the self.

Status for the adult white male in America depends primarily on work: "Occupation is the supreme determinant of human careers."[3] Through performance of a *specific* work-role, men relate themselves to other men. Moreover, vocation determines the person's *general* social status, i.e. his standing in the larger society, and ultimately his conception of the world. "The broker sees the *Ding-an-Sich* as real estate," runs a line from Auden.

Occupation contains the "categories of thought," the conceptual system, which integrates the institutional order.[4] Time is measured in work-terms, space is shaped by work-needs, daily life is scheduled by work-demands. Personal identity derives from work rather than kinship, politics, or religion. Question: who are you? Answer: I am a sociologist. Work, not faith, moves mountains, justifies existence, explains the ways of God to Man. Hell is worklessness. "Whoever complains on account of hard work does not deserve to live," writes an unemployed man in Warsaw in the 1930's, "He commits an awful sacrilege. He does it without knowing, because he has not experienced the numbness of an idle life."[5]

Historically, the work-ethic may be waning, but most men still spend most of their waking hours on the job. Surveys indicate 90 per cent of the population would want to work, even if it were not financially necessary.[6] "The burden of leisure, long the exclusive curse of the rich," comments Dan Wakefield, "is now the darkest threat to the well-being of the working man . . . a great emptiness, [a] more sinister and formidable enemy than Henry Bennett's goon squads at Ford plants in the 1930's."[7] Where hunger and rude necessity may have been the work-incentive of previous centuries, today, says Levenstein, "men work to stave off meaninglessness."[8] Betty Friedan traces the identity crisis of contemporary woman to the lack of significant work, of purposive activity.[9]

When the ends of action are blurred and ambiguous, anomie ensues. Anomie is both a social condition and a psychic state, a general aimlessness accompanied by feelings of emptiness. Louis Wirth describes anomie as a "social and emotional void"; de Grazia equates it with "separation anxiety"; while Merton stresses the idea of normlessness. The awkward word *meaninglessness* can serve as a common denominator of these differing perspectives.[10]

Meaning is an act not an idea. Belief becomes meaning only when it impels and structures conduct. Meaning is *self*-generated, flowing from the person's active participation in the social process. The self, as pictured by George Herbert Mead, is both an "I" (a subject) and a "me" (an object). The "me" is the image which others have of the self; the "I" is the actor who responds to that image. The "me" is the self as a role-occupant. There are as many "me's" as there are social roles, but there is only one "I." While the "me" is socially determined, the "I" remains free, or at least chooses the "me" presented to the world. The "me" is the self as defined by others, but the "I" eventually selects the others (the reference group) who define the "me." Created by society, the self also creates its own society. "After the self has arisen," says Mead, "it can provide for itself its own social experiences."[11]

When communication breaks down, the self cannot validate its existence as a "me": we label this syndrome *dissociation*. The self is left *without* a social role, and personal disorganization results.[12] But encapsulation *within* a social role may prevent the person from acting as an "I": this syndrome we label *envelopment*. Dissociation implies disorganization; envelopment a rigidity of organization which inhibits spontaneous action.[13] Both conditions render the self impotent, that is, powerless to act, thus engendering the meaninglessness of anomie.

Since in our culture work is a main motive for action, and therefore a primary source of meaning, suicide rates should bear some relation to occupational roles. But the actual connection between work and suicide is immensely complex and cannot be deduced from grand sociological theory. Relevant analysis must begin with dull statistics.

The relation between occupation and suicide has not been adequately studied. Piker surveyed a large number of suicide attempts but was unable to compute rates because his classification did not correspond to city census statistics; von Andics understood the relevance of occupation but her work is useless from a statistical standpoint; Dublin and Bunzel, in 1933, presented *one* occupational table based on 1930 British data; Henry and Short correlated suicide with income but not with occupation.[14] The statistical data in this chapter were first presented in 1958; since then Breed has published a significant paper on suicide and occupational mobility.[15]

The present chapter is a study of occupation and suicide in Tulsa, Oklahoma. Official suicide statistics are sometimes wildly inaccurate, and because the "universe" of suicides is small, the misreporting of only a few cases vastly distorts the calculation of rates. In an effort to correct recording errors we checked each death-certificate listing of occupation against the city directory listing and stories in the local press. Thus we obtained a reasonably exact picture of the occupational status of some 95 per cent of the male suicides who were Tulsa residents between 1937 and 1956.

Tulsa is a city of over 250,000. Tulsa County is almost exclusively urban with less than 3 per cent of its population listed as "rural-farm." Virtually all of the county's population is concentrated within the Tulsa Standard Metropolitan Area. While it is impossible to know whether the suicide pattern for Tulsa corresponds to that of American society as a whole, Tulsa is a rather typical, mid-western city. Founded about 1900, it has grown rapidly and is now a managerial center for the oil industry. Its employed male population in 1950 was divided almost equally between white- and blue-collar workers, 31,592 and 30,477, respectively. The population of the metropolitan area remained almost constant during the 1930's, with 11 per cent of employable males listed as "seeking work." In the early 1940's, war industry—mainly aircraft manufacturing—and the general national prosperity revived the economic life, unemployment declined, and the population of the metropolitan area increased by 28 per cent, from 193,363 to 251,686, in the decade of the 1940's. During the 1940's home ownership increased from 56 to 65 per cent, placing the city ninth in the nation in the number of homes which are "owner occupied." The median annual income for employed males in 1950 was $3016. Between 1950 and 1956 the metropolitan area

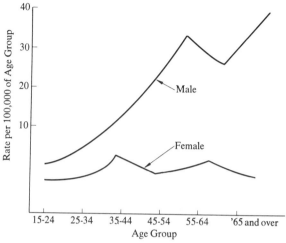

Figure 1. Suicide by Age and Sex

grew by 50,000. Oklahoma City, 100 miles to the west, is of comparable size (325,352) but has a somewhat lower average income, more murders, fewer suicides, and substantially less alcoholism than Tulsa. In ranking 105 American cities by 1936-45 suicide rates, Porterfield and Talbert place Tulsa (rate 14.3 per 100,000) in 39th place, and Oklahoma City (rate 10.2) in 89th place.[16]

During the twenty years between 1937 and 1956 at least 426 residents of Tulsa County over 14 years of age committed suicide. The average annual rate is 13.0 per 100,000; the adult white male rate (27.0) is over four times as high as the female rate (6.6) and ten times as high as the Negro male rate (2.7).

Figure 1 presents a differential pattern of rate increase by age and sex. The female rate attains its zenith in the 35 to 44-year-old period and then declines; the male rate rises continuously and reaches its peak after 65, suggesting an association between occupational role and suicide.

Table 1 gives the suicide rates for males in the standard (census) occupational categories. It is revealing to compare the rates by five-

Table 1. Suicide by Occupation Category for the Adult White Male Population of Tulsa County, 1937-1956

Category	1937-1941			1942-1946			1947-1951			1952-1956			TOTAL 1937-1956	
	No.	Pop.[a]	Rate per 100,000	No.	Pop.[b]	Rate per 100,000	No.	Pop.[c]	Rate per 100,000	No.	Pop.[d]	Rate per 100,000	No.	Average Annual Rate per 100,000
Professional Managerial	36	11,462	63.0	19	13,962	27.3	20	18,851	21.2	30	20,759	29.0	105	35.1
Sales-Clerical	9	10,988	16.4	7	11,352	12.4	6	12,111	9.9	5	12,831	7.8	27	11.6
Craftsman (Skilled Labor)	7	7,975	17.7	8	9,757	16.3	6	14,537	8.3	12	15,987	15.0	33	14.3
Operatives (Semi-skilled Labor)	10	7,645	26.1	8	8,530	18.7	12	10,339	23.2	8	11,366	14.0	38	20.5
Unskilled Labor	5	2,535	39.4	4	2,945	27.2	8	3,020	53.0	6	3,380	35.4	23	38.7
Service	4	2,427	33.0	3	2,677	22.5	1	2,431	8.2	4	2,502	32.1	12	23.9
Retired	9	2,000	90.0	8	2,000	80.0	7	2,215	63.0	13	2,415	100.8	37	83.4
Unemployed and Unclassified	8	...	...	6	...	...	1	...	...	5	...	...	20	...
Agriculture	2	5,688	7.1	1	5,688	3.5	2	3,637	11.0	2	3,590	11.1	7	8.1
Student	6	8,064	13.9	0	8,064	...	3	9,562	6.3	5	10,131	9.9	14	7.5
TOTAL	96			64			66			90			316	
Average Annual Rate	34.0			23.1			22.4			27.2			27.0	

[a] 1940 census.
[b] Population estimate of the Oklahoma Employment Commission.
[c] Estimated Population over 65 and not in labor force (not given in 1940 census).
[d] 1950 census.

12

year intervals. During World War II suicide rates throughout the nation dropped to the lowest point since 1917, and Tulsa County followed the national trend. For all males the rate for the half-decade between 1942 and 1946 was 32 per cent below the 1937-41 rate, whereas the female rate during this time rose by 7 per cent. Moreover, it appears that occupational groups reacted differently to the war and its accompanying prosperity: the combined suicide rates for professional-managerial, service, and unskilled workers dropped nearly 40 per cent while the sales-clerical, skilled, and semi-skilled rate declined by about 20 per cent. Over the entire twenty-year period it appears that both extremes of the vocational hierarchy exhibited a high suicide rate, while the middle groups maintained a fairly constant and low rate.

Schmid and van Arsdol suggest the possibility that blue-collar workers have a higher suicide rate than white-collar workers.[17] Our Tulsa findings, however, do not support this contention. For the combined professional-managerial and sales-clerical population the average annual rate was 24.6 as opposed to 19.6 for manual workers. There seems to be a qualitative as well as quantitative difference between the white- and blue-collar suicide (see Table 2). The former is more likely to be a premeditated act, whereas working-class

Table 2. Suicide in the White-Collar and Blue-Collar Worlds*

	White-Collar (Professional-Managerial and Sales-Clerical)		Blue-Collar (Skilled, Semi-skilled, and Unskilled)	
	No.	Per cent	No.	Per cent
Single, widowed, divorced, estranged	43	30.8	44	42.5
Murder + Suicide	3	2.8	15	16.0
Residence outside city limits	4	3.2	17	18.0

* Data on estrangement and murder + suicide were taken from the Tulsa *Daily World* and Tulsa *Tribune.*

suicide is more impulsive: six times as many murder-suicides occur in the blue-collar world. While the average age of the two groups is roughly comparable—48.2 for the white-collar suicide, 45.2 for the blue-collar suicide—the latter's family life is more likely to be disorganized.

Eighteen per cent of the blue-collar suicides as opposed to some 3 per cent of the white-collar suicides lived outside the city limits but within the county. Many of the manual workers were recent rural migrants not yet adjusted to urban life.[18]

Within the professional-managerial category, professions have the lowest rate, followed by salaried managers and officials, and finally self-employed proprietors, who have the highest rate. Pharmacists and physicians have unusually high rates, while engineers and accountants rank low. Among certain professions—authors, editors, and reporters (population 150), the clergy (population 285), teachers (male population 463), college professors (population 115)— no suicides occurred. Nurses have an incidence of suicide six times that of females in general, while women sales-clerical workers have a rate below that of the general female population. In blue-collar occupations, cab drivers have a rate four times higher than that of the general male population, while truck drivers fall below the mean. Though the size of our sample precludes generalization, the data presented in Table 3 may be suggestive.

But the greatest strain of all—for the male—derives from lack of occupation. Over the past twenty years the retired have a suicide rate of 89.0, almost five times that of the adult male population and twice that of all males of the same age group. While the female rate declines slightly after 65, the male rate increases sharply, as is shown in Table 4.

Suicide is an ultimate expression of accumulated self-contempt. Psychiatric theories often trace the origin of self-hatred to guilt generated by early childhood experiences.[19] It is our contention that both guilt and self-contempt are rooted in anomie which results in the inability to act, i.e. impotence. Whether turned inward on the self or outward on the world, destructiveness is the "outcome of an unlived life."[20]

Table 3. Suicide by Specific Occupation, 1937-1956*

	White-Collar				Blue-Collar		
Occupation	No.	Pop.	Rate	Occupation	No.	Pop.	Rate
Pharmacists	6	162	120	Cab Drivers	7	402	86.9
Physicians	5	309	83	Welders	5	974	25
Nurses	6	776	38	Machinists	4	1,154	17
Lawyers	4	544	36	Truck Drivers	7	2,847	12
Engineers	6	1,953	15	Mechanics	8	3,776	10
Accountants	3	2,054	7	Carpenters	2	1,804	5

* Data from *Seventeenth Census* . . . , 1950, Vol. II, Part 36, pp. 206-7. The actual rates would be somewhat higher than those given here as the population has grown 28 per cent since 1940.

The relationship between self-destruction and anomie is revealed in the suicide rates for the aged. As Figure 1 shows, the male rate rises continuously throughout life with a sharp increase after 65 while the female rate declines after 40. Theories which trace all suicides to the insecurities of childhood must explain why the effect of early life diminishes with age for the woman but increases for the

Table 4. Suicide by Age and Sex of the Adult White Population in Tulsa County, 1937-1956

	Population 14-64			Population Over 65			% Rate
	No.	Pop.[b]	Rate	No.	Pop.	Rate	Change
Male[a]	257	74,776	17.1	56	6,402	42.6	146.0
Female	96	81,207	5.9	7	7,024	4.9	1.7

[a] Three of the male suicides were of unknown age and are not included in this table.
[b] Average population of the 1940 and 1950 censuses.

man. Nor is suicide due to the weariness of long life, for women over 65 have a rate below those under 65 (Table 4). Without denying the influence of early socialization and the physiological strains of aging it appears that the suicide of the elderly male is connected primarily with the loss of occupational status. The suicide rate for men increases nearly one and a half times after 65; moreover, the *retired* male over 65 has a rate almost twice that for all males of the same age. Retirement in our society is a virtual excommunication. Men with no history of sickness develop chronic illnesses after retirement. It is certainly plausible to suggest that such unemployment is a primary and not merely precipitating factor in the suicide of the aged male. To be without work is to live without purpose.[21]

Work, however, provides no absolute immunity against suicide, and it appears that the quality and extent of anomie vary by standard occupational categories—used here as ideal types. The type, an abstraction, does not fully describe all (or any) of the particular cases subsumed by it. It does, however, serve as an index to social roles.

Occupational Type (from Table 2)	Average Annual Rate per 100,000
I. Professional-Managerial	35.4
II. Sales-Clerical	11.6
III. Skilled Workers (Craftsmen)	14.3
IV. Semi-Skilled Workers (Operatives)	20.5
V. Unskilled Labor	38.7

Each of the types above must be viewed in relation to the others. Factors "causing" suicide in I or V will also be at work with II, III, or IV. But our task is to find specific differences between the types which may account for the observed variation of suicide rates.[22]

"The whole occupational sphere," Talcott Parsons writes, "is dominated by a single, fundamental goal, that of 'success.' "[23] The idea of success is derived from a larger conceptual framework which defines the nature of man in terms of the active mastery of existence.

The determining factor in the distribution of suicide by occupation is the relationship between the self and the success ideology.

Anomie as Dissociation (Type V). The unskilled laborer lives a hand-to-mouth existence, both physically and psychically. As a casual worker, employment for him is sporadic even in prosperous times; routines for the organization of everyday life are either absent or ineffective. Discontinuity in the occupational sphere coupled with the absence of the regulating mores of the wider society creates an atmosphere of pervasive disorder.[24]

Type V individuals have not internalized the success ideology and have no subculture of their own to draw on for orientation. (This is especially true in Tulsa, where there are few ethnic communities.) In an individuated culture the person without dominant, long-range goals becomes increasingly the victim of whim and egoistic impulse. He has little rationale for the delay or regulation of response. Here we have the picture of an "I" without a "me"—a desocialized personality. Devoid of a coherent conceptual structure, the individual cannot sufficiently organize his world so that he can act effectively within it. That which cannot be integrated into the conceptual system—the strange, the unknown—is a source of anxiety and produces two characteristic reactions: flight and aggression. Anxiety rather than frustration by external circumstances is the primary source of the aggression of type V. Incapacitated by anxiety, the suicide either withdraws into apathy or finally strikes out at the world impulsively —one-third of the suicides of type V occurred in conjunction with unpremeditated murder.[25] Having exhausted his resources for coming to terms with a threatening chaos, the individual annihilates the world by killing the self.

Integration (Types IV, III, and II). With reference to the conceptual system of the social, these three types represent a middle ground between the dissociation of type V and the total involvement of type I.

Insofar as V and IV are distinguishable categories, the dividing line between them is the concept of success. There is a certain co-

herence in the life of the semi-skilled worker: regularity of employment, some participation in associations (e.g. unions), and at least
a nominal membership in the community. For the semi-skilled
worker success comes to mean immediate gains in income rather
than advancement to a managerial position. Nevertheless, type IV
workers have the goal of raising the personal and family consumption level: success means a new car, home ownership, possibly a
bank account, freedom from debt.[26]

With type III the drive for an active mastery of existence is more
clearly revealed. All of V and many of IV occupations are "jobs" as
distinct from "trades." Men drift into jobs but they learn a trade,
which calls for specialized training.[27] The individual motivated to
learn a trade has to some degree internalized the success philosophy.
His craft, moreover, may bring some satisfaction to the urge for creative activity. Both factors combine to reduce anomie: the suicide
rate for type III was the lowest of the manual workers during the
twenty years covered by this study.

Type II has an unusually low suicide rate. More conservative in
political and economic philosophy than the manual worker, type II
maintains a middle-class style of life with its emphasis on propriety,
restraint, and (a somewhat illusory) individual responsibility. Like
the craftsman, the sales-clerical person is disciplined by his occupational role, and the fact that he works directly with people may give
him a sense of meaningful participation in society. Martin Needleman's recent study indicates white-collar workers show an extremely
low degree of anomie (as measured by the Srole scale) and generally find their work and way of life satisfying.[28]

Anomie as Envelopment (Type I). With lower-grade manual
workers, especially type V, anomie seems to be associated with a
fragmentation of the conceptual scheme and "results from man's activity lacking regulation . . . ultimately [the product of] society's
insufficient presence in the individual."[29]

The success concept supplies a general framework of orientation
for types IV, III, and II, but a large segment of nonoccupational be-

havior is relatively unrestrained and spontaneous. But in type I the self is almost completely enveloped by the success ideology and presents the paradox of what may be called institutionalized anomie, i.e. meaninglessness arising from normative regulation itself.

Almost the whole of life for our type I (professional-managerial) people is structured around the idea of success. But as Melvin Tumin wrote in the 1950's, "the emphasis has now shifted from the importance of work and striving to the urgency of *appearing to be successful* . . . [and] being successful is measured by power and property one openly consumes."[30] Success is no longer defined by action but by the possession of prestige symbols, which signify "belongingness" and serve as protection against the anxiety of disapproval. But the ideology of the success is believed all the more fervently. For if the symbols of success and prestige have no meaning then the world itself is a chaos. The hold on reality is too tenuous to risk examination of the metaphysical validity of the success symbols, and the way of life they symbolize. Questioning threatens the foundations of the psyche. Consequently, people deliberately blind themselves to the real meaning of the symbols and thing symbolized. There is a concomitant paralysis of the critical faculties: the person cannot sufficiently detach himself from the prevailing institutions (values) to gain an objective view of the world. Psychologically, he is not free to examine his own motivations. Since he does not know himself as an "I" he cannot trust his own judgment or act on his own convictions. Enveloped by the culture he has no life of his own as an "I," but everywhere meets a "me" he must conform to. Max Scheler anticipated the emergence of this personality type, which was devoid of "authentic fellow feeling" but still identified with others. Life acquires then a "tendency to dissipate itself in a vicarious re-enactment of the doings of one or more other people. His very acts and decicions are determined by demands inherent in the other's conception of him."[31] Arthur Miller's Willy Loman breaks apart when his customers stop smiling back: failure as a salesman means failure as a self.

When occupational types, I through V, are arranged on a continuum, the bimodal distribution of suicide stands out clearly. At V is a disorganized way of life becoming more coherent as we move toward I with increasing involvement in the success ideology; moving from I toward V we see a diminishing rigidity, a relaxation of the success demands, as presented in the following diagram:

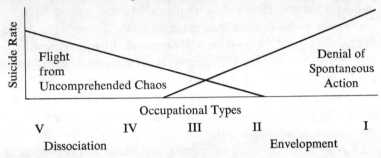

Although occupational status is but one component of the total social setting, it is an essential key (in our culture) to the relationship between self and society. Occupation tends to create both by selection and by the nature of the role itself either a dissociated or an enveloped personality. Both dissociation and envelopment immobilize the self, producing the meaninglessness of anomie.

3

Anxiety as the experience of anomie: inferences drawn from suicide biographies

> . . . someday I want my son to know his dad was not insane but just afraid of life.
>
> Suicide note of an unemployed filling station attendant, *Tulsa World,* Jan. 22, 1947.

Suicide is a meaningful response to meaninglessness, a last effort of a victim to become an actor. Hamlet, "sicklied o'er by the pale cast of thought," has "lost the name of action." But he can still "take arms against a sea of troubles and by opposing end them," thus terminating the drift toward total dissolution. After a serious suicide attempt which left him blind, Peter Putnam wrote:

> The extreme negation of life, [suicide] is the sole positive control over life, the only irrevocable decision a man can impose upon his future. Through complete selfishness, it confers utter selflessness . . . although it is a symptom of a diseased mind, it is entirely rational. To the individual living in perfect isolation, it is the only logical escape from the suffering of isolation.[1]

The isolation of the suicide is self-created, not externally imposed. In the downward spiral of despair, the person cuts himself off from others to gain greater control over "reality": by the contraction of awareness the perceptual world is *narrowed* to manageable dimensions. This choking off of sensation is both a cause and consequence of anxiety—Angyal notes the word anxiety derives from a root for "narrow."[2]

Anxiety is the subjective side of anomie. Confronted with chaos, the person panics. The strange and unstructured situation sets off an alarm reaction which can evoke three essentially different responses: fear, anger, and anxiety. In fear, says Jurgen Ruesch, the person consciously identifies threatening objects, and avoids them; in anger, he seeks to overwhelm or destroy the endangering stimuli. Both anger and fear lead to action which terminates the alarm response. But in anxiety, the person is unable to act, immobilized, while the alarm mechanism continues to operate, leading eventually to the disorganization of the individual.[3]

Anxiety arises out of the paralysis of self. Conflict of roles, extrusion from an established pattern of action (e.g. retirement), loss of status or love object, protracted isolation, crippling perceptions of personal inadequacy—whatever incapacitates the self generates anxiety. Prolonged anxiety depletes the vital energies of the organism, produces the "inner deadness" which precedes the actual death of the suicide. And because suicide itself is an act—something the person can *do* about his suffering, his immobilization—the very conception and plan of self-imposed death may alleviate anxiety and bring tranquility at the end. As Kobler and Stotland put it, the person takes on a suicidal identity, and in preparing for death "achieves a kind of equanimity and stability of behavior . . . life achieves a new goal: its own end."[4]

Ultimately, the suicide is defeated by his strategy for handling anxiety. In suicide case histories two defenses against anxiety stand out: flight and denial. In flight the person dissociates; he cuts himself off from others in order to reduce threatening demands on the ego but therewith he deprives himself of the feedback necessary to sustain the sense of self-worth. Denial is an almost opposite reaction: refusing to recognize his own distress, the person nullifies his own perceptions. "Denial disclaims the external world . . . as repression disclaims the instincts," says Lewin.[5] The dissociated person becomes disorganized: runs in all directions at once. But denial entails a rigid organization of self: the person encases himself in an envelope as a shield against anxiety. Dissociation represents loss of control, envelopment, over-control, but both end in the destruction of autonomy, of self.

The aim, and function, of the self is management of anxiety. As the self dissolves, anxiety returns, and suicide may become the "only way out"—the phrase recurs with startling frequency in suicide notes. To present the argument schematically:

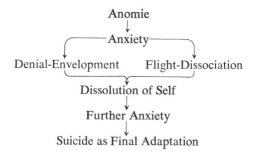

Of course there are numerous adaptations to anxiety: compulsiveness in work, in sexuality, or in religiosity; psychosomatic illness, alcoholism, psychoses. The suicide seems to search for other avenues of escape and finally happens upon the idea of self-liquidation as the "only way out" of the collapsing enterprise of life.

The terms "envelopment" and "dissociation" were used in the previous chapter as temporarily useful categories for explaining the statistical correlations between occupation and suicide. The suicidal person is often a disorganized deviant who makes a mess of every life-situation—family is discordant, work irregular, interpersonal relations destructive—the classic picture of anomie as de-regulation.

But on deeper probing we were struck by the "normality," organization, and "rationality" of many suicides. A disorganization hypothesis—such as the Gibbs and Martin theory of status-integration—could account for the suicide of "bottom people" who were clearly outside the normative framework of the culture.[6] But "top people" are not anomic in the disorganized sense of the word. The very organization of the lives of upper-status suicides seemed to contribute to the mood of meaninglessness which brought on the act of self-annihilation. The top people seemed to lose autonomy, they had no life of their own—hence the concept of envelopment as an opposite of dissociation. Envelopment could be construed as a social condition operating through the psychological mechanism of denial: the person damps out his own feelings—the "I"—in order to comply with the demands of others and conform to the image of the "me" which they present to him.

But neither dissociation nor envelopment can be understood statically, and so mysterious an act as suicide cannot be reduced to arithmetic. Therefore to gain a different, deeper grasp of the suicidal biography we turned to the Tulsa press, which reported on 319 of the 426 suicides occurring between 1937 and 1956. About 20 per cent of the stories directly quote suicide notes, randomly scattered over the entire period and throughout the status hierarchy. Some 15 to 30 per cent of the suicides of each major occupational category, excepting students (60 per cent) and retired people (2 per cent), left some kind of written message. Files of the Tulsa Police Department were checked and found to contain a few notes but little else of sociological interest. Our material does not lend itself to a quantitative content analysis, and our method is simply "a process of looking at events until they become luminous," as Willard Waller would say.[7]

The suicide is groping for a way out of anxiety and its concomitant stress; often the process is conscious, occasionally unconscious. "Just in case there is some doubt why I did this," a 19-year-old physics student writes, "I am making this explanation. I am a suicidal maniac. I have no logical reason for wanting to die, but have an uncontrollable desire to die" (*Tulsa World,* Jan. 1, 1937). Like the alcoholic who unknowingly craves drink because it relieves tension, so the idea of death may become an irresistible Nirvana for the suicide. "I will be at ease now," writes another young Tulsa suicide, "At least it can't be any worse. I'm just so tired I want rest now" (*Tulsa World,* Jan. 22, 1947).

Flight is the simplest response to anxiety. If one is scared one runs. But the suicide usually cannot define what frightens him; he is "just afraid of life," consequently he avoids life, isolates himself from others, dissociates. In numerous Tulsa suicides dissociation culminates in total aloneness: the victim lives alone, has no local kin, friends, or organizational ties. Usually the total isolate does not bother to leave a note; occasionally the note will be addressed to whom it may concern. Thus a 36-year-old bartender who lived by himself in a furnished room wrote: "to whom . . . please give my body to medical research. My belongings to the Salvation Army" (*Tulsa Police Files,* Dec. 2, 1954). A 60-year-old pensioner without family, friends, or job explains simply: "Just tired of living" (*Tulsa World,* September 11, 1956). The decomposed body of an unknown woman lies in a field; twelve cents and a note are found in her purse: "There is no other way out. . . . A year ago there was but I did not have the money to buy the help of an intelligent doctor. He said I need a change to help myself. I have been defeated at every turn in the road. I can no longer see my way ahead" (*Tulsa World,* August 31, 1943). A cab driver walks to the railroad tracks, drinks poison, leaves a note: "To the only friend I ever had in the world. I love you. Forgive and forget" (*Tulsa Tribune,* March 18, 1939).

Dissociation and drift often take a physical form. A 49-year-old auto-polisher committed suicide in 1953 in Tulsa. Earlier he had operated a pipe and supply firm; then he had been a policeman in Borger, Texas; he had moved to Tulsa from South Gate, California; before that had worked as a guard at the Flamingo Hotel and Club in Las Vegas, Nevada. He had been on a drinking spree immediately before his suicide; his wife had left him ten days earlier. He wrote: "2:00 p.m. This is my last words. Dorothy I love you. You will never know how much. I haven't worried about you for you wanted to go. But it was too much for me" (*Tulsa Tribune,* Nov. 20, 1953).

But sometimes the suicide does not relinquish his claims on a loved one so easily. There is an enraged suicide who is connected to others through his hostility. Suicide is often an act of aggression against a loved one, usually the spouse. Thus a 46-year-old laborer wrote, "Send my clothes to mother, you____," and he cursed his former wife for doublecrossing him (*Tulsa World,* May 28, 1938). After writing the note the man accidentally encountered his wife in front of his hotel and shot her.

A 62-year-old unemployed iron-worker wrote: "I want someone to report this trouble to the law for this thing has 'murde' me. . . . Please inviscate clearly Vina Smith [his wife] is the meanest woman on earth. I want Mrs. Keaton to have everything I've got. She is just a friend. Bye, bye. Ike Smith" (*Tulsa Police Files,* Dec. 5, 1941).

In a similar vein is a note from a 44-year-old truck driver, leaving a war bond for his wife: "Here is another bond for you, I hope you enjoy spending it!" Another note read, "She got all my money and then had them fix the summons to beat me out of everything else. Boy what a frameup. They are all alike to the bottom, as the song goes" (*Tulsa World,* Jan. 1, 1949). In more elegant language the estranged wife of a prominent attorney left the same message: "Devotion then desertion. What made you do it? How could you be so cruel. You of all the others! God forgive you. In despair, your devoted wife" (*Tulsa Tribune,* Aug. 8, 1939).

Finally there is the "berserk" suicide consumed by blind fury. A former deputy sheriff who at the time of his suicide was an army private at home on leave killed his divorced wife, her roommate, and then himself. To his army major he wrote: "This crime is bad but as you know the army teaches us to kill. I was honest and upright and done the best I could. These people asked for it. P.S. I was dressed in full O.D. at the time." Another note addressed to the sheriff read, "Don't try to keep this gun. My boy needs the money. It will bring something . . . P.S. The army teaches us to kill." Actually the army deserves little credit for teaching this man to kill: two months earlier he had blasted his wife's apartment with a shotgun, but legal charges were dropped so he could enter the service. A third note was closer to the unfortunate truth of the matter: "Them that don't like me are the ones that know me—P.S. This is the same caliber [of gun] that Gleason [the county attorney who had killed himself a year before] went by. You don't have to be in combat to give your life to your country." (*Tulsa World,* April 1, 1943). The life of this 38-year-old man was marked by violence, instability, and marital discord (twice divorced). Neither folkways, mores, nor legal sanctions could curtail his destructive impulses. The murder-suicides in our study were of this same general character, though none of the others left such revealing notes. Usually the murder-suicides do not leave notes. Indeed, the murder is the note.

Most rational men can imagine misery sufficient to drive them to self-murder. Cicero says when the play ceases to please we should serenely quit the theater.[8] Occasionally suicides do depart in just such a spirit. Fearing the recurrence of a stroke, a 52-year-old unemployed worker writes his brother: "This is the best way out if I can make it. Don't tell anyone what happened. Tell the folks I left town. Let the county plant me . . . Had another light passout while listening to the ball game [on the car radio] . . . so here goes" (*Tulsa Police Files,* July 28, 1956). But there are others, unwilling to go that gently, who seem determined to take down all the other players and the theater too. Wahl says the suicide regresses to a stage of infantile omnipotence where the self and the other merge, and the person annihilates the self in order to destroy the world.[9] In killing the self the person is killing the other, and vice versa. The dissociated suicide loses the capacity to take the role of the other; for him the other has no autonomous existence. Professing great love for his wife and fearing she would leave him, the husband killed her, saying, "If I can't have Mary no one else can have her. She is dead

and I'll soon be with her." Then he killed himself (*Tulsa World,*
July 11, 1943).

The dissociated are disorganized outsiders, loners, usually with
no fixed or stable place in the social order. Often, however, the suicides are thoroughly integrated into the social structure, seemingly
"normal" by cultural standards. Thus an outstanding civic leader,
a vice-president of a paper company, and a member of the Shriners,
the Lions, the American Legion, the Advertising Club, the Sales
Executive Club, the Chamber of Commerce, and the Episcopal
Church, killed himself leaving the note: "All work and no play isn't
worth it. Ruth [his wife] is the finest of mortals . . . all her life is
spent for others. I thought I was tough but a man (or a woman)
can take just so many adversities. Goodbye sweetheart; see you in
heaven" (*Tulsa World,* April 19, 1943). Allegedly the man had not
suffered any obvious adversities, had no domestic, financial, or
health worries. He was not a social isolate or an economic failure,
and was still relatively young—forty-nine. The press described him
as a "bluff, hearty man with hundreds of friends . . . a man of unfailing good humor and personal vigor, his suicide incredible." Who
knows what inner agony this man endured? Is there a more ruinous
obligation than to have to be a man of "unfailing good humor"—
what more explicit denial of reality?[10]

The "enveloped" person denies his dependence on others while
maintaining a superficial and manipulative sociability, traits which
equip him for success in the corporate structure. But the drive to the
top often leaves him emotionally desiccated. In 1939 a prominent
petroleum engineer, the editor of the *Oil and Gas Journal,* poisoned
himself. The notes he left seemed irrelevant on first reading but became significant for what they *failed* to say.

One read:

> To whom it May Concern—Please notify Mrs. Catron at the
> Catron Drug Store, 910 W. Admiral Blvd., telephone
> 2-1947, of my act and ask her to inform Dorothy (my
> daughter).

The only address I have of my son is care of radio station WLLD, 201 No. Wells Street, National Sales Office, Chicago, Ill.

Turn my body over to the R. A. McBirney Funeral Home. Please have a simple funeral with burial at Rose Hill, if possible.

Signed

————L. E. Bignell

P.S.: A statement of my financial affairs will be found in a loose leaf black covered book in the second right hand drawer in the little desk at my office at 209 Mideo Bldg.

A second note:

Dear Dorothy and Frank. A statement of my financial affairs is attached, in addition to the money there are 2 typewriters in the office. The small desk and chair also belong to me. There are some papers and pictures in the large desk that are mine.

In the 2 book cases in the office room 209 there are numerous books and literature. I should like for the technical books to be turned over to the technical department of the Tulsa Public Library. I should like for Roy L. Ginter to select such volumes as he may like for his files.

At my apartment 612 No. Osage Ave. are my personal effects. Use your own judgment as to what may be done with the clothing. This about completes the inventory of my effects. I do not have a will because it is not necessary if my affairs are settled according to the statement attached.

I am tired trying. I simply want the rest I cannot have in this world. Forgive me and may God succor and help you both to carry on.

Affectionately,
Father.

Another note:

You will all form your own opinions and believe what you want to believe regardless of the facts so why should I try to make any explanations of my acts.—Bignell.

Has it been absurd? . . . Sixty-three years . . . "A long fool's errand to the grave?" Bignell refuses to philosophize; he cannot bring his despair into consciousness. Nietzsche says the thought of suicide has saved many lives. Reflection on the infinite tragedy of death eases the finite pain of life. But Bignell does not think about death, only of the details of dying . . . what to do with the body . . . books . . . chairs . . . clothing. Not a Prince Hamlet but like Eliot's Prufrock:

> "Deferential . . .
> Politic, cautious, and meticulous."[11]

Rarely is the suicide a brooding metaphysician. But a young student enunciates what the less articulate seem to feel but cannot verbalize: "The things I have lived for are dead. My soul is dead; it is for me to join it" (*Tulsa Tribune,* Oct. 9, 1939).

The suicide is haunted by an undefined feeling of loss, a sentiment frequently stated, more often implied. After an automobile accident left him blind in one eye, a wealthy 46-year-old owner of a lakeside resort wrote: "Jean: This eye, loss of weight, loss of reason and other losses—too much, Bill" (*Tulsa World,* Nov. 15, 1947). But deeper than any physical loss is the sense of slipping, of losing control. "I've lost my nerve and just can't go on," wrote a 47-year-old civil engineer (*Tulsa Tribune,* June 17, 1939). Another engineer, aged 42, wrote: "I have worried too much about matters that were of no great importance and am losing my mind. I have felt myself slipping for some time and the nervous and mental stupor is more than I can bear" (*Tulsa World,* July 1, 1940).

In the fiercely competitive "oil culture" of Tulsa, "slipping" is an irreversible disaster; failures seldom get a second try. For the "enveloped" personality, loss of status is tantamount to loss of self. In 1940 a once-wealthy independent oil producer named Holmes shot himself, explaining, "Financial reverses—that's all." But his biography contains a deeper story. In 1920 he sold his seat on the New York Stock Exchange, came to Tulsa for the oil boom. In 1927 he was severely injured in an oil rig explosion which killed two of his workers. Finally, wiped out by the recession of 1937, he moved to San Antonio, Texas. But he returned to the scene of the old oil derrick for the last act, left a note which read: "On this spot 17 years ago nature tried what I am going to try—nature muffed—hope I don't" (*Tulsa World,* Sept. 16, 1940). Like Melville's Captain Ahab, who would "strike the sun if it insulted me," Holmes, in pursuit of the ever elusive "black whale" of oil, scored a final triumph over nature by his act of self-annihilation. Defiant to the end, Holmes alone made the final choice, and by killing the body preserved the self, refusing to be dragged down to the psycho-social death of economic ruin.

Is the reason for suicide present adversity or past deficiency; external crisis or internal failure? Posed as an either/or the question is unanswerable. In the long, convoluted, always bewildering chain of causation which ends in self-murder the external and the internal are inextricably bound. "Purely" external factors as remote as sunspots, barometric pressure, and seasonal change exert a "precipitating" influence on suicide. And certain social forces are as external as the weather.

Forced to quit work at age 65, men often develop emotional and physical disorders simply as a result of idleness. Some retired men in our study—one an office worker, another an oil pumper—who worked for one company for over 40 years, broke apart when their jobs were over. Retirement was an endless Sunday afternoon. But in other cases retirement may be an effect rather than a cause; not company policy but some other difficulty compels the independent businessman or farmer to give up his work.

Loss of a love-object, grief over the death of a spouse, sometimes appear as a purely external cause of suicide. Explaining she has "quit living" since the death of her husband, a 36-year-old housewife wrote her sister, "I am going to ask your forgiveness. I have tried to live since he died but find it impossible. It is the only way out" (*Tulsa World,* Oct. 6, 1942). Had he lived, would she have found some other reason to kill herself? Who knows? But in most cases not loss through death but separation motivates the suicide. "I can't live without you," a 23-year-old bar-maid writes her ex-husband. "I'd rather be dead or in hell or anywhere" (*Tulsa World,* Nov. 19, 1943).

Not the external condition as an objective reality but the subjective definition of the situation determines human action. Loss of work—unemployment—seems occasionally to be a cause of suicide. But in 1940 Tulsa had an official unemployment rate of 10 per cent of the labor force; during the 1940's the rate dropped to 2 per cent; until 1956 it remained under 5 per cent. Yet the working class suicide-rate is relatively constant over the years 1937-56. Professional and managerial workers, on the other hand, show a rate of 65 per 100,000 for the 1937-42 period as opposed to a 20-year average of 35 per cent. For the worker the depression meant fear—the tangible threat of physical deprivation—while the business class faced the anxiety of status-loss. The meaning of the loss is determined by the subculture of the "actor." In the 1930's a man who once dealt in oil royalties is peddling novelties and silk hosiery. Trying for a comeback and failing, he writes a former business associate, "As you know, there is only one thing for me to do. I made a grave error. There is no chance for me here now" (*Tulsa Tribune,* May 28, 1941). When the factory closes and a lathe-operator is "thrown out of work," he does not attribute his unemployment to his own "grave error." Men can endure necessity if it is not of their own making.

Consider again our Mr. Holmes. He is broke but not destitute. Once the president of Holmes Oil Company and a member of the stock exchange, he could surely locate a clerical or janitorial job. But how can he live in the oil world—the only world he knows—and not be reminded of *his* failure? Holmes and his reference group define his bankruptcy as a self-created calamity. While he had no more control of the laws of the market in 1937 than the laws of nature, which exploded his oil derrick in 1927, he is socialized to assume responsibility for what happens to him. To reach the top a man must display supreme and fanatical self-confidence, he must shape the outer world to suit his inner will. If he sees his rise as due to his own effort, how then can he blame his fall on anyone else? The rules of capitalist individualism dictate self reliance. Holmes does not make the rules; they come to him from outside, an external agency molding his conduct. But the rules are also inside, they constitute the structural beams of the self. Without the rules the self collapses, anxiety sets in. No one can live for long without an identity. Unable to act as an oil man, Holmes chooses an active death over a passive survival as clerk or peddler. As a suicide he is still dominant and defiant.

The self-murder of any particular person remains forever a mystery. Was Holmes a suicidal personality, acting out some demonic death-wish? Had he weathered his "financial reverses" would he then have invented some other pretext to justify his self-destruction? Who knows? Suicides like automobile accidents can be predicted on an actuarial basis, but no individual suicide can be anticipated. Even the suicide attempt is a poor predictor of actual suicide. Pokorny followed up 617 attempts over a 14-year period and found only 3.4 per cent finally killed themselves; Stengel and Cook estimate 10 per cent of those who do kill themselves have made previous attempts.[12] How many men look into the abyss and finally, like Hamlet, turn back?

Unlike Hamlet, the real suicide is not concerned about hell; he has been there already. Death has to be an improvement. The Tulsa notes are devoid of religious speculation, except for occasional references to the hereafter. "No one responsible except myself," writes a 34-year-old welder, "I hold no enmity against anyone. If there is a heaven and hereafter, I may find it, who knows?" (*Tulsa World*, May 4, 1951). A little enmity might have saved the man's life, aroused the anger which would have driven the organism into action and thus banished anxiety. Usually the suicide wants to take full credit for his act; seldom does he blame anyone else for his failure; rarely can he express, or experience, anger. He sees himself as having made a mess of his life, or says, "I guess I just should never have been born" (*Tulsa World,* June 7, 1955). A middle-aged laboratory technician attributed his suicide to a raw deal from an oil company, but concluded the note with a surprisingly mild castigation: "If American oil companies do people like they do me, God will not continue to bless them" (*Tulsa World,* Nov. 2, 1948). The company is not defined as an exploiter but a "God-blessed" institution, and therefore immune to criticism and attack.

The whole institutional apparatus of contemporary culture—corporations, governments, churches, schools—is devoted to the pacification of the aggressive impulses through the inculcation of a belief in the benevolence of the existing social order. Thus conflict is minimized and anxiety maximized. Since he seldom confronts an institution which decisively opposes him, the person has nothing to press against, to protest, to overthrow. Hence he loses perspective on the object world as a reality separate from the subject world, the self. "Awareness of the boundaries between self and object," says Rollo May, "is precisely what breaks down in anxiety."[13] Here too is the ultimate anomie—boundlessness.

4

Danger, anxiety, and courage: suicide, black and white

> Man prefers to abandon life when it is least difficult
> EMILE DURKHEIM, *Suicide*

Danger activates the organism. When life is jeopardized, man embraces it with total passion. In the duress of war the suicidal tendency subsides. Coal miners, who work in constant danger, exhibit the lowest suicide rate of any occupational group. In German concentration camps suicide was less frequent than in the general population, and neurotic and psychosomatic disorders disappeared.[1] In America, blacks have a substantially lower suicide rate than whites.

Anxiety is both the triggering mechanism and the predisposing condition for suicide. Anxiety depletes the emotional reserves and produces the nervous exhaustion which gives rise to the will to die. The decision to die alleviates anxiety.

Anxiety is the product of anomie, of the experience of the unstructured. Even the animal manifests anxiety when placed in a milieu where it is unable to react to stimuli in an ordered way. The organism can meet fear directly either by attack or flight, but anxiety is a formless threat without precise location. "We can look at the cause of the fear which actually lies spatially before us," writes Kurt Goldstein, "[but] anxiety attacks us from the rear, so to speak. The only thing we can do is to attempt to flee from it without knowing where to go, because we experience it as coming from no particular place." Fear mobilizes the person, compels a rational contact with the outer world, sharpens perception. "Whereas anxiety paralyzes the senses and renders them unusable, fear drives them into action."[2]

Danger converts anxiety into fear which can be met with courage, bringing self-affirmation. "The immediate actual danger has anxiety reducing power," says Paul Tillich. "It produces courage instead of neurosis. Neurosis develops if one cannot come to grips with the source of danger, with the threat of non-being."[3] Concentration-camp victims were often able to bear enormous physical stress, and in spite of malnutrition showed great resistance to sickness and exhaustion. Edgar Trautman reports the case of one simple woman who explained her endurance by saying, "Fear gave me the strength." Living in persistent fear of death does not diminish the desire to live, writes Trautman. "It rather stimulates the urge for survival and makes the daily struggle for life the purpose of life itself."[4]

White culture, anxiety-ridden, forces the black to live in fear. To survive, blacks develop courage and solidarity. Friendship ties are stronger in the black than the white community, according to Prudhomme's 1938 study, and persecution has created a "social oneness" which diminishes the self-destructive impulses.[5] As the protagonist in Ralph Ellison's *Invisible Man* explains, all blacks are kinsmen because "we were burned in the same oven."[6] For four centuries the black in America has lived in almost daily confrontation with the existential challenge: not only to survive physically but to prevail psychologically in a society which defines him as a pariah. Acceptance of the culture's definition of Negro would destroy him; resistance to the dominant society may have given life a meaning it lacks for the white. Jean-Paul Sartre describes a similar situation in France in 1942:

> We were never more free than during the German occupation. We had lost all our rights, beginning with the right to talk. Everyday we were insulted to our faces and had to

take it in silence . . . Everywhere . . . we encountered
the revolting and insipid picture of ourselves that our op-
pressors wanted us to accept. And because of this we were
free. Because the Nazi venom seeped even into our
thoughts, every accurate thought was a conquest . . . And
the choice that each of us made of his life and of his
being was an authentic choice because it was made face to
face with death.[7]

By body count the Germans are still ahead, but no *single* act of
Nazi cruelty surpasses the savagery of the southern white. As late as
1916 a black was burned at the stake in downtown Waco, Texas (a
city of 100,000 people), and burnings in the rural areas of the South
continued into the 1930's. Between 1859 and 1959, some 5000
blacks were illegally executed, thousands more were killed with due
process of law, and perhaps nearly 100,000 were murdered with im-
punity. Blacks were lynched for every conceivable "offense"—killing
a cow, refusing to dance on command of a white man, "leering" at
a white woman, testifying in court in support of a black defendant.
Burning was a frequent form of lynching, and even Southerners con-
ceded the uncanny courage of the victim. Consider the rather typical
case reported by the *Kissimmee Valley (Florida) Gazette* of April
28, 1899:

SAM HOLT BURNED AT STAKE

Fully 2,000 people surrounded the small sapling to which
he was fastened and watched the flames eat away his flesh,
saw his body mutilated by knives and witnessed the con-
tortions of his body in his extreme agony.

Such suffering has seldom been witnessed, and through it
all the negro uttered hardly a cry. Those who witnessed
the affair saw the negro meet his death and saw him tortured before the flames with unfeigning satisfaction.

Holt went to the stake with as much courage as anyone
could possibly have possessed on such an occasion and the
only murmur that issued from his lips was when angry

knives plunged into his flesh and his life's blood sizzled in the fire before his eyes.

Then he cried, "Oh, my God! Oh, Jesus."

Masks played no part in the lynching. There was no secrecy; no effort to prevent anyone seeing who lighted the fire, who cut off the ears or who took the head.

Not even the bones of the negro were left in peace, but were eagerly snatched by a crowd of people drawn from all directions, who almost fought over the burning body of the man, carving it with their knives seeking souvenirs of the occurrence.

On the trunk of a tree nearby was pinned the following placard, "We must protect our southern women."[8]

Still the black race survived, even flourished—does the higher fecundity of blacks indicate an unconscious life-maintaining effort generated by the threat of death? Noting the rise of the European birth rate in World Wars I and II, Raymond Aron said, "The anguish of disasters revived the will to live."[9] The principle seems universal to the biological world: under adverse conditions organisms multiply more rapidly than in lax or easy circumstances.[10]

Adversity may have given the black a durable identity, enabling him to withstand strains that break the white. During World War II military rejections for psychological reasons were 50.3 per 1000 blacks and 70.6 per 1000 whites.[11] Jaco's thorough study shows whites in Texas have a mental disorder rate twice as high as that of blacks.[12] Alcoholism rates are nearly twice as high for whites as for blacks.[13] Kardiner and Oversey speak of a deep scar left on the black psyche by the caste system and wonder how far their findings would also apply to the lower-class white, adding that "the situation of the latter cannot possibly be as bad."[14] However, the suicide situation is worse: in Tulsa white unskilled workers have a rate of 38 per 100,000, semi-skilled workers, 20 per 100,000. as opposed to a total black suicide rate of 4 per 100,000.

Throughout the twentieth century, black Americans have had a

Table 5. Suicide Rate per 100,000 for Nonwhites and Whites in the
United States, 1949 to 1963*

| | Nonwhite | | White | |
	Male	Female	Male	Female
1949-51**	6.1	1.5	18.5	5.3
1955	6.1	1.5	17.2	4.9
1956	6.1	1.6	16.9	4.8
1957	6.8	1.4	16.5	4.6
1958	7.0	1.8	18.0	5.1
1959	7.4	1.9	17.8	5.0
1960	7.6	1.9	17.1	5.3
1961	7.2	1.9	17.6	5.3
1962	7.2	2.2	17.8	5.9
1963	7.9	2.2	17.8	6.3

* From Table 1-20, Deaths and Death Rate for Each Cause by Color and
Sex: United States, *Vital Statistics of the United States,* Vol. II–Mortality,
Part A (Washington: U.S. Department of Health, Education and Welfare, for
years listed.

** Data for 1949-51 from Jack Gibbs, and Walter Martin, *Suicide and Status
Integration* (Eugene: University of Oregon Press, 1964), 62.

suicide rate substantially lower than that of any other ethnic group.
Table 5 shows the suicide rates for white and nonwhites between
1919 and 1948. The nonwhite population of the country is composed of 19 million blacks and 1.5 million others. Other nonwhites
have a lower rate than the white population but higher than the
black population: in 1959 the suicide rates per 100,000 were:
American Indian 11.5, Chinese 13.1, and Japanese 6.9.[15] In the
Deep South the black rate is around 2 compared with 10 for whites;
in the northern states the Negro rate is two to three times higher
than in the South, though still lower than the white rate. The nonwhite rate in the northern cities is not substantially higher than in
the southern cities. Consider the following rates per 100,000 taken
from Dublin's recent work:[16]

By selected states:

	Total	White	Nonwhite
Alabama	7.5	9.9	2.0
Mississippi	7.0	10.3	2.4
Georgia	9.4	12.1	2.7
Louisiana	8.2	10.7	3.0
New York	9.7	10.0	6.0
Illinois	9.6	10.2	3.8

By selected cities:

	White	Nonwhite
Houston	13.9	4.6
Atlanta	16.0	3.2
Birmingham	17.0	4.4
Baltimore	13.1	4.6
New Orleans	8.2	1.7
Cleveland	14.1	4.0
Los Angeles	19.9	10.3*
Philadelphia	12.8	5.6
Detroit	14.1	3.9
San Francisco	30.6	6.6
New York	10.2	6.7
Chicago	11.5	3.6

* Possibly due to large Chinese and Japanese population, classified as non-white.

The nonwhite suicide rate appears to increase in the 1950-63 period. as Table 5 indicates. But national census data must be taken lightly. Martin Gold's rates on nonwhite suicide in the 1930's are approximately the same as the official rate of the 1950-63 years.[17]

In the northern cities it appears that blacks under age 35 have a suicide rate comparable with that of whites of the same age range, but the black rate in later life declines while the white rate increases. Ronald Maris has assembled interesting data on Chicago, as presented in Table 6. Dublin's national data do not disclose quite so sharp a drop of the nonwhite rate with age as Maris's data suggest. But our data from Tulsa indicate that suicidal acts—both completed and attempted suicide—cluster very much in the under 40 population.

Table 6. Suicide Rates per 100,000 Population by Sex, Age, and Race, Cook County, Illinois, 1959-1963*

| | Males | | Females | |
	White	Nonwhite	White	Non-white
Age	White	Nonwhite	White	Non-white
0-14	–	–	–	–
15-24	6.4	5.1	2.2	3.7
25-34	10.9	11.7	6.2	–
35-44	14.8	11.0	7.4	4.4
45-54	22.5	–	8.6	3.6
55-64	28.2	–	7.9	–
65-74	36.7	–	8.6	–
75-84	52.0	–	9.4	–
85 and over	61.6	–	–	–

* Source: Bureau of Statistics, Illinois Department of Public Health, Springfield, Illnois. From Ronald Maris, "Suicide in Chicago: An Examination of Emile Durkheim's Theory of Suicide" (Unpublished Study, 1966), 118.

Table 7. Suicide by Sex and Race for Adult Population of Tulsa Metropolitan Area, Oklahoma, 1937-1956[a]

| | Actual Suicide | | | Attempted Suicide[b] | | | Rate Difference |
	No.	Pop.	Rate per 100,000	No.	Pop.	Rate per 100,000	Per cent of Attempt over Actual
White Male	316	81,178	18.8	293	75,788	20.3	7.9
White Female	103	89,207	5.7	537	82,041	33.9	494.
Negro Male	6	6,801	4.4	12	6,331	10.0	127.
Negro Female	1	8,332	0.6	55	7,600	38.1	6,250.
	426			897			

[a] Population statistics from U.S. Department of Commerce, *Sixteenth Census of the United States: 1940, Population,* Vol. II, Part 5; and *Seventeenth Census of the United States: 1950, Population,* Vol. II, Part 36 (Washington: U.S. Government Printing Office, 1952), 200-201; 244.

[b] Data from Tulsa Police Files include only reported attempts of those living within city limits; therefore, base population is smaller than for actual suicides. Attempts cover only the years 1938-1956.

Table 8. Female Attempted Suicides,* 1938-1956

| | White | | Black | |
Age	No.	Per cent of Total	No.	Per cent of Total
15-24	157	32.7	23	53.4
25-34	146	30.4	17	39.5
35-44	98	20.4	1	2.3
45-54	53	11.0	1	2.3
55-64	19	3.9	0	0.
65 & Over	7	1.4	1	2.3
	480	99.8	43	99.8

* Fifty-seven white and 12 black attempts were of unknown age.

Data from Tulsa between 1937 and 1956 show a white male rate of 18.8 contrasted with a black male rate of 4.4. Only one black woman killed herself during this period, but there were at least 55 Negro female attempts as opposed to 12 black male attempts (see Table 8). Suicide attempt data from the files of the police department are highly unreliable because of under-reporting. Still it is of interest to note that of those reported, 94 per cent of the black female attempts as opposed to 63 per cent of the white female attempts occur before the age of 35, as shown in Table 8. The overall statistical configuration of suicidal acts by age, sex, and race for Tulsa is given in Figure 2, a picture quite similar to the national pattern.[18]

Suicide is clearly related to the life cycle: points of age-status transition—from youth to adulthood, from maturity to old age—are times of anomie, where the old rules of conduct no longer apply and new ones have not yet been crystallized. But the crisis of aging has a different meaning for whites and blacks, men and women.

Suicidal behavior makes an abrupt appearance around the age of 13; we discovered only one case of attempted suicide prior to that age. However, at the age of 13 three suicides occurred, and thereafter both attempts and suicides increased for both races and both sexes. Although it is impossible to compute rates by yearly age cate-

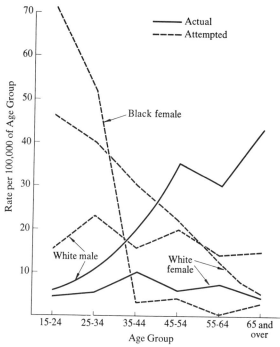

Figure 2. Attempted and Actual Suicides, by Age, Sex, and Race, Tulsa, 1936-1956

gory, Table 9 gives the frequency distribution of adolescent suicidal acts.

Self-destruction presupposes self-awareness. The self is always in the process of formation, but true self-consciousness dawns, rather traumatically, with adolescence. And with puberty comes the "statistically sudden" onset of suicide. We examined the records of 1327 attempted and actual suicides in Tulsa and found only one case under age 13. If suicidal behavior had a gradual onset one would expect to find at least a few cases scattered through the earlier years.[19]

What happens during adolescence, this "infancy of our higher nature," as G. Stanley Hall called it? Gerth and Mills see adolescence,

44   SUICIDE

Table 9. Frequency of Recorded Adolescent Suicidal Acts, Tulsa, 1937-1956

Age	Black Attempts Male	Female	Black Actual Male	Female	White Attempts Male	Female	White Actual Male	Female
0-12	0	0	0	0	0	0	0	0
13		1					3	
14	0	0			1			
15		1				7	1	
16		5			3	7	1	1
17		3			3	14	2	
18		4			2	18	2	
19		2		1	2	27		3
20	1	1	2		4	16		
21					6	16	6	3
TOTAL	1	17	2	1	21	105	15	7

not childhood, as the most important period in the life history of the person in our society.[20] Not until the age of 12 to 14 does the person become fully aware of himself as an object. Self-consciousness is itself a source of anxiety, and makes possible a new and qualitatively different response to the "primordial anxiety" laid down by earlier experience.[21] The young child can either blindly rebel or silently suffer, but he cannot envisage eliminating the self as a solution for his distress.

The crisis of adolescence is both biological and cultural. Sexuality brings the urgent necessity to interact with another human being, a situation filled with psychic peril. In addition the person must, through willful effort, establish an orientation to an adult world which has not yet been experienced.

Adolescence is anomie: a veritable status-wilderness. Impelled to act but bereft of meaningful rules to follow, the self is flooded with anxiety. Typically, the male "acts out"; the female "acts in." The aggressive behavior of the delinquent boy is often a quest for danger, an effort to win his "red badge of courage." Male delinquency rates for both black and white are several times higher, and attempted suicide rates several times lower, than female rates. Sexuality entails new responses for which the past offers no reliable precedent, a threat which may stimulate regression.[22] In attempting suicide, the young woman makes herself helpless in order to elicit help. Statistics indicate a sharp drop in female attempts once the turmoil of coming of age is worked through in the early twenties.

While the anomie of adolescence bears equally hard on the white and black female—judged by the statistics of our study—the menopausal trauma appears to be unique to the white woman. Suicidal acts for black females do not increase in middle life. The identity of the white woman is built on the wife-mother role, and when children grow up and leave home she is rendered obsolete, with a resulting rise in both suicide and mental disorder rates.[23] Like her counterpart in folk society, the black woman passes from the role of mother to grandmother, escaping the despair of uselessness. In the southern Negro family, says Frazier, "the grandmother is often more important than the mother."[24] Even in the northern urban family the grandmother is a common feature and can "always earn her keep as caretaker and nurse for the grandchildren, though the aged father is much less welcome."[25] Even so, the black male handles old age better than the white—if the suicide rate is an index. The white male rate increases steadily throughout life, and sharply around 65, while the black male rate appears to decline in later years.

Adolescence is suicidiogenic for white males but not for black males (see Table 9). Fully 90 per cent of the young (under 21) male suicides in Tulsa were from middle- or upper-class families. Usually they were model-boy types, not delinquents: one was an Eagle Scout; several were outstanding students; one was a fraternity pledge; most of those aged 17 to 21 were college students. Few had experienced dire deprivation; many were victims of parental overprotection. A 17-year-old after a week away at college returned to

Tulsa afflicted with homesickness and killed himself as "the only way to avoid further anguish to my parents" (*Tulsa Tribune,* Sept. 15, 1938). A 21-year-old recent Yale graduate shot himself "at his palatial family home," immediately after returning from a ride in the convertible his grandfather had given him as a graduation present (*Tulsa World,* Aug. 4, 1953). Privileges of status may deprive the person of the opportunity to test himself and develop the competence for coping with hard realities.

The anomie of ostensibly favored youth is captured by the Japanese novelist, Osamu Dazai, who killed himself at the age of 38. "I have never known . . . 'hunger,' " says the protagonist of *No Longer Human.* When asked what he wants his first impulse is always to answer, "Nothing." People tell him how lucky he is, but he himself feels like he is suffering in hell. He would even prefer prison to "groaning away sleepless nights in hellish dread of the 'realities of life.' " He feels his unhappiness stems "entirely from my own vices," and that he has no way of fighting anybody. "If I had ever attempted to voice anything in the nature of a protest, even a single mumbled word, the whole society . . . would undoubtedly have cried out flabbergasted, 'imagine the audacity of him talking like that.' "[26] David Reisman speaks of the neurotic as one whose life is *insufficiently* complicated,[27] who therefore creates crises in order to have a battle to fight and hence a reason for living. The suicide may conjure up the ordeal of death because there is no other *definable* complication in his life.

Black people in America are compelled to live with clear and present complications. The lot of the black is hard, but he can legitimately blame society for his suffering. His crime, says Helen McLean, "lies in being born a Negro . . . fate (an impersonal situation) and not he, is responsible. Therefore the guilt of his hostility can be externalized."[28] The enemy is outside the ego, like an enemy in war.

Because blacks live in a world of objective danger, they can ill afford the luxury of self-deception. After observing the South, the psychiatrist Robert Coles was surprised that the extreme hardship of the Negroes' lot produced so little emotional illness. The Negro cannot flee danger, Coles writes, "danger is everywhere, a never ending consequence of his social and economic condition." Coles found that Negro children were often lonely, isolated, and afraid, "but they knew exactly what they feared, and exactly how to be as safe as possible in the face of what they feared." In the end the children seemed to gain "an abiding, often tough sense of what is about them in the world, and what must be in them to survive. Survival required facing reality. "You can't run away from being black," Coles was told.[29] Constantly faced with the antagonism of the surrounding society, the Negro does not have the opportunity to forget who he is.

By contrast, the white person is often encouraged to be other than he is, enticed into a world of make-believe. White culture not only permits but recommends "running away"—flight and denial—as a primary adaptation to threat. The white is victimized by the American dream, by the pursuit of an ever receding happiness; he grows impatient with frustration and intolerant of pain. For the white, the prospect of future improvement makes the actual present more difficult to bear, while the black learns, in Durkheim's words, "that certain sorrows can be endured only by being embraced."[30] Of course these sweeping generalizations do not apply to all blacks or all whites and are made merely to suggest that differences in value orientation in the two sub-cultures may have a bearing on the suicide rate.

Historically, blacks in America have been less suicidal than whites. The difference is a function of the social situation, not ethnicity. The black bourgeoisie experiences the same anomie as the white.[31] Today in the northern cities the black suicide rate approximates the white rate as conditions of equality are approached. In Mississippi the white rate is five times the black rate (10 as opposed to 2 per 100,000), while in New York the ratio is 10 to 6; in Chicago the rate is the same for black and white males under 30. Usually the greater the hostility toward a group the lower its suicide rate will be. Jews in nineteenth-century Europe living in a climate of anti-

Semitism were substantially less suicidal than Christians. Members of oppressed minorities have to develop ego-strength, to withstand the derogation of the dominant majority, a strength which confers a certain immunity to suicide, and presumably other anxiety disorders. "Misfortune has its uses," says Schopenhauer, "for, as our bodily frame would burst asunder if the pressure of the atmosphere were removed, so, if the lives of men were relieved of all need, hardship and adversity; if everything they took in hand were successful, they would be so swollen with arrogance that, though they might not burst, they would present the spectacle of unbridled folly—nay they would go mad."[32]

PART TWO

THE CITY

Mind takes form in the city; and in turn urban forms condition mind . . . the city records the attitude of a culture
and an epoch to the fundamental facts of its existence.
. . . With language itself, it remains man's greatest work
of art.

LEWIS MUMFORD, *The Culture of Cities*

5

The city: matrix of civilization

> The present is saturated with the past and pregnant with
> the future.
>
> LEIBNITZ

The city is both a symbol of hope and sign of failure. To St. Augustine heaven is the City of God, while to Shelley, "hell is a city much like London." Throughout history the city appears in this dual aspect, at once sublime and sinister.

The first cities were sacred places where men gathered for worship, according to Fustel de Coulanges. The formation of the city was not a commercial enterprise but a religious act: "Every city was a sanctuary; every city might be called holy."[1] Out of the city grew the high culture of the ancient world. "Reason and reflective thinking were born in the city," writes R. E. Park, "They came, if not into existence, at least into vogue, in Athens."[2] The ancient city was a total community: a religious nucleus, a political union, a center for social intercourse. Socrates preferred urban life to the empty countryside because, as he said, "Men are my teachers." Socrates was "unmistakably an urban man," says Alvin Gouldner, "His philosophy was one of the first real fruits of urban civilization."[3] The city is the matrix—the term derives from the Latin for "womb"—of civilization.

51

But the city is also a cesspool of corruption and cruelty. The Judeo-Christian conception of the city from the first Biblical denunciations of the whore of Babylon to the twentieth century is summarized by the Reverend Josiah Strong: "The first city was built by the first murderer Cain, and crime and vice and wretchedness have festered in it ever since."[4]

If civilization begins with the city and the extrication of man from the confinements of communal life, it often ends there too, with a depletion of the vital energies of a people. Lewis Mumford, following Patrick Geddes, outlines six stages in the genesis and decline of the city. First the village, or *eo-polis,* grows into the town, *polis,* an association of villages. Then comes the city proper, the mother-city or *metropolis,* with a maximum release of cultural energy as in Platonic Athens, Dantean Florence, Shakespearean London, Emersonian Boston. But with the metropolis comes "an individualism that tends to disrupt old social bonds without creating new order on a higher plane"; the city fails to absorb and integrate disparate cultural elements. Thus the stage is set for the *megalopolis,* swollen out of all human proportion, with "industry divorced from life utility; life itself compartmentalized, dispecialized, finally disorganized and enfeebled." Consensus destroyed, the city resorts to coercion in an "attempt to recreate order by external military [and police] means" —hence the fifth stage, *tyrannopolis,* followed inexorably by *necropolis,* the city of the dead.[5]

Since the 1930's, when Mumford wrote, the downward cycle has continued. In his 1969 campaign for mayor of New York, Norman Mailer said:

> Our cities, close to inoperative, heavy, sullen, dangerous as wads of oil soaked rags, wait for conflagration and massive applications of law and order which will produce sabotage and underground movements in reaction. The spectre of a hundred cities as corrupt, as occupied as Saigon is near to us. The condition of civil war is near to us. Yes, the economic condition of this country is kin to a junkie who de-

pends on the military industrial complex for a fix. So, just as the children of an addict wither or run wild, so do cities accelerate into their poverty, their rebellions, and their ongoing sense of dread.[6]

Megalopolis——→Tyrannopolis——→Necropolis. Population grows beyond manageable proportions; the self-regulating community breaks down; official force and threats are used to maintain law and order which in turn generate counter-force, lethal conflict, further alienation. Those who can, flee the city, as in Rome in the fifth century A.D.; the rest remain to riot and rot. Pointing to the decline of the birth rate in the late nineteenth century, Oswald Spengler says the "last man of the world-city" does not care to reproduce because he "no longer wants to live," has taken a "metaphysical turn toward death."[7] The phenomenon can be explained without recourse to mysticism. Under the stress of extreme overcrowding even animal populations lose fertility and become violent. If confined at densities greater than they are prepared to tolerate, guppies will attack and eat one another—a virtual fratricide. Toads can survive years of captivity when kept under conditions in which they do not see each other too much, but when crowded they actually starve to death in the presence of an abundance of food—as V. C. Wynne-Edwards points out in a chapter significantly entitled, "Socially Induced Mortality."[8] In an essay which decisively influenced both Oswald Spengler and R. E. Park, Georg Simmel argued that the "intensification of nervous stimulation" which inevitably accompanied urbanization undermined the "sensory foundations of psychic life."[9] In the small town one responds to almost everyone else with some kind of emotion and feeling; in the city it is necessary to disengage, develop a reserved and blasé attitude in order to preserve the psyche. Norman Mailer describes New Yorkers as they "push through acrid lung-rotting air and work their way home, avoiding each other's eyes in the subway."[10] Often we hear of people assaulted in full view of bystanders who fail to lift a hand to help the victim. Simmel saw this deliberate indifference to others as characteristic of urban life.

. . . the nerves find in the refusal to react to their stimulation the last possibility of accommodating to the contents
and forms of metropolitan life. The self-preservation of certain personalities is bought at the price of devaluating the
whole objective world, a devaluation which in the end un-
avoidably drags one's own personality down into a feeling
of the same worthlessness.[11]

Following the lead of Simmel and Durkheim (in the *Division of
Labor*), American sociologists turned to demography and ecology
for an explanation of the nature of urban life. Park thought of the
ecological process as shaping the cultural superstructure of urban society: "The organization of the city, the character of the urban environment and of the discipline which it imposes is finally determined
by the size of the population, its concentration and distribution
within the city area."[12] Drawing on Park, Simmel, and Durkheim,
Louis Wirth reasoned that "as the number of people interacting
[dynamic density] increase, social relations become superficial and
segmentalized" imparting a "schizoid character" to the urban man.[13]
Density necessitates a division of labor, thus diminishing the area
of shared experience, while the sheer number of social contacts
precludes the intimacy of rural life. Men move in and through a variety of social circles, never deeply involved in any of them. "No
single group has the undivided allegiance of the individual," says
Wirth. Since men live amongst strangers, moral sanctions lose their
meaning.[14] The anonymity and transience of urban life engenders a
sophisticated and calculating self-centeredness. Tradition breaks
down, and the removal of communal restraints on exploitative behavior leaves men to survive or perish in a ruthless, individuated
struggle for existence. Kingsley Davis reiterates the Park-Wirth
thesis: when the city is too large to be a primary group, secondary
social controls emerge with "an atomization of the constituent individuals" of the urban world.[15] The demographic-ecological theory
can be represented schematically as follows:

$$\text{dynamic density} \longrightarrow \begin{bmatrix} \text{division of labor} \\ \text{HETEROGENEITY} \\ \text{mobility} \end{bmatrix} \longrightarrow \text{anonymity} \longrightarrow \text{anomie}$$

Still the demographic-ecological framework has never proved completely satisfactory as an explanation of the urban way of life. The theory is culture-bound, for it assumes all cities correspond to the American model. Moreover, the conceptual scheme of ecology contains serious logical contradictions, as Ruth Alihan has shown.[16] Finally, the definitive work of Walter Firey demonstrates that the "laws" of ecology are not "natural" but cultural phenomena, the product of social institutions.[17] In a chapter on "localized anomie" Firey shows that the deterioration of communal and kinship solidarity, typical of the American city, is a function of the economic system rather than urbanism as such. Furthermore, Firey sees the economic order itself as the product of the value system of a contractural society. Far from being an independent variable, the ecological complex is itself the creation of an institutional matrix. For instance, the medieval city built around the institution of Catholicism had a different spatial pattern and social life than the American city structured mainly around the institutions of capitalism.[18]

Sociology, by focusing on the visible, "geophysical" aspects of the urban environment, is describing effects rather than analyzing causes. As Don Martindale puts it in a brilliant preface to Max Weber's *The City*, ecological studies have established the properties of the various zones—natural areas, habitats—but paid little attention to the life that produced those properties: "An extraordinarily patient study was made of the scene of the crime, the criminal was largely ignored."[19] Still, Park always insisted the city was a "state of mind," not merely a collection of people or an assemblage of material things. To get at the institutional roots of the urban mentality it is essential to turn to history.

Science itself is historical, as Teggart says, "it seeks to explain how things come to be as they are."[20] Political science could not ac-

count for the conduct of, say, the United States Congress by studying only the behavior of congressmen in 1970. Some knowledge of
the past of Congress is required to understand its present action. But
urban sociology today is written as if the American city had no past
—and the product is "weary, flat, stale and unprofitable," except perhaps to professors and publishers. Several sociologists have written
on the pre-industrial city.[21] But the 25-page bibliography of the 1957
edition of the Hatt and Reiss *Reader in Urban Sociology* contains
scarcely a reference to the nineteenth-century American city. This is
especially unfortunate because the transition from a rural to an urban society began immediately after the Civil War and reached
fruition in the decisive period between 1890 and 1910, when the
"core culture" which has more or less prevailed in America since
then came into being.

The late Howard Becker worked out a typology of the Greek city
using what he called the "culture case study" method.[22] Despite the
relative abundance of historical data, sociologists have seldom attempted a case study of the American city. Historians, on the other
hand, have studied the city, but are hesitant about generalizing and
constructing typologies. The following three studies are an attempt
to deal in some detail with the evolution of the American city and
the emergence of anomie as seen in one city: Buffalo, New York.
Buffalo is only one case—but what occurred here occurred to a
greater or lesser degree throughout the American urban world.

Demographically, economically, and culturally Buffalo's development is typical of the American city. A mere village in 1810, a small
town by the 1830's, nearly a metropolis by mid-century, it spreads
out into a megalopolis in the twentieth century. Between 1810 and
1850 the population doubled each decade, growing from 1508 to
42,261 (Table 10, Chapter 6 gives data on growth since 1850). In
1900 the city numbered 352,387; by 1960 some 450,000 though the
metropolitan area (city + suburbs) contains over one million people. The first settlers were New Englanders moving west. In 1830
some 10 per cent of the population was foreign-born, of mainly Ger-

man and Irish stock. By 1860 nearly half the population was German—30,000. Polish immigration began in the 1880's and 1890's; Italians came in large numbers at the same time. By 1914 the foreign-born constituted one third of the population. The black population was negligible in the nineteenth century—between 500 and 1000; was about 2000 in 1910, grew to 5000 by 1920; 14,000 in 1930; 18,000 in 1940; 38,000 in 1950; and 73,000 in 1960. While Buffalo was once called a Polish city, there is today little to distinguish it from other heavy-industry centers of the Northeast. Pittsburgh, Cleveland, Detroit, and Chicago differ from Buffalo only in degree, not kind. The institutional forces which shape the city are translocal in character and produce an almost identical end-product. Even in the 1880's Lord Byrce observed that American cities differ from one another chiefly in that some are made of bricks and wood and others are made of wood and bricks.

The history of the nineteenth-century city, someone said, is the history of an illness. But as the following three chapters indicate, the city is more the victim than the source of the disorder.

6

The location of anomie: a culture case study of urbanization: Buffalo, New York, 1810-1910

Our home is in the city's dust and strife
From its too feverish air we breathe our life
Ours is no soft commune with field and sky,
Not ours in depth of summer wood to lie,
And take from Nature's ever lavish hand
The stores of pleasure there at our command
From all her life and bloom we dwell apart
The year's sweet fall, the coming of her springs,
All have the strange, sad feel of distant things.

DAVID GRAY, Buffalo poet and newspaper editor, 1873

The city embodies the profound contradictions of our time, a paradox of organized chaos, of regimented individualism. A monolith devoid of inner coherence, the city's "parts" seem unrelated to the whole. Lewis Mumford summed it up: "external regularity; internal disruption."[1] The fragmentation of the modern mind, reflected in art and philosophy as well as social pathology, is associated with urbanization.[2] In the city, says R. E. Park, "man gains his freedom but loses his direction"; urbanization "secularizes society and individuates the person." More a population aggregate than a community, the city is functionally integrated through the cash nexus, but there is "no communication and no consensus . . . human relations are symbiotic rather than social."[3] Anomie is the essence of urbanism as a way of life.

When the American city was young it imbibed the dreamy uto-pianism of the surrounding culture. Established as a trading post by the Holland Land Company in 1802, the village of Buffalo (pop. 1500) was burned by the British in 1813, grew to a population of 2000 by 1820, then quadrupled during the next decade after the completion of the Erie Canal in 1825. Buffalo was designed by Joseph Ellicott, who had assisted L'Enfant with the planning of Washington, D.C. Ellicott laid out the main streets as spokes radi-ating from a semicircular wheel. In the semicircle was his private es-tate, which he donated to the town as a public park. Ellicott gave the city valuable waterfront property upon which piers were to be built and rented at a profit to support city government and thus obviate the necessity for taxes—municipal socialism 75 years before the word came into currency. The city accepted Ellicott's gift, chopped up the estate and sold it to businessmen, ran gridiron streets across the basic radial design, producing a chaos of parallelograms and trapezoids, and allowed private interests to grab the waterfront. Far from having a source revenue, the city found itself paying rent to the pier-owners by the 1870's. In the 1860's a kinsman of Ellicott's lamented that "a little of our Yankee love of straight lines" could not have been allowed to give way to the wishes of a man "whose soul was bound up in the prosperity of this town . . . his name will not now be linked with the city."[4] But history is nothing if not ironic. By the 1950's the Ellicott district was a dense, decaying slum. Ellicott's end is emblematic of the fate of the visionary in America. Disillusioned by the rejection of his bold and imaginative plan for the city, he hanged himself in 1826. If he could see Buffalo today he would have no reason to regret his final act.

But the 1830's were confident years, when Tocqueville's happy republic still absorbed the morning sun.[5] The happy republic, like the dancing bear, did after all perform and, to the astonishment of the rest of the world, ordinary men proved capable of managing their ordinary lives.

When Harriet Martineau visited Buffalo in the 1830's she thought it the least desirable place of residence in the free states—"the very nostrils of hell."[6] But another English diarist, Captain Marryat, thought of the city of Buffalo as "one of the wonders of America— judiciously planned . . . with wide streets . . . lofty and substantial buildings, made of brick or granite . . . five or six very fine churches, a handsome theatre, a townhall, market, three or four hotels . . . a harbor full of shipping and magnificent steam boats."[7] Marryat, an English gentleman, noted that the "lower people" in Buffalo were much less civil in their behavior than their eastern counterparts, and "appear to think of rudeness as a proof of independence."[8]

During the 1830's, Marryat estimated a 100,000 newcomers passed through Buffalo each year, a third of them Europeans, the others were Americans coming from the east coast. "They poured westward like an army of locusts," said a Buffalo intellectual at the time, "to devour the broad acres of the national domain."[9] From this flood of pioneers derived the prosperity of the town. And from the beginning Buffalo, as the press proudly put it, was "imminently a business city."

> Everybody is actively engaged . . . there are no loungers or gentlemen loafers among our population. Every newcomer is warmly welcomed for all feel that there is room for more. [The motto] "Each man for himself, but all for Buffalo," has made us what we are. (Editorial, *Buffalo Commercial Advertiser,* May 11, 1837)

Although a commercial center, the city had a strong sense of social solidarity in the 1830's and '40's. Everyone knew virtually everyone else. "I recognized and was familiar with every person of all ages," writes one citizen of the time, "every dwelling and other building—and every brick in the pavements."[10] The mayor was expected to hold "open house for all comers" on New Year's Day;

housewives might borrow anything from "an egg to a piano" from a next-door neighbor. One writer speaks of the community as a "band of brothers and sisters"—doubtless an exaggeration. Nevertheless, both necessity and common values created a kind of mutual dependence which is seldom found in the contemporary city. Eight months of the year, from April to December, were devoted to business but the other four months of the ice-bound winter, writes a local resident, Mrs. Poole, "were quite generally given up to social enjoyment. . . . One never expected to be without several friends on any evening where there was not an important social affair taking place. . . . It was not uncommon to write three hundred or four hundred invitations to a party."[11] Mrs. Poole describes the society as "full of ceremony and courtly usage, at the same time quaintly provincial." By the mid-1830's the top people were beginning to put on airs—a source of amusement to a radical newspaper editor, Thomas Low Nichols, reporting on a ball for General Winfield Scott:

> All the aristocracy of Buffalo was there, and such an aristocracy . . . we counted four sons of blacksmiths, two peddlers, seven smugglers, nine brokers and brokers' clerks . . . a variety once glad to follow respectable professions as house painters, carpenters, tailors and bricklayers . . . [who now] turn up their noses at their grandfathers, their fathers, and even their former selves. (*The Buffalonian*, February 5, 1837)

Judging by the press—and other writing from the 1830's—a sizable portion of the population was quite articulate, widely read, and conversant with the leading ideas of the time. The bookstore was a center of intellectual life, and the public lectures at the Young Men's Association were a popular winter pastime. The simple but not uninteresting social life of the time is revealed in the diary of a young woman written in 1838:

> Jan. 1 . . . prepared for callers but need not have taken so much trouble for we only received about a dozen calls. . .

Jan. 8 . . . the reading society . . . Scott's Waverly novels.

Jan. 10 . . . lecture on the "The Progress of Literature in the 13th and 14th Century" . . . enough to make you go to sleep, you could scarsely understand what was said.

Jan. 14 . . . This morning we all went to Church . . . I went again this afternoon.

Jan. 17 . . . lecture at the YMA . . . on astronomy . . . at 2 a.m. a fire on Main Street . . . It was not a very grand fire and was soon extinguished.

Jan. 21 . . . I have attended church all day . . . met General Scott.

Jan. 24 . . . lecture on Animal Magnetism . . . crowded to overflowing . . . a number of audience were made converts . . . others considered it all a hoax.

Jan. 25 . . . a party.

Jan. 29 . . . a home burnt.

Jan. 30 . . . went shopping.

Feb. 2 . . . fireman's ball . . . General Scott and staff were there . . . not home until after 12.

Feb. 12 . . . to Mayville [nearby village] . . . beautiful sledding.

Apr. 19 . . . exhibition at church . . . scholars acquitted themselves well . . . crowded with spectators. Our Episcopal clergyman, Mr. Baldwin, was present and I fancied that he looked quite sober to see what a concourse of people any little novelty could congregate together, while with all his preaching he could scarsely get more . . . than a couple of pews.[12]

Of course there were outsiders, e.g. an anomic waterfront element who would scarcely find their way to the lectures of the Young Men's Association or the Episcopal church. But the open frontier siphoned off the transients and "riff-raff," and the resident population retained its democratic illusions of classlessness, thinking of itself as simple folk possessing that sense of equality which Tocqueville made the key to the American character.

The extremes of wealth and poverty were less pronounced than in subsequent decades. Few people lived off the unearned increment of capital; the owners of property were usually the managers of their holdings. Most establishments employed no more than twenty or so workers; manufacturing (ship-building, iron-working) was still a handicraft.[13] Like the merchant, the artisan served a small personally known clientele, and there is no record of serious and sustained labor trouble (though there were occasional riots). The workers, as Professor Horton comments, "were not aiming at working-class solidarity but tried rather through individual exertions to rise above their class and enter business or the professions."[14] Classes were not segregated ecologically; of the four residential wards of the city the assessed value of real estate was approximately the same in each— $2,500,000.[15] A businessman's "word was as good as his bond," and merchants freely borrowed money from one another when low on cash.[16] As late as 1840 the city council had no fixed time to meet; members simply gathered in a local tavern or hotel when there was business to be discussed. Buffalo had only one paid policeman until the mid-1840's and did not have a uniformed police force until 1866. Seemingly informal (primary group) control was sufficient to maintain order and carry on the business of the community (but more disorder could be tolerated in this early period, when the social structure still had a certain looseness about it).

Faith in man has seldom soared higher than in the three decades prior to the Civil War. Although preoccupied with commerce, Buffalonians always found time to reflect on the wonders of progress and the grandeur of democracy. A lecture on "Human Progress" at the Young Men's Association "brought out the largest and most intelligent auditory" of the season in 1848. The press felt the lecturer was absolutely right when he said "our race was growing wiser and better . . . and the plainest Bethel church and the humblest school house in our land, were evidence of a higher civilization than all the power which built up the Egyptian pyramids" (*Buffalo Morning Express,* Jan. 6, 1948). In June 1848 the mayor led a parade in support of Parisian revolutionaries, and on July 4th read the Declaration of Independence to the assembled citizenry of Buffalo. Mere mention of the word "democracy" triggered an inner exultation. When Zachary Taylor and Millard Fillmore (a Buffalo lawyer) were elected to the highest offices in the land in 1848 the *Express* could hardly contain itself:

> This is the coronation day of free men. On this day is presented a spectacle never before witnessed since the world began. Three million voters, representing more than 20 million free people are today engaged in the duty of selecting their head servants for years to come. The wildest dreams of ancient Republicanism never approached this sublime consummation. (*Buffalo Express,* Nov. 7, 1848)

America's demonic genius for self-deception was already preparing for its triumph. Millard Fillmore, Buffalo, and the rest of the country assumed the problem of slavery would vanish if no one thought about it. The editor of the *Express* did not permit himself to wonder about some ten million unfree blacks who were excluded from the "sublime consummation" of 1848. Fillmore insisted he did not believe in the equality of black and white; he opposed slavery not on moral grounds but only because it gave the South an unfair economic advantage. Nor did the spokesmen of the happy republic perceive the growth of a white *"Lumpenproletariat,"* for whom the theoretical right to vote meant nothing without minimum economic security. In 1848 a demonstration of 500 unemployed Buffalonians demanding work or bread was handily dispersed by the militia—and dismissed by the press with a sermon on laziness.

By the late 1840's the community was losing its cohesion. "The introduction of the railway brought strangers of every condition and kind to our doors," writes Mrs. Poole; "that exclusiveness which the locality, surroundings, climate and conditions of the times forced upon us was now at an end, never to return."[17] Both the sources and the profundity of the change eluded most of the observers of the time. There was an imperceptible tightening of class lines, a gradual closing of the avenues of social ascent, a solidification of the power of the ruling elite.

While the change did not come overnight, by the late 1860's the

Table 10. Population, Property, and Crime in Buffalo, 1850-1908

		Property*				Crime**	
		Real		Personal		Arrests per 1,000	
Year	Population	Millions of Dollars	Per capita Dollars	Millions of Dollars	Per capita Dollars	Male	Female
1850	42,261	15.3	352	2.03	48.2	—	—
1855	74,214	27.3	368	6.66	99.5	55.0	13.3
1860	81,129	28.1	298	5.89	72.5	49.1	17.3
1865	94,210	25.8	274	7.73	82.2	113.5	48.2
1870	117,714	30.8	262	6.54	56.0	100.0	30.4
1875	134,557	34.9	260	6.10	45.6	—	—
1880	155,134	81.7	525	7.52	48.4	99.0	18.3
1885	205,400	99.9	483	8.46	41.2	75.5	13.5
1890	255,664	151.3	591	11.0	43.2	121.0	17.3
1895	304,025	220.2	720	14.3	47.2	131.0	13.3
1900	352,387	223.0	635	9.4	26.7	—	—
1905	376,587	241.9	645	7.4	19.7	104.0	13.3
1908	400,641	269.4	636	7.3	18.4	160.0	13.9

* Data on Property Valuations from Truman C. White (ed.), *Erie County* (Boston: Boston History Company, Publishers, 1898), 441; and the *Proceedings of the Board of Supervisors of Erie County* for the years 1900, 1908. Data can only be regarded as a rough estimate.
** Rates are based on data from *Proceedings of the Board of Supervisors of Erie County,* 1875-6, for the years 1855-75; and from the *Annual Reports of the Buffalo Police Department* for the years 1876 through 1908. Again the data must be taken as only approximations.

outlines of a new society were clearly visible. At the top of the social pyramid were families of great wealth; at the bottom, a detached and indigent proletariat, the so-called "dangerous class."

As a response to the presumed danger from the lower class, the arrests for both major and minor crimes escalate sharply after 1866 (Table 10). By the 1870's around 5 per cent of the population was receiving poor relief from the city. Of the 7696 on relief in 1879, 17 per cent were native-born Americans, 36 per cent were Irish, 30 per cent German, and the remainder of miscellaneous European stock.[18] Vagrants were sent to the "poor farm" for thirty days; petty thieves received as much as sixty days in the workhouse for such crimes as stealing a coat or a pair of boots.[19] This was the age of the vagabond when tramps roamed the country as "pitiful caricatures of the pioneer."[20]

Some sense of the time can be gained from a review of the chronic labor trouble of the period. Railroading was the primary industry of Buffalo, and in 1877 when wages were reduced from $1.50 to $1.38 a day (12 hours) a major strike was precipitated. The local press insisted that the "strikers' rebellion" must be put down, and for that purpose the state militia was finally called to the scene. After the return to normalcy the press seemed puzzled that neither the railroad nor the employees "consider that they owe any sort of allegiance to each other." Of course the workers "had a right to decline to work at the reduced pay, but there their rights ceased." However just their complaint, there can be no toleration of the strikers' course, "for the right of a person to employ laborers to work at any price they may agree upon without interference is one without which society cannot exist" (*Buffalo Express,* July 21, 26, 27, 1877). Although the press assumed the 1877 strike would "make the corporations more solicitous to avoid giving occasion for strikes in the future," the same scene on a larger scale was re-enacted in 1892. After the local police proved unable to subdue 700 striking railroad switchmen, 8000 troops were dispatched to Buffalo. The switchmen finally capitulated, saying they could not fight the U.S. Army and half a dozen corporations too, but for several days martial law reigned; the saloons were closed (often at bayonet point), and the streets of the city were deserted. The railway workers were the first to unionize and later the crafts followed suit, saying simply: "We organize because we must." Concentrated capital created conditions in which it was no longer possible to bargain on an individual basis.

The decade of the 1890's was the high noon of Buffalo capitalism. The city boasted sixty millionaires, twice the number in all the United States in 1850. Congruent with the prevailing myth, men were said to have acquired their fortunes through hard work, thrift, and individual genius—the virtues of the Protestant ethic. One writer contends that none of the Buffalo millionaires inherited great wealth, and the assertion contains a kind of literal truth; there was no great wealth to inherit in 1850. But inherited position had a decisive effect on individual destiny. The ten richest families had been well established in the city since 1840. Between 1860 and 1890, when the fortunes were made, the population of the city trebled—from 81,000 to 244,000—and the businessman or landowner already established in the community was bound to prosper. Without question the rich got richer, and there is some evidence that the poor got poorer; during the period the per capita personal wealth appears to decline (see Table 10). A more intangible change also occurred; men came to look differently on wealth and poverty. Increasingly, business and labor inhabited different social worlds. Writing in a Buffalo union publication, Samuel Gompers stated the case clearly, "Modern society is based on one simple fact, the practical separation of the capitalist class from the great mass of workers. It is not so much a difference in industrial rank as social status . . . a distinction scarcely noticeable in the United States before the previous generation."[21]

By the 1890's the separation acquired even a physical or ecological dimension. Upper-class families, of Anglo-Saxon origin and Protestant religion built three- and four-story palaces along Delaware Avenue.

> This fashionable section was only a small part of the city [writes Mable Dodge Luhan], but it seemed to us the only real Buffalo . . . On Delaware Avenue you knew everyone you met on the street but people never talked to each other except of outward things. There was hardly any real intimacy between friends and people had no confidence in each other . . . they neither showed their feelings nor talked about them . . . In those days only the outermost rim of life was given any conscious attention.[22]

The life of the upper class was somber, humorless, utterly separate. Consider the lines from a wealthy woman:

> Like thee old Oak, I too, have stood apart,
>   Beaten by winds, forsaken and forlorn
> I stretched my arms to unresponsive air
>   I said in bitterness be strong my heart!
> Now life's delusions from my soul are torn
>   I too can storm and isolation bear.[23]

By the 1880's the small and literate patrician element looks with longing to the past, a spirit embodied in Buffalo's most accomplished poet, David Gray. A Buffalo newspaper editor for thirty years, a radical abolitionist who was later a power in the Democratic party, a learned man fully conversant with the scientific thought of the day, Gray could speak with equal force to the intellectual and business community. In 1863 he grasped the fact that the country was in the midst of a revolution "which may last the lifetime of any of us and result algebraically speaking in X. Such things have been in world history before, and why not again? Man is not a whit wiser or better animal than he was when Greece and Rome, successively, crumbled away in blood."[24] Gray saw the happy republic finally dissolve in the corrupton of the 1870's. After Tilden was defrauded of the presidency in 1876, Gray withdrew from public life. Gray had been slated for a minor ambassadorial post in the Tilden administration, but it was not the thwarting of personal ambition which led to his despair. Like Henry Adams, David Gray experienced the "degradation of democratic dogma" and spent his last years in a bewildered revolt against progress, industrialism, and the city. For Gray, the city was the symbol of the conquest of man by his own creation. "What do the young know of David Gray?" asks James Gluck in a memorial address:

> . . . editor of the *Courier,* the author of a few poems, a man of literary tastes, of scholarly habits, somewhat exclusive, reserved in manner, whose later years, dominated by peculiar religious vagaries, were passed in enfeebled physical and mental health, until his death by a railway accident put an end to the trials of his friends and the sufferings and aberrations of himself. The end was strangely emblematic of the struggle during life. The material elements of our civilization—its rush and roar and turmoil, of which the on-rushing railway train was at once so striking a type and a representative—were too powerful for the fine and delicate spirit; they first bruised his mind and then killed his body.[25]

Gray was a pre-Civil-War American, unable to survive in the bleak and ruthless "progress" of the '70's. But most of the "new rich" greeted the future with brassy optimism. Progress meant money, and money was the sacred value around which all else revolved. As Mrs. Luhan says of her grandfather: "He had a sense not only of the importance but the holiness of money."[26]

Money was the cornerstone of the polity as well as the economy. Thrift was the highest civic virtue, and at the dedication of the new city and county hall in the 1870's seemingly the noblest words the orator could find were these: "The people . . . have secured a building at less cost than has been expended for any similar structure in this country."[27] The theme is reiterated on every ceremonial occasion, even down to the present. Thus from the 1870's on the annual message of the mayor to the city council begins with a *ritual of frugality*. In 1875 Mayor Dayton told the council, "For the first time in years the questions of government—municipal, state and national—are now considered as ones of finance and political economy. Men everywhere are . . . governing their action by business principles."[28] Even Grover Cleveland, whose rapid rise to national fame began as a reform mayor of Buffalo, climaxed his first address to the council in this vein: "We are . . . trustees and agents of our fellow citizens, holding their funds in sacred trust."[29] The philosophy of politics as business reaches something of a high point in 1895 when Mayor Elam Jewett told the council, "Enterprises are attracted by a wise conservative and business-like government . . . To me the city of Buffalo appears to be, not a political hive, but a vast business corporation."[30] Except for the abortive effort at reform between 1898 and 1920, when plans for municipal socialism (city ownership of utilities) were seriously promoted by even the local business class, there has scarcely been a departure from the creed of laissez-faire capitalism.[31]

Around the turn of the century the economic base of the city was changing. Ownership and control of key industries were passing to outside interests.[32] The formation of the Lackawanna Steel Company in 1901 was the prototype of subsequent industrial development. The company was founded with a capital investment of $30,-000,000, 17 per cent of which was local. Ten years later local ownership had dwindled to 7 per cent. Only two of the twenty-man board of directors were Buffalonians, but the company was handed a *carte blanche* by the city. No building restrictions were imposed, and there was no protest against health and safety conditions, even though there were as many as 4000 injuries a year and one fatality a day in a work force of 6000. By 1906 the steel works covered 1500 acres and had an authorized capital stock of $60,000,000 (doubled since 1901) and in that year alone sold over $28,000,000 in products. Yet the employees, mainly Polish and Slavic immigrants, worked twelve hours a day, seven days a week, at wages ranging from ten to twenty cents an hour.[33]

Worse than wage slavery was the threat of unemployment. From the 1870's on unemployment rates were abnormally high, and the census of 1900–a prosperous time–provides the figures shown in Table 11. Baffled by unemployment the *Express* comments:

> Several families were found with no fuel and obliged to stay huddled together in bed to keep from freezing to death . . . in sub-zero weather. . . . [They] haven't enough ingenuity to find or make employment for themselves . . . it never occurred to the unemployed Poles to get a sled and go to the lake for fish. . . . But what's anybody going to do about it? They need help just as much as if they were clean. (*Buffalo Express*, Feb. 10, 1893)

Table 11. Unemployment for Males over 10 Years of Age in Buffalo in 1900

| Occupation | Number in Labor Force | Unemployed | | | | |
		1-3 months	4-6 months	7-12 months	Total	Per cent
Professional	5,081	161	136	74	371	7.3
Domestic and Personal Service	23,681	2,712	4,198	1,356	8,266	35.3
Trade Transport	34,330	1,354	1,705	666	3,725	10.9
Manufacturing and Mechanical	42,354	4,383	3,969	1,685	10,037	23.4
TOTAL	106,340	8,675	10,108	3,817	22,600	19.8

Data from Department of Commerce and Labor, Bureau of the Census, *Occupations at the Twentieth Census*. Special Reports (Washington: U.S. Government Printing Office, 1904) p. 432.

With heavy industry came the slums, where, in Hobbesian style, the life of man was "nasty, brutish and short". The Buffalo of 1910 was a replica of Upton Sinclair's *Jungle*. Fifty to sixty people crowded into ten-room houses in the steel districts, and sometimes boarders could not rent rooms but only spaces on beds for a night or day turn. Ninety-four per cent of the Poles of Buffalo had an income of less than $635, the estimated living wage for the time, and the Hungarian settlement held "the astonishing record of 10,000 human beings without a single bathtub" (*Buffalo Express,* March 15, 1910). One observer notes that:

> at night gangs roam the streets and come toward each other . . . roaring at the top of their voices. When they meet they start fighting simply for the sake of fighting which has become a sport for these people. They use clubs, knives and revolvers. . . . Police are called but refuse to come to the area. . . . Children have no place to play except with the pigs and goats who wallow about in the slime and swamps. (*Buffalo Express,* April 7, 1907)

While the lot of the craftsman had improved, the unskilled factory worker, isolated from the larger community and unprotected by union power, was hardly more than a piece of machinery. The personnel policy of Lackawanna Steel was both a cause and a symbol of this new way of life.

> Of the five or six thousand employees [writes the *Buffalo Times*], everyone is so recorded that not a man can loaf or beat his time a minute without the heads of different departments being cognizant of the fact and his wage cut accordingly. . . . When a man is hired, a card record is taken . . . and he is given a number. . . . After assuming this number the laborer loses his name and thereafter is known only by the figures on his coat. (*Buffalo Times,* Sept. 11, 1904)

While material conditions have improved since 1910, with the further regimentation of the work force still others have "lost their name," become a cipher in a ledger.

Outwardly placid, the nineteenth century closed on a note of foreboding. Metaphorically speaking, the century ended at the Pan American Exposition in Buffalo when a Polish "anarchist" assassinated President William McKinley.[34] The act seemed to materialize the secret fears which the wealthy had harbored for twenty years. Earlier, Buffalo Congressman James O. Putnam had warned: "We are rapidly becoming a nation of great cities. In them gather the dangerous elements of society. In them anarchy hatches its plots of murder and lights its revolutionary fires . . ."[35] The prophesy was more a projection of guilt than a rational assessment of the radical movement; nevertheless, the Buffalo of 1900 was anything but confident. "The Gilded Age," as Professor Horton remarks, "was an age of innocence only for sheltered dowagers and debutantes; it was an age of apprehension."[36]

In the 1840's the young men of Buffalo were advised that success came only through a wise self-reliance and was "incompatible with all presumption upon Destiny and excluded all dependence on Adventitious Circumstance."[37] By the turn of the century the advice seemed all but irrelevant; the lives of most people were shaped by circumstances quite beyond their own control. For the working class, unemployment came like a natural disaster, unrelated to the actions of men. Even the merchant class, supposedly the incarnation of individual initiative, owed its affluence as much to the mysterious dynamics of population growth and industrial expansion as to its own efforts. Success was largely the consequence of being in the right place at the right time with the right connections. In addition, there was the fortuitous gyration of the business cycle, which, conceived as beyond rational control, actually became so. More than ever, chance seemed to rule the affairs of men.[38] With the separation of the social classes it became increasingly difficult for either class to gain a rational comprehension of the actions of the other. With the emergence of the trans-local corporation, remote authorities could make decisions affecting the lives of thousands who had no alternative but acquiescence. A people who a century earlier had conquered nature was now unable to master its own creation—the social environment. "The steel town," writes Lewis Mumford, "was an environment much more harsh, antagonistic and brutal than anything the pioneers had encountered."[39] Both individually and collectively, men seemed impotent in the face of the urban problem.

In the progressive period in Buffalo (1900-1920) there was an heroic effort at municipal reform, which in the end accomplished little. Once the labor movement was co-opted into the corporate structure, the energy for social transformation was dissipated. In the 1890's labor was explicitly socialistic, calling for collective owner-ship of all means of production and distribution as well as higher pay and an eight-hour day. In Buffalo by 1910 the wages of crafts-men had been raised substantially, but the proposals for collective ownership were abandoned. Henceforth, the American Federation of Labor asked for its members nothing more than "the right to sell their labor to the best advantage of themselves"; far from revolutionary, "the principle upon which organized labor is founded . . . is the best bulwark of society against the threat of socialism."[40] The demand for radical reform subsided as the principle of self-interest, the spirit of capitalism, prevailed.

Since its foundation the American city has been dominated by an economic institution—first the market, then the corporation. Neither local political institutions nor religious institutions were able to regu-late economic activity; indeed, both merely reinforced the existing system. The key to the city is the economic institution:

First, the business ideology was clearly embodied in municipal or-ganization. From the 1870's onward the objective of local govern-ment was the creation of a climate favorable to business enterprise, which meant minimal taxation and control. If the purpose of the city was to stimulate investment, what better incentive than a compliant, administration? Given this definition of the situation, it was inevi-table that the "spirit of graft and lawlessness," as Lincoln Steffens called it, should assert itself. "In all the cities in 1900," said Steffens, "the better classes—the businessmen—are the sources of corruption, but they are so rarely pursued and caught that we do not fully real-ize whence the trouble comes."[41]

Under laissez-faire capitalism the city could play at best only a regulative not a productive role in economic life. As early as 1873 the socialists had proposed public works programs to solve the unemployment problem, but the most Buffalo offered the indigent was the county poor farm. Private charities were left to cope with all the problems created by starvation wages, immigration, and unemployment.

Second, the industrial corporation as the main employer of men determined their style of life in countless ways. First it created an "employee mentality," a submissiveness quite at odds with the ideal of self-reliance. Occupying a role of passive subordination eight or twelve hours a day did not condition men to take an active part in a democratic community. There was an active and anarchic rebellion, an aggression bred of frustration and expressed in crime, but little interest in social reconstruction. The insecurity of wage-labor and unemployment also contributed materially to the high crime rates of the urban slums. The slum was the product of industrial capitalism; it was created *in* not *by* the city. As we have seen, it was corporate policy (of the railroads in the nineteenth century and the steel mills in the twentieth) which precipitated the bitterest labor trouble in Buffalo. Given the premise of profit-making it was inevitable that wages should be cut to the subsistence level. For the middle class, status in the corporation was beginning to replace status in the territorial community as the primary bond upon which one's fate depended. Since its ownership was translocal, the corporation had only a nominal and pecuniary interest in the city of Buffalo. In the nineteenth century the local capitalist elite, while amassing wealth, still took pride in the city, and established organizations of enduring benefit to the community: a remarkable park system, a museum of natural history, art galleries, libraries, and the historical society. But as the power and autonomy of the local elite declined, the city lost much of its color and high culture. Wyndham Lewis describes the Buffalo of the 1930's as "a dark and massive patch upon the landscape, with a gilded thread [Delaware Avenue] running down the middle . . . around which oceans of aliens surge and stagnate."[42] Since then even the gild has gone.

Finally, the ecology of the city is a product of economic institutions rather than sub-social, biotic competition. A "cultural institution"—the railroad—blocked the development of a "natural" harbor for seventy-five years. The spatial order of the American city is rational only in serving the ends of profit for property holders. In the context of the needs of the community, land use may be quite irrational. For instance, the city of Buffalo has been desperately deficient in park space for forty years, yet more and more public land is sold to private interests.[43] This is not an expression of the natural law of ecology but the cultural law of profit.

The disorder of urbanism is a function of the order of capitalism. Just as the ecology of the American city is primarily a creation of the institutions of capitalism—property, contract, profit—so too the social life of the city bears the unmistakable impress of this unique mode of economic organization. In the development of capitalism, social relations were turned into commodity relations. Both labor and land became items for sale, and property was the agency through which men were "integrated" into the social system. Those without property were without status—outsiders, aliens—and they were the ones who inhabited the inner city where disorganization was most pronounced. Unemployment, poverty, wage labor, and the boom and bust cycle of business enterprise were the real *sources* of anomie. The city only collected the wreckage.

The individuation of the city was a product of both organization and disorganization. For Park the model of urban individuation was the Polish peasant in Chicago, emancipated from the bonds of the folk community. This was an individuation by default, a result of *de*-socialization. But another form of individuation filtered down from the top of the social pyramid. The philosophy of individuation was embodied in the mores of the ruling elite of the nineteenth-century American city. Individualism was both an ideology—a defense of power—and an ideal. The maxims of individualism were not learned accidentally: from childhood on one was socialized to stand alone, to view all dependency as a form of weakness, to aspire to self-reliance. The principle was imbibed through religion (Protestantism), politics (democracy), and above all economic life (market capitalism). It expressed itself in the priority of private over public life and in the tendency of Americans to isolate themselves from the larger community.

Ironically, *the institution of individualism produced as its unintended consequence the regimentation of urban life.* Individualism precluded the possibility of the formation of enduring solidarity, of co-operative action. It sapped the vitality of the labor and socialist movements, created "the spirit of graft and lawlessness" which Lincoln Steffens called the American spirit. Individualism provided the legal fiction of the corporation-as-person, enabling the large business organization to regulate the life of the community to suit its own purposes. Efforts to bring corporate power under public control were defeated in the name of individual freedom. In pursuit of profit the corporation regimented the labor force and rationalized the productive, distributive, and consumption process. Initially a philosophy of revolt, individualism became a source of compliance. So long as the individual had the illusion he himself was advancing he had no reason to question the System, even though it deprived him of identity.

Anomie is the terminal stage in the unfolding of the ethos of individualism, a drama acted out in the theater of the city but not inherently linked to urbanism. Historically, Western individualism was a rebellion against the sacred authority of the communal society of the Middle Ages: Protestantism, capitalism, and democracy were its primary expressions and created the institutional context and the driving force of the urban-industrial revolution of the nineteenth century. The principle of individualism found its supreme manifestation in capitalism (both Protestantism and democracy still contained communal elements). The rupture of social bonds, the chronic industrial and commercial crises, the continuous antagonism between capital and labor—traits which Durkheim isolated as symptoms of anomie—flowed from the same source, the institution of capitalism. The American city, in both its physical contour and its inner spirit, is a realization of the value system of capitalist society.

7

Revolution aborted; society sacralized: class war in Buffalo, 1910-1920

> No one, unafflicted with invincible ignorance, desires to preserve our economic system in its existing form.
>
> WALTER LIPPMANN, *Drift and Mastery*, July, 1914.

All institutions have their ultimate foundation in consensus, a shared commitment to a conceptual scheme or value system.[1] Without a minimal allegiance to its aims and rules no institution can operate; an institution is an authority structure. Power is a derivative of an institutional office, or "command post" as Mills put it.[2] Power is a function of organization; the power of the chief flows from the allegiance of the tribe, from consensus. But when that consensus begins to dissolve—the condition of anomie—a struggle for power ensues, resulting in conflict. The source of conflict lies in the process of institutional dislocation. As institutions lose grip on their participants and their public they become coercive, and coercion intensifies the antagonism of those already alienated from the system. Moreover, the condition of anomie invites exploitation—the extension of power by force. The process can be observed in the declining phase of ancient and medieval society; both personal and collective conflicts increase with the deterioration of consensus, the growth of anomie.[3]

Every functioning society is integrated by a nuclear institution;

the history of the Middle Ages is the history of Catholicism, and the past hundred years of Western life can be written in terms of the transformation of the institution of capitalism. Between 1860 and 1900 the capitalist consensus reigned supreme, at least in America.[4] More than merely an economic system, capitalism was an ethos, a faith, a way of life. Capitalist theory and ideology provided the rationale for the political order as well as the organizing principle of industry, i.e. production for private profit. The capitalist was the hero of imaginative literature (e.g. the novels of William Dean Howells) and popular culture (Horatio Alger). The virtues of hard work, thrift, and sobriety were preached and often practiced. Yet the very triumph of industrial capitalism brought in its wake a profusion of social problems—crime, pauperism, unemployment, and labor conflict which verged close to class war. Developments of the late nineteenth century followed rather closely the Marxian paradigm, and while there may have been a minimum of class consciousness in America there was no absence of class struggle.[5] A relentless drive for profits intensified exploitation and gave rise to riots and strikes which were suppressed by the police and military authority of the state, thus solidifying the workers into a labor movement.[6] The drive for profit produced a disastrous fluctuation of the business cycle, with periods of overexpansion and prosperity followed by bleak times of contraction and business failure. The system exhibited all the rational irrationality of warfare. The industrialist was a "captain of industry," the workers were his unwilling troops, and his chief task was to discipline them. Initially industries fought each other, but by the late '90's they had entered an unspoken truce and jointly fought the farmer, small business, labor, and the general public. The result was a near-anarchy, a war of each against all.

There were three major responses to this "war": the conservative capitalist elite sought to perpetuate it, occasionally turning it into a national war (1898, 1917); the reformists (populists, progressives, trade-unionists) wanted to fight a limited war; the revolutionaries (anarcho-syndicalists, I.W.W., socialists) sought to turn the Hobbesian war of each against all into a class war of some against others. The reform elements accepted capitalist ends but sought rules to restrict the power of monopolies and thus restore the free competition of the marketplace. This objective animated the "trust busting" and regulative legislation of the period.[7] Similarly, trade-unionism pursued capitalist goals of higher wages, shorter hours—the market philosophy of more for less—and rejected political objectives which would alter basic property relations.[8] Numerically, smaller but more influential than is often recognized today, the revolutionaries wanted to transform, not reform, society by building working-class solidarity on the co-operative principle as a means to abolish the competitive profit system of capitalism. Between 1900 and 1920 the reform forces won certain battles—income and inheritance taxes, strengthening of antitrust laws—but in the end lost the "war." In 1919 the Wilson administration's plan to retain control over the railroads and to establish public ownership of communications was defeated, and in the same year the Supreme Court ruled that U.S. Steel did not constitute a trust. By 1921 the capitalist elite had been able to liquidate radicalism, roll back the tide of reform, and consolidate a new position of dominance—one that has not seriously been threatened since then.[9] But the capitalist elite could no longer justify itself in terms of the traditional capitalist ethic—rags to riches, every man a capitalist. Rather, it found its justification in the concept of Americanism. Americanism was implicitly identified with capitalism—the open-shop crusade of the 1920's was known as the "American plan" —and became the accepted rationalization of capitalist power. This is not to suggest that an all-powerful elite forcefully imposed its will on a resistant public; nor on the other hand did the people enthusiastically embrace the new Americanism. Rather, the power of the capitalist class after World War I was so overwhelming as to deter the very thought of opposition. In 1919 the public was weary from the frustration and futility of reform and opted for the simple alternative of disengagement; it "returned to normalcy" with a vengeance (Harding was elected by one of the largest pluralities on record).

The people preferred the imagined certainties of the past to the confusing present and the problematic future.

The decisive "battles" of this "war" between the forces of reform, revolution, and reaction were fought out in the American city between 1910 and 1920. While the outcome of the "war" is known already, a re-analysis of the campaign may throw light on the problems of conflict and conflict resolution. The present chapter deals with some of the skirmishes that occurred in the city of Buffalo. We can see in this microcosm the forces which were shaking the whole urban industrial world.

The primary source of data for this study is the newspaper file. For the sociologist, concerned with the behavior of groups and collectivities, the newspaper is an indispensable source; it is as close to a living history as one is apt to come. The newspaper is not the product of a single mind but a collective creation, a daily record of the public life of the community. Newspapers, of course, reflect the ideology of their publishers, but the news is distorted more by selection than by deliberate falsification. Important events are sometimes ignored, but where there is a competing press that danger is diminished. The decade of 1910-20, before the syndicated column, radio, TV, and the national newspaper chain, was in many ways the great day of American journalism. At that time Buffalo had six dailies (as opposed to two in 1970), and thirteen major weeklies—four German, one Polish, one Italian, and the remainder English. In addition there was one German and one Polish daily. Of the six dailies the *Express* is the most reliable and substantial; in its prime it was regarded as the *New York Times* of Buffalo. Politically, the daily press ranged from center to far right (*The Commercial*). The Democratic papers were mildly reformist; the Republican papers were more conservative. While none of the papers were pro-labor they differed in their hostility to unionism; *The Commercial* equated the closed shop with Bolshevism; the others were more temperate. The Catholic press was strongly anti-Socialist but mildly, and occasionally vigorously, pro-labor. Little remains of the Socialist press. The *Arbeiter-Zeitung* had a long history in the community and early connections with the De Leonite Socialist Labor party. It seemingly flourished between 1912 and 1916, when circulation increased from 2750 to 7500, but ceased publication during the war. Copies of the *Buffalo Socialist* between 1912 and 1914 have been preserved; the paper continued until 1919 under the name of *New Age,* but no copies of it are available. On major issues the press follows the current of opinion of the whole nation, with the Republican papers acting as the local pace-setters and the Democratic ones following suit. Generally, the opinion of the *Express* became in time the opinion of Buffalo. Table 12 gives data on the principal newspapers used in this study.

Table 12. The Buffalo Press, 1910-1920*

| Newspaper | | | Circulation | |
(Daily)	Year Established	Political Affiliation	1912	1919
Express (morning)	1846	Republican	36,927	37,473
Enquirer (evening)	1891	Democratic	30,000	30,674
Courier (morning)	1828	Democratic	44,021	41,497
News (evening)	1880	Republican	93,572	107,142
Times (evening)	1882	Democratic	54,158	57,787
Commercial (evening)	1831	Republican	7,500	10,000
(*Weekly*)				
Catholic Union and Times	1872		15,000	22,000
Live Wire (J. of Chamber of Commerce)	–	–	3,650	4,340
Buffalo Socialist	–	Socialist	2,750	Ceased publication
Arbiter-Zeitung	1886	Socialist	–	Ceased publication
			(1914) 7,500 (1916)	

* Data from N. W. Ayer, *Directory: Newspapers and Periodicals* (Philadelphia: N. W. Ayers and Sons, 1912, and 1919)

With a population of half a million, the social life and political climate of Buffalo in the decade of World War I were typical of the American city of the industrial heartland, differing in detail but not in contour from Cleveland, Pittsburgh, Detroit, or Chicago.[10] Toward the close of the century the city was dominated by a capitalist elite, described by Professor Horton as "the noblemen of America," with both the trappings and the substance of power:

> . . . the power of the community in commerce and industry was concentrated in the banks. The men who wielded that power thought of themselves as capitalists and referred to themselves as such with conscious pride. Their pride was justifiable. They belonged to a class that had made itself the dominant power in the country, turning by force of intelligence and character the greatest battles of the century to its advantage. This class had supplanted the Southern aristocracy and had made the United States, on the whole, submissive to its will. . . . In their economic affairs they were anxious lest they leave any stone unturned in their attempt to strengthen and extend (their power). . . . In their political affairs these fresh and zestful capitalists were as alert and vigilant as in their economic concerns.[11]

Some index of the capitalist command of political life in Buffalo is indicated by the voting record of the city—and the vote is always only the one-tenth of the iceberg above the surface. Although 60 per cent of the city were blue-collar workers, with another 20 per cent in the lower white-collar ranks, Buffalo voted Republican in every national election between 1892 and 1932, except 1912 when the Taft-Roosevelt split gave a plurality to Wilson. In 1896, McKinley, the forthright spokesman of the capitalist class, defeated the great commoner Bryan by a handy two to one. (Table 13 gives an overview of the Buffalo vote from 1896 to 1920.) The rising Democratic vote indicates the growing spirit of reform, yet the ideology of the two parties was essentially the same. Eugene Debs said in a Buffalo speech in 1908, "The Republicans want the capitalist system as it

Table 13. Presidential Vote in Buffalo, 1896-1920*

Date	Total Vote Cast	Republican	Per cent Total	Democratic	Per cent Total	Socialist	Per cent Total
1896	59,122	35,739 (McKinley)	60.5	23,383 (Bryan)	39.4	—	—
1900	66,527	34,720 (McKinley)	52.2	31,807 (Bryan)		—	—
1904	62,777	34,408 (Roosevelt)	54.9	28,369 (Parker)	45.0	—	—
1908	77,436	40,210 (Taft)	52.1	35,992 (Bryan)	46.5	1,234 (Debs)	1.6
1912	65,951	20,769 (Roosevelt)	35.5	26,192 (Wilson)	39.8	4,207 (Debs)	6.9
		14,433 (Taft)	18.8				
1916	99,000	52,000 (Hughes)	52.5	45,000	45.4	2,000 (Benson)	2.2
1920	123,915	78,447 (Harding)	64.5	32,734 (Cox)	26.8	12,734 (Debs)	10.5

* Compiled from data from *Buffalo Express* for years cited.

is; the Democrats want the capitalist system as it was" (*Enquirer,* Oct. 2, 1908). Debs said the choice was between:

> Wall Street and Taft
> Or Tammany and Graft.

While Debs's own showing in 1908 was not impressive, it represented a gain over 1904, and in the next four years the Socialist vote increased fourfold both locally and nationally. In 1912 Debs drew a larger crowd (9000) in Buffalo than did any of the other candidates, and some of his more ardent supporters were actually surprised when he did not win the presidency. Moreover the Socialist vote was a party vote, and in Buffalo Charles E. Russell, Socialist candidate for governor, ran slightly ahead of Debs (4207 vs. 4457). "After the election," says one student of the subject, "there was not the usual fading of interest."[12] The party was beginning to take root in the community and by 1913 had seventeen locals, a central office, a biweekly newspaper, and had begun construction on a socialist school and a labor lyceum.

The strength and influence of the socialist movement cannot be assessed by the vote. Their numbers were small, but they had a revolutionary spirit which gathered momentum between 1912 and 1914, a spirit personified in Debs: "We ask no quarter, and we grant none; we ask for no compromise and become stronger with each defeat."[13] Although the local Socialists were less articulate they were equally defiant. "A good thing about your work for the socialist movement," the *Buffalo Socialist* told its imaginary capitalist readers, "is that every time you fire a man you make him hate the system—the capitalist system—you make him class conscious" (Nov. 30, 1912). To the conservative trade-unionist it said: "Talk of a living wage is tommyrot. If you were not getting a living wage now, you'd be dead. The Chinese get a living wage. The socialist wants you to get all you produce, and you're entitled to it" (Nov. 9, 1912). In its rhetoric, at least, the Socialist party repudiated the whole society demanding not only better wages and working conditions but:

> . . . the emancipation of the whole people through the ab-
> olition of the profit system and the substitution of the So-
> cialist commonwealth . . . The main purpose of the So-
> cialist Party is to fight the battle of labor against grasping
> capitalists and employers—to put human life above the
> sordid scramble for dollars. And its ultimate aim is to sub-
> stitute a sane system of cooperative production, democrati-
> cally administered, for the present planless system which
> enriches the idle few at the expense of the great multitude
> who produce all the wealth of the world. (*Buffalo Socialist*,
> August 9, 1913)

The respectable community alternatively ignored and ridiculed the Socialists, but one eminent Buffalonian wrote in *Harpers* in 1911:

"Socialism is a movement of such a nature . . . as seems likely to break suddenly, someday into avalanches and floods."[14]

To alert Buffalonians 1913 must have seemed the beginning of the floodtide. As a year of labor unrest it is comparable only with 1877, 1892, and 1919. MacTeggart's thorough study of Buffalo labor history indicates that there was an average of less than two strikes a year between 1824 and 1917. In 1913, thirteen major strikes were recorded and the most notable of these involved 1700 street railway workers and 2300 national guardsmen. The strike was initially organized by the man who was editor of the *Buffalo Socialist* (and also vice president of the Proletarian Club).[15] Maximum wages of streetcar workers amounted to 28 cents an hour for a man of nine years' service, and some employees worked as many as eighteen hours a day for $1.80. When the strike was called the company imported 500 strike-breakers from Chicago and Philadelphia, and the local police force was increased by 250 uniformed men. Still unable to establish car service the company pressed city officials to call out the national guard (both the sheriff and the mayor refused but a local judge was prevailed upon to sign the order activating the guard). No strike before had so directly affected the total population of the city, and the public reaction was a mixture of alarm and delight—which did not necessarily follow class lines. The excitement was a welcome relief from the tedium of daily life. "All Buffalo flocked to Main Street in hope of excitement," wrote the *Express*.

> The crowds were as dense as appeared on election nights in the days before voting machines . . . a moving mass of people . . . one double procession of automobiles. Trucks were fitted with seats offering joy rides for ten cents. . . . A trip of a patrol wagon would attract a following of easily a 1000 men and boys screaming and yelling. . . . The surging crowds poured through the side streets making the night hideous with their noise.
>
> • • •
>
> The crowd was made up largely of the idly curious out to see rather than to take part in whatever trouble occurred.

> Fathers and mothers regardless of their own or their children's safety brought them out in baby buggies or toted them along by hand . . . dozens of young hoodlums passed insulting remarks and acted in a way which ought to have been sufficient to drive decent people off the streets. . . . The young girls were out in force also, chattering and giggling. . . . (April 8, 1913)

But the next day rioting took a more serious turn, "revolver shots were exchanged between the police and the mobs . . . the police chief's car was the target of a fusilade of bullets, though no one in the machine was hit" (*Express*, April 9, 1913). The following day the entire 4th National Guard Brigade—2300 men—policed the city, but their efforts, said the *Express*, "were met with jeers. . . . Troops with fixed bayonets held no terrors for the disorderly elements." Finally, the troops fired on the mobs; the *Express* describes the scene:

> "Fire!" came the command. A dozen rifles cracked. The crowd scattered and a woman came reeling down the bank. There was another spit of bullets from the other side of the bridge, and a boy got one of them in the arm. The crowd thronged to the area. The soldiers followed with fixed bayonets and drove the throng back to the curb. More than one felt the butt of a rifle against his ribs . . . and one received a bayonet thrust in the hand. (*Express*, April, 10)

No fatalities resulted, but the firing on the crowd tilted public opinion to the side of the strikers, after it had become apparent that neither the police, the military, nor the strike-breakers could operate the street-car lines. Even the *Express* demanded that the company accede to the strikers' demands, which had been reduced to the issue of union recognition.

> . . . a question of union recognition is a minor matter. If the strikers as their leaders say, are willing to go back to work provided the union is recognized, then the company has no right to deprive the city of safe transportation. . . . The business of this company is to furnish transportation, not to fight a sociological question. (April 11, 1913)

In the meantime the socialists had been eased out of the strike leadership, and the conservative AFL element was recognized; the situation returned to normal (without pay increases). Under the caption: "Wicked Loss to Business" the *Express* (April 12) totaled up the cost of the strike:

Total cost of troops (paid by county)	$40,000
Fares—15,000 a day	90,000
Damage to cars	10,000
1,000 Strikebreakers at $2.50 a day	28,000
Wages	25,000

During the remainder of 1913, twelve other strikes occurred—car workers of the railroad, street-car laborers, store clerks, delivery drivers, teamsters, truck drivers, icemen, railway-express men, machinists, taxi-drivers, baggage helpers, plus an abortive strike of school children.[16]

Throughout the country 1913 and '14 were years of unrest and unemployment; in Buffalo vagrancy arrests rose from 969 in 1910

Table 14. Male Arrests in Buffalo, 1910-1921*

Year	Total Arrests	Vagrancy	Murder	Disorderly Conduct	Assault	Drunkenness	Burglary	Larceny (Grand)
1910	20,130	969	7	3,638	919	8,960	299	398
1911	22,181	1,081	7	3,696	962	8,957	306	428
1912	24,532	1,333	12	2,911	1,058	11,330	334	469
1913	25,790	1,104	8	2,984	1,379	11,214	312	431
1914	30,686	1,931	5	2,354	1,502	13,713	407	307
1915	28,643	1,661	8	3,779	1,451	10,772	358	450
1916	32,586	1,450	15	4,028	1,639	13,910	280	443
1917	32,901	1,598	21	4,274	1,685	14,205	380	658
1918	33,067	1,196	25	4,444	1,523	13,315	469	636
1919	28,314	1,664	18	4,498	1,348	8,853	384	564
1920	22,214	1,247	17	1,160	1,373	7,334	331	670
1921	23,269	2,426	22	842	1,640	8,655	345	614

* Data from Annual Reports of Buffalo Police Dept. for years cited. The population of the city was 423,715 in 1910, 506,775 in 1921.

to 1931 in 1914; in this period the total number of arrests increased by 50 per cent (see Table 14). Although it is difficult to generalize about trends in crime, Table 14 parallels rather closely the pattern Arthur Wood found for Detroit.[17] Arrests reached a high point in 1917 and 1918, but the upward climb had begun earlier.

With the outbreak of World War I the economic picture improved almost instantaneously. "The war had been in progress only one week," writes Dickman, "when Buffalo producers began making extensive preparation for a boom in the export field. . . . Steel was soon operating at or above capacity and more grain passed through the port than ever before in history."[18] All of the daily papers except the *Times* (published by a Bryan-Democrat) were united in their support for loans to belligerents. "The proposition is essentially simple," said the *Express*, "the question for us to decide is whether we would rather refuse credits and go without the trade or grant credits and keep the trade. We cannot refuse credits and keep the trade." The loans were justified by the local press because "business not politics was behind them." The question of which Europeans benefit . . . "is of little interest to Americans compared with the fact that it will be a great benefit to the United States" (*Express,* Sept. 28, 1915). Economically, the war could not have come at a more opportune moment. Up to the time of U.S. entry (April 1917) $1,500,000,000 had been lent to the Allies and $27,000,000 to the Central Powers—which amounts were spent in the United States. In the last year of neutrality, exports, for the United States as a whole, jumped from $2,500,000,000 to $4,300,000,000. By 1916 there was "a continuous and extraordinary prosperity."[19]

From the outbreak of hostilities the press, first subtly and then overtly, promoted the idea of U.S. intervention, but the public was slow to respond. On August 4, 1914, the *Express* called for increasing U.S. strength to full wartime levels. On the other hand, the local Socialists were holding peace meetings six months before that date, and in mid-August 1914 conducted an open-air meeting to protest the war at which "3,000 people listened with interest but displayed no great enthusiasm" (*News,* August 16, 1914). Toward both war and peace the public was apathetic. "It never entered into discussion," writes the local historian Sweeny, "not even into our thoughts, that we had need to take sides in such a conflict. The announcement by the umpire . . . at the Ferry Street ball park occasioned about the same relative interest as the telegraph dispatches from French and Belgium battlefields."[20] The neighborhood press ignored the subject entirely, and "the mayor's [annual] message of 1915 contained no mention of the war or its local effects. His communication of 1916 was likewise barren of war reference."[21] The people "went their war-listless way," says Sweeny, but:

> On November 3, 1915, Joseph Choate, former American ambassador to England held a meeting at the Bankers Club in New York City. . . . Every American city was invited to participate through its mayor. . . . Addressing the meeting the mayor of Buffalo said, "Buffalo . . . is solidly in favor of the great enterprise which inspires our coming together . . . 450,000 of us stoutly favor every reasonable effort looking to national preparedness. . . ." While neither the mayor's speech nor the occasion for it attracted any great amount of attention here at home . . . the mayor did not delay putting the city in entire accord with the plans of the *National Security League.*[22]

The main function of the National Security League, composed locally of men of high status from different segments of the community, was to promote sentiment for military preparedness. The pomp and drama of the preparedness parades and rallies delighted the populace, but as Sweeny reflects, sadly; "the interest was largely recreational . . . opinion was divided on the question of whether the trouble might reasonably be expected with England or Germany."[23] In one such demonstration the Buffalo *Courier* could detect "the vibrant spirit of American nationalism" (Nov. 15, 1915). On the other hand the *Express* later wondered: "With all the popular enthusiasm for preparedness it is strange that membership in the local regiments of the national guard should have fallen off to an extent which threatens the disbandment of these organizations" (Jan. 3, 1916). While the press and powerful voices in the national elite were urging a belligerent policy,[24] it was clearly the peace issue that elected Wilson in 1916 by the narrowest vote of any President prior to Kennedy. When local troops returned from Mexican border duty in March 1917 patriotic fervor was at such a low ebb that the *News* was moved to ask: "Are we decadent . . . indifferent to everything save personal business pursuits?" (Mar. 14, 1917).

Patriotism increased after the declaration of War but was still insufficient to inspire much volunteering for active service, and it was necesary to resort to conscription. Although the Socialist party lost some of its top leadership in the split over the war, its electoral strength increased. In 1917 Morris Hillquit came close to winning the mayoralty of New York City, and in Buffalo the Socialist candidate for mayor in the primary polled 14,200 as opposed to 14,400 for the Republican and 17,000 for the Democratic candidate. (The Republican won in the run-off as a result of Socialist support.) In Rochester the socialists won half a dozen city and county offices. The high vote was attributed to the anti-war sentiment (*Express,* Oct. 17, 1917).

For Buffalo, World War I meant a maximum of prosperity with a minimum of hardship. About 20,000 residents served in the armed forces, and of these some 951 were either killed or died of disease. The war had an integrating effect: "There was no east side, south side, west side or north side—only Buffalo," says one historian, "Personal affairs were secondary. Buffalonians will never forget the stirring, inspiring, self-sacrificing days of 1917-18."[25] Profits and wages were equally inspiring, as Table 15 indicates. In July 1917 the official publication of the Chamber of Commerce observed: "Gargantuan as the task of subduing the arrogant autocracy has proven to be, nevertheless it appears to be progressing satisfactorially," and added as an afterthought, "The slogan 'business as usual' has been expanded to 'better business than usual' " (*Live Wire,* July 1917, p. 189).

Table 15.   Manufacturing in Buffalo, 1909-1919*

Year	No. of Establish- ments	Average No. of Wage Earners	Value of Products	Wages
1909	1,753	51,412	218,808,000	28,727,000
1914	2,225	54,416	247,516,000	34,818,000
1919	2,093	75,899	634,410,000	95,702,000

* Data from 14th *Census of U.S.: Manufacturers,* vol. VII, 1919 (Washington: Government Printing Office, 1923), p. 232.

But as the year wore on there was a mounting and diffuse anxiety. "German spies and plotters," says Sweeny, "were thick in all sections of the country."[26] Even before war was declared the Chamber of Commerce and the city council had urged the mayor to call up troops to guard the waterworks. The mayor refused, but he organized a volunteer police brigade "purely for the patriotic purpose of serving their city in the case of riots or uprisings. . . . After daily toil in the banks, offices and in shops (says Sweeny) the police reserve patrolled the streets . . . and many meritorious arrests were made by the members."[27] There seemed to be an urgent need for those on the home-front to participate more directly in the war effort. The Liberty-Loan campaign and the home-defense brigades partially filled this need; in addition there was spy-hunting. "Do not wait until you catch someone putting a bomb under a factory," advised *Live Wire;* "Report the man who spreads pessimistic stories . . . cries for peace or belittles our efforts to win the war. Send the names of such persons . . . to the Department of Justice. . . . The fact that you made the report will not be made public. You are in contact with the enemy today, just as truly as if you faced him across No Man's Land" (*Live Wire;* July 1918, p. 149). However, Sweeny noted that "Buffalo, happily, escaped the stain of any great amount of disloyalty among its citizens . . . [local] German propaganda took the form of interpreting the war as a capitalist war and sought to foment resistance to the draft. That was effectively and vigorously suppressed."[28]

By an easy transmutation the "radical" replaced the "Hun" as the primary enemy. In fact, as early as September 1917, the *Live Wire* warned: "The I. W. W. is an element more dangerous to the peace and prosperity of the United States than is Germany and her allies." The category of radical initially included the I. W. W.s and the anarchists, and later all those who opposed the war—including pacificists and conscientious objectors. Locally, the I. W. W. had no organization and apparently the Socialists were too numerous to molest, though technically they were liable for arrest under the Espionage Act. However, for fear of alienating the radical vote the press was almost civil in its discussions of socialism. The *Express* made the unheard of concession that "We are all more or less socialists now days. Some of us call our socialism by the name of State Regulation or Municipal Ownership or Organized Benevolence. But it is socialism pure and simple as distinguished from the individualism of Herbert Spencer" (*Express,* Oct. 18, 1917).

The year 1918 began calmly enough with the sage advice from the Chamber of Commerce that "if we could attain sanity in all things, there would be no more difficulties (*Live Wire,* Jan. 1918, p. 1). However, when peace broke out, hysteria rose. On November 14, 1918, the *Express* carried a banner headline: BOLSHEVISM THREATENS ALL EUROPE. . . . On December 8 the headlines read: UNEMPLOYMENT GREATEST DANGER TO THE NATION NOW . . . "and it will come with attendant misery at a time when anarchistic tendencies are cantagious." These two headlines told the story of what was to come in 1919.

Despite its opposition to the war—perhaps because of it—the Socialist party, locally and nationally, was stronger at the beginning of 1919 than at any time before or since. The number of registered Socialists in Buffalo increased from 2000 in 1916 to 5000 in 1919, and the party could muster a vote of around 15,000 between 10 and 15 per cent of the electorate. And it was not the actual size but the potentiality for growth, both nationally and locally, which most disturbed conservative elements. Socialist rallies, speeches, even party feuds, were given good press coverage, and the *Express* noted that "the party's last [1918] labor day picnic had had 10,000 in attendance" (*Express,* Dec. 22, 1918). Although the *Express* was mainly interested in fighting European Bolshevism, it was not happy about the domestic radical scene. "The idea that any body could really entertain such a project as an armed insurrection to overthrow the republic of the United States—the best government on earth—impresses most Americans as so absurd as to be worth only a derisive laugh. . . . There is not going to be a revolution in the United States. There is not going to be a reign of terror. But there may be some forcible demands for those who do not like the United States to get out and stay out" (*Express,* Jan. 3, 1919). The demands were not long in coming.

Unrest continued throughout the year and in September 1919 a nation-wide steel strike (involving 365,000 workers) occurred and was billed as an attempt to Bolshevize the steel industry.[29] Buffalo was a steel city, and in the fall of 1919 radicalism was very poignantly in the air. The Socialists held nightly street-corner meetings as did the Minute Men, whose objective was to counteract Bolshevik propaganda, and even the Communists were able to get 400 votes in the primary municipal election.[30] Buffalo was then governed by four city commissioners and a mayor, and the election of 1919 to select three commissioners was fought on the issue of socialism. To the surprise of everyone (including the Socialists) the Socialist candidate got the high vote of 47,000 followed by the Republican party candidate with 42,000 and an Independent Republican with 39,000 (*Express,* Nov. 5, 1919). The election so alarmed a leading banker that he cancelled a $14,000,000 offer to buy the controlling interest in the street railway company—although the press took the election with equanimity after the initial shock wore off. The *Express* excused its own complicity in the election of a Socialist:

> The conservatives will blame the newspapers for not con-
> ducting a campaign of silence. The conservatives ought to
> have taken warning after the primaries, realized that Per-
> kins [the socialist] was a dangerous opponent, and gone vig-
> orously to work to bring out the vote against him. . . . The
> newspapers are potent at times but not omnipotent. In fact
> there are well authenticated instances of candidates with
> every newspaper in town against them . . . winning. You
> can't kill a man by ignoring him. But responsibility has
> cooled many a hot-head. May that be true of Perkins. (Nov.
> 5, 1919)

Locally, the "counter-revolution" was gathering momentum, and
the concept of dangerous radicalism was expanding to include not
only the anarcho-syndicalists but the Communists and Socialists—and
those with "tendencies" in that direction. On November 21 the *Commercial* warned: "Outraged Patriotism To Rise Up in Righteous
Wrath To Crush Foul Plot against Nation." On December 30th the
headquarters of the Communist Party was raided by the State Lusk
Committee, and twenty men and two women were arrested. The
Express thought:

> The raid will probably have considerable effect on the self-
> deceived, both those who are in the Communist party and
> the large number who are on the outside looking in. Radi-
> cals for fun and particularly parlor Bolsheviks may exam-
> ine a little more closely the actual location of the deadline
> which may not be overstepped with prudence by those who
> wish to retain a standing as American. . . . The arrest of
> local radicals conveys a warning which goes considerably
> beyond the limits of their party membership. (December
> 31, 1919)

Two days later the nation-wide raid on the radicals by U.S. Attorney General Palmer resulted in the arrest of 136 in Buffalo. The
city was not unpleased with its showing, which compared favorably
with 300 each for New York and Detroit, 120 each for Philadelphia
and Chicago. (The poor showing of Chicago, capital of American
radicalism, was due to the fact that the county sheriff, jealous of

federal authorities, made a pre-emptive raid sending the radicals into hiding.) The Justice Department issued warrants for 250 in Buffalo, but only 105 were finally served.

Sociologically, one of the more interesting features of the raid was the citizen participation which it involved. "More than 200 policemen," noted the *Commercial* "were aided by as many citizens, members of civic organizations such as the Chamber of Commerce, Rotary and Kiwanis and other clubs" (Jan. 3, 1920). The information for the raid was supplied:

> . . . by a secret committee of citizens which has been working day and night since last spring. . . . Just how powerful this organization may be is shown by the fact that all of the evidence [for both the Lusk and Palmer raids] was furnished by the committee. . . . All the photographic copies of membership cards, which so astounded the alleged members of the Communist party . . . were secured by the committee. . . . For the raids on Friday, 221 names were submitted to the government by the committee . . . and of these 80 or 90 were finally brought in. It was brought out that the citizens committee had had paid investigators keeping track of alleged radical activities here. Members of the committee and these investigators got memberships in the Communist party and got in at meetings, securing names and other information for the raid on the branch of the Union of Russian Workers here in November. How much money was contributed to the investigation is not known . . . but $25,000 has been subscribed by Buffalo men for the purpose of investigating the local radical press. (*Commercial,* Jan. 6, 1920)

On January 5 the *Enquirer* printed a list of 125 citizens who took part in the raid. By tracing out the means in various source books it was found that this group was predominantly upper class. Seventy-two per cent of the names appeared in *Dau's Blue Book,* which describes itself as "a compilation of the most prominent householders."[31] The *Social Register* listed 24.8 per cent of names; 52 per cent of those appearing in the *Blue Book* were listed as members of the

Chamber of Commerce; 45 per cent were members of the leading men's club. The *City Directory* revealed that approximately 70 to 80 per cent of the "raiders" were officials of manufacturing corporations. Of the eight men singled out by the *Express* as the organizers of the raid and given special commendation by the federal authorities, one was a former president of the Chamber of Commerce and general production manager of a radiator manufacturing concern, two were officials of a forge company, two were stock brokers, another in manufacturing, and one a member of the school board and the business manager of the *Commercial* (*Express,* Jan. 3, 1920).

Today the raids sound like an episode from the Keystone cops. "One hundred automobiles were assembled in the center of the city at 4. p.m.," writes the *Enquirer,* "and started on a dash of red hunting which radiated throughout Buffalo and the surrounding towns:

> Drivers were supplied with copies of federal warrants and while the police officer watched the prisoner the organization member searched his home for radical literature and explosives. In one man's room was found a shotgun and other weapons . . . along with some 1914 Russian war bonds. In another apartment was found a picture of Leon Trotsky and some I. W. W. papers . . . in still another a picture of the local socialist lawyer. . . . A detective came to the station with arms filled with alleged radical literature but the publications were all in Polish and he was unable to make any translations. . . . The jail was crowded with 205 radicals—greatest number of prisoners in years said the jailor—The chief of police looked them over and said: "A fine looking bunch they are. It's too bad we can't line them up against the wall there and shoot them" (Composite quote from the *Enquirer* and the *Commercial,* Dec. 31 through Jan. 4).

Yet the raids were deadly serious. Throughout the country some 10,000 radicals were jailed. *Nation* magazine called it "an unprecedented outburst of terror and terrorism."[32] While the Red Scare came to its dramatic climax between November 1919 and March 1920 it did not begin or end then.[33] Anti-radicalism became institutionalized, a kind of permanent counterrevolution built into the legal system in the form of criminal syndicalism laws, into the investigative and police apparatus of federal, state, and local governments, and into the voluntary organizations of the business class.[34] The Red Scare terminated a decade of class conflict and ushered in a time of repression and apathy.

The period 1910-20 was a decade of conflict, the climax of a crisis germinating for thirty years. Developments analogous to those described above occurred throughout the urban world: Buffalo was only a mirror of the larger culture. Rarely had a decade of American life been so riddled with strife and dissension. Arrests for violent personal crimes in Buffalo and seemingly throughout the nation began to rise around 1906, reaching a peak in 1918, afterwards (to 1940) receding.[35] The suicide rate for the nation reached its high point for the twentieth century in 1913.[36] Crime and suicide are individual manifestations of a collective discord—of anomie—and signify an unconscious repudiation of existing society. In the political sphere the "repudiation" became articulate as an organized attack on the institutions of capitalism, an incipient class war.

In the years between 1866 and 1890 the authority of capitalism was virtually unchallenged if not unquestioned. But from the early 1890's to 1914 there was a restless agitation for some kind of limitation on the power of the capitalist class. Yet even during the epoch of trust-busting the concentration of capital continued unabated.[37] The public image of big business may have been soiled by ten years of muckraking, but its power was not seriously threatened by the reformers.

Yet by 1910 the "ruling class" or power eilte was immobilized by the inner paralysis of the capitalist system. External and legal restraint on capitalist power could be circumvented easily enough. But the business class was as powerless as anyone else when confronted with the business cycle. Big business had full access to coercive powers—the police and military were available as strike-breakers, etc. But force could not create jobs, or run industry, or win elections. Coercion was useless against labor and tended to solidify rather than destroy the union movement. The elite could, for a time, inhibit, but it could not initiate action.

Between 1912 and 1914 the crisis of capitalism deepened. In the years between 1902 and 1906 the growth rate of the total economy was 7.6 per cent, declining to 4.6 for the years between 1910 and 1913; in 1913 both the production and consumption of goods dropped sharply.[38] Unemployment and crime increased, locally and nationally (see Table 14). Throughout the country strikes flared in bitter violence (Paterson, Lawrence, Ludlow), and took on an alarmingly political coloration. The problem was deeper than a worsening of "existential conditions." Actually wages increased slightly between 1911 and 1915 and unemployment was a customary feature of working-class life. It was the "definition of the situation" rather than the objective reality which had changed. Years of reform and revolutionary agitation had altered expectations. Men no longer bore their lot as "fate," and what had once been endured as sacrifice came to be seen as exploitation. In the 1890's economic collapse was no real threat to established society because there was no formulated alternative to capitalism. By 1912 there was not only a vigorous radical movement—international in scope—with a new model for the organization of society, but a significant defection of the intellectuals who were rapidly losing faith in the ideology of capitalism. "The battle does not lie against crusted prejudice" wrote Walter Lippman in July 1914, "but against the chaos of the new freedom."[39] Two weeks later the outbreak of World War I put an end to the chaos.

The war in Europe brought an instant prosperity to America, creating an immediate and inexhaustible market for agriculture and manufacturing. For the upper class the war was not only an economic venture but an opportunity to reassert its "rightful" leadership of the community. The war opened up a sphere of action and power to compensate for the paralysis of the upper class in the realm of politics and economics.

For the upper class the war was a holy crusade, but the general public was for the most part indifferent to the lofty appeals to save civilization. A sizable and organized minority actively opposed the war, and the high 1917 Socialist vote (25 per cent of the electorate in most cities) pointed to a significant anti-war sentiment.[40] The popularity of the war sprang from prosperity rather than patriotism; for the majority, it was more a spectator sport than a historic mission. But the sense of drift was ended, and progressives took solace in the belief that the war was "administering the *coup de grâce* to the old capitalism."[41] In actuality, the war restored the old capitalism. Wilson's timid experimentations with social and economic planning were scuttled early in 1919. Talk of a new freedom vanished in a concerted onslaught on the old freedom.

By 1919 the business class was in clear if insecure ascendancy after a twenty-year retreat. But its new position of dominance had yet to be ratified by public consensus. Moreover, corporate capitalism was threatened internationally by the spread of Bolshevism and the designs of the League of Nations; domestically by the return of the pre-war chaos, unemployment, the high cost of living, the increased power of labor (resulting from war gains), and the indefinable threat of radicalism.

The fear of radicalism had some objective basis, or so it seemed at the time. The electoral strength of the Socialist party had grown, not declined, during the war years and the Socialists had made headway in the labor movement.[42] (See also Table 13.) Even within the conservative AFL the Socialists could muster 33 to 45 per cent of the votes and several times came close to deposing Gompers. More ominous still was the 1919 steel strike, masterminded by William Z. Foster and left-wing Socialists who came to constitute the Communist party. Significantly, Catholic labor—at least in Buffalo—also took credit for the strike.

But the real source of the Red Scare of 1919-20 was the fear of an idea, not a movement. As a local immigration official inadvertently put it: "A man cannot have radical ideas and become the kind of citizen we want in this country" (*Buffalo Enquirer,* Jan. 20, 1920).

The specter of Bolshevism only provided the pretext for a campaign which had been under way—and underground—for several years.[43] As early as 1916-17 the I. W. W.'s were "the victims of a determined conservative campaign to stamp out radical social and economic ideas . . . a drive with all the earmarks of class war."[44] The liquidation of the I. W. W. was accomplished by the simple expedient of the systematic removal of its leadership by imprisonment. Next came the left-wing Socialists, with the imprisonment of Debs and the top leadership of the party for opposition to World War I. Next came the right-wing Social Democrats—the expulsion of five legally elected assemblymen from the New York legislature and of Victor Berger from Congress. To contend that the Socialist party would have been tolerated had it supported the war, or had it not, in its enthusiasm for the Russian revolution, gone too far to the left, is to misread the facts. Gompers's AFL supported the war and never missed an occasion for patriotic proclamations, yet it was as badly mauled as the Socialist party. According to Murray, the AFL lost one-third of its membership between 1920 and 1923 as a direct result of the Red Scare, "a staggering loss not recouped until after the crash of 1929."[45] After labor came the liberals, who were not imprisoned but intimidated; writes Arthur Schlesinger, Jr., "If but few had actual indictments hanging over them, all felt a sentence suspended over their enthusiasms, their beliefs, their innermost thoughts."[46]

The Red Scare was both a source and a symbol of the restoration of capitalist power; it marked the end of the organized opposition to the corporate order. The reform movement was bankrupt before the 1919 hysteria, its social basis eroded by the decline of the "old" middle class. Progressivism was a rebellion of the local merchant class against the translocal corporation. But by 1920 even retailing was coming under corporate control (the chain store), and manufacturing was concentrated in a few giant cartels. In Buffalo between 1913 and 1919 the value of manufactured products declined (see Table 15). The old middle class was consigned to a second seat in the power structure. Although the number of wage-workers increased sharply during the war, the trade-union movement was no match for organized capital. The AFL had never been an opponent of capitalism and in fact prided itself on being the main bulwark against socialism. But in 1919 big business was in no mood for accommodation and launched its aggressive open-shop campaign—"the American Plan"—which nullified labor's wartime gains.[47] While the forces of reform were on the wane, the revolutionary movement was simply obliterated in the 1920's. The Socialist vote in 1920 for Debs was 902,000, but in 1928 Norman Thomas polled only 268,000, and the Communist vote for Foster amounted to only 48,000.[48] The decline of the Socialist movement was due to a variety of factors: direct suppression, dissension and distrust over the issue of patriotism, and the business prosperity of the 1920's. While the unemployment remained high (10 to 15 per cent of the labor force) and agriculture was depressed, the dominant minority prospered and was able to suffuse the 1920's with a mood of optimism, contrasting sharply with the discontentment of the progressive era. Alan Valentine speaks of the year 1913 as "a preface to the Age of Anxiety as well as a postlude to the Age of Complacency."[49] The sequence could almost be reversed. The 1920's was the most complacent decade on record. Both major parties regressed to the ideological infantilism of pure *laissez faire*. Between 1900 and 1920 progressive republicans and liberal democrats alike advocated some form of governmental regulation of the economic process. In the 1920's political leaders simply closed their eyes to the contradictions of industrial capitalism, sowing seeds of the disastrous results to be reaped in the '30's.

In 1920 corporate capitalism was unopposed but still unsupported; it had power but needed a principle to make legitimate its rule. "Power is a fact," writes A. A. Berle, "but it is also a fact that the human mind apparently cannot be wholly or permanently inhibited from asking certain questions. . . . There is . . . no instance in history in which any group, great or small, has not set up some theory of the right to power."[50] In an earlier period private property was the legitimizing principle of capitalism, but with the dominance of the corporation, property recedes into the background, and the "public consensus . . . indefinite, completely unorganized, without traceable form . . . becomes the final arbiter of legitimacy."[51] The essence of the new consensus was Americanism, which was manufactured during the war and extended to legitimatize the corporate order. In the late 'teens an Americanization crusade was launched as a "constructive" anti-radical measure, designed primarily to assimilate the immigrant.[52] But Americanism came to mean more than assimilation; it meant above all else a belief in the sanctity of the prevailing order of society. As an Americanism speaker told an immigrant audience in Buffalo: "If you have not found your share of happiness here [in America] something is wrong. Our history proves that there is nothing wrong with our institutions, so the individual must be wrong" (*Buffalo Express,* Jan. 30, 1920). The statement is an exaggeration of the basic thesis of Americanism: the social system is sound; any defects must therefore be attributed to the person. The whole historical tendency toward secularization was beginning to be reversed in the 1920's. To describe the antithesis of secularization, Howard Becker coined the term "sacralization," "the process by which societies are tightened, hardened, reintegrated and restored."[53] The idea of Americanism was the sacralizing principle of the system of corporate capitalism which has dominated American society since the 1920's.

As a social system or institution capitalism has been characterized by a drive for limitless expansion. Yet by 1913 American capitalism was immobilized: the growth rate was declining, and unemployment, business failures, and labor discontents were rising. The capitalist class constituted a powerless elite, unable to operate the institutional machinery it theoretically commanded. As the system faltered, conflict increased. Opposition to the old order mounted and became organized as a political force. Many and diverse elements clamored for reform; even revolution was a distinct possibility. But the vast infusion of state-capital (i.e. defense spending and war loans) in

World War I restored the capitalist elite to its traditional leadership of the community. However, opposition to capitalism grew even during the war years, and after the war, chaos returned. The patriotic hysteria generated by the war provided the pretext for the liquidation of radicalism, although the campaign had been under way long before. The war itself undermined the forces of reform—the "old" middle class was relegated to a subordinate role in the social structure and trade-unionism was unable to withstand the opposition of organized capital. The Red Scare of 1919-20 not only neutralized the opposition to corporate capitalism but continued as a kind of permanent counterrevolution. In 1920 corporate capitalism was unopposed but still unsupported by public consensus. The new order was "sacralized" or sanctified by the mystique of Americanism, which replaced the older Protestant ethic as the ideological foundation of corporate capitalism.

8

Crime as a response to the anomie of war: the configuration of arrests in Buffalo, 1830-1970

> What do you think of the war?
> Which one?
>
> Interview with local hoodlum, *Buffalo Times*, August 5, 1914

Crime is by definition a social phenomenon and its extent and character vary with the "metabolism" of the larger society. "The cause of crime," writes Clarence Jeffry, "is in the legal and social institutions, not the individual offender."[1]

Violence in the animal world bears a resemblance to crime in human society. Animals, like men, are social by nature, live in communities, abide by "mores" (conventional codes), similar to an "institution" in being a pattern of collective action learned through socialization and passed on over generations. Contrary to the ideas of the Social Darwinians, animals are normally rather serene and nonviolent, at least when measured against men. But the animal uprooted from its natural community either grows belligerent or sulks in despair, like his human counterpart, and the disorganized animal society usually exhibits an excess of contention.

The simplest animal social structure is the pecking order, or dominance hierarchy. When the pecking order of a flock of chickens is upset, fighting increases, food consumption and egg production drop.[2] Generally, dominance hierarchies serve to restrain and regulate intra-group conflict. After observing baboons in their natural habitat, Washburn and de Vore noted that in troops "where the rank order is clearly defined, fighting is rare." The usual effect of the hierarchy, once relations among the males are settled, is to decrease disruptions in the troop. The dominant animals, the males in particular, will not let the others fight. When bickering breaks out, they usually run to the scene and stop it. Dominant males thus protect the weaker animals against harm from inside as well as from outside the group.[3] Correlatively, disruption of the hierarchy foments strife, a struggle for succession: Haddow observed that "prolonged and severe fighting always broke out [in monkey bands] after a large male had been shot."[4] Normally, monkeys manifest a high degree of maternal and paternal care. But under anomic conditions there is a Hobbesian war of each against all. Transporting a colony of 100 Rhesus monkeys from India to an experimental laboratory-island near Puerto Rico, C. R. Carpenter observed that the "instinct" of mother—and father—love virtually disappeared: females fought the infants away from the food supply (even though food was plentiful), and several mothers killed their own children. On the new island more infants were killed by the adults than died of all other causes. Hostility was pervasive; fighting incessant. However, after about a year on the new island the community re-established itself and the agitation subsided.[5] Thomas and Znaniecki described a similar process of organization-disorganization-reorganization in the transplantation of the European immigrant to America.

According to V. C. Wynne-Edwards, animal societies evolve conventions—codes of law—to safeguard the general welfare of the group, "especially against the anti-social, subversive self-advancement of the individual."[6] Compliance with the code is the result of social pressure and appears to be "the exact counterpart of what we recognize in our own behavior as moral conduct." If the code—the social tradition—is rendered inoperative, lethal strife ensues, mortality rates climb. So too on the human scene: anomic populations are violent, e.g. the murder rate in "disorganized" America is twenty times higher than in "organized" England, where the "pecking order" (the class structure) and conventional codes are more intact.

When informal pressure (ostracism, ridicule, gossip) fails, then the human community resorts to the threat of physical punishment to coerce conformity to the social code. At that moment crime is born. Crime is any act or personal condition which calls forth formal and official punishment.[7] In the primitive society, the peasant village, or even the American small town, custom and convention are usually sufficient to guarantee the continuity of the social system. But in the heterogeneity and anonymity of the metropolis, or in times of social upheaval, the community seeks to maintain order through the imposition of legal restraints and thus transforms deviant behavior into crime.

Crime—against persons, property and public order—flouishes under conditions of institutional dislocation, of anomie.[8] When individuals do not feel morally obligated to adhere to the rules which protect (in fact, create) private property, an increase in larceny is to be expected. And in the anomic situation personal violence is common because men feel they can no longer rely on the community for protection and "take the law into their own hands." The frontier violence —of the wilderness or the urban jungle—derives from the presumed necessity for self-defense, as Thomas and Znaniecki explain: "The murderer does not feel himself backed up in his dealings with the outside world by any strong group of his own . . . . [he takes recourse] in the idea of self-redress. . . . In short, the immigrant . . . feels as if he is in a human wilderness, with nobody and nothing but his physical strength to rely upon."[9] Viewing the contemporary scene, Jackson Toby comes to a similar conclusion: "predatory crime occurs when social vigilance is reduced."[10]

In a similar vein John Dollard explains the relationship between violence and social disorganization among the Negro population of the South: "The personal security of the Negro is by no means so well guaranteed by the law as is that of the white person. [Negro men and women] are frequently armed. . . . Apparently we have here a kind of frontier where the law is weak and each person is expected to attend to his own interests by means of direct personal aggression and defense."[11] Moreover, Dollard continues, there is a differential application of the law. The dominant white caste "condones Negro violence" because it weakens the solidarity of the Negro group and makes it less resistant to white domination. This "tolerance of violence," Dollard says, "is not a conscious policy . . . but pragmatic, unformalized and intuitive." However, it is "functional" for the maintenance of the caste system. A similar situation could be found in the nineteenth-century industrial slum, where working-class violence was permitted, if not encouraged, as a means of atomizing labor solidarity. Criminal violence is both a cause and effect of anomie.

But punishment also grows with the spread of anomie. Crime is defined by punishment, and the crime rate is a function of both criminal action and police action, which could be stated as

$$CR = CA \times PA.$$

This simple formula calls attention to the interdependence of the variables which make the end product called "crime." The total amount of crime increases in times of social upheaval because the establishment, threatened by loss of a supporting consensus, resorts to law to maintain *its* order. For instance, in the age of the bourgeois revolutions, from roughly the sixteenth century to the nineteenth century, a collapsing aristocracy tried to save itself through recourse to police-juridical intimidation. In England the break-up of feudalism, the enclosure movements, the commercial expansion, and the beginnings of the industrial revolution, "all took place within the shadow of the gallows," says E. P. Thompson; "the class war was fought out in terms of crime and punishment."[12] Hanging, jailing, and flogging were the weapons of the upper class; crime, riot, and mob action were the responses of the people. In thirteenth-century England there were only ten or fifteen capital offenses on the books and the death penalty was in fact rarely used. By the sixteenth century there had been an extraordinary increase in the number of death sentences; in the reign of Henry VIII (1509-47) an estimated 72,000 vagabonds were hanged, often in rows of 300 to 400 at a time.[13] Public execution was justified as a deterrent—a means of terrifying others into willing submission—but in actuality aroused further antagonism. Violent punishment bred ever more violent crime. By the eighteenth century the number of capital crimes had risen to 218, and the death penalty was imposed almost exclusively for economic offenses. In 1785 there were 97 executions in London and Middlesex—one for murder, 43 for burglary, the remainder for assorted property crimes like forgery and horse-stealing.[14] But the ruthless arbitrariness of eighteenth-century jurisprudence did not make the population more law abiding. Instead it created that profound disdain for authority which became the moral foundation of Anglo-American democracy.

While hardly paradise, the new American Republic did free men from some of the horrors of law and order. "The prevailing attitude of lawlessness [in the colonies]," as Goebel and Naughton put it, "subsequently underwent transfiguration into the spirit of liberty."[15] Colonial codes specified some 10 to 20 capital offenses, as opposed to over 200 in England, and the death penalty was seldom carried out. More executions occurred in London and Middlesex in 1785 than in Massachusetts between 1780 and 1900.[16] In colonial New York there were 140 executions between 1664 and 1776—of these, 39 were slaves involved in alleged conspiracies in 1712 and 1741. "It is patent that there prevailed in New York Province," Goebel and Naughton write, "if not greater compassion at least greater reluctance to take life than in England."[17] Whipping was an approved "afflictive penalty," often coupled with carting—the offender was put in a cart and drawn around town to be ridiculed and abused by the public. The culprit was "thereby rendered infamous," that is, identified as a public enemy—a powerful incentive to leave town. But only 250 whipping-carting cases are recorded in the 112-year history of the colony of New York.[18] Drunks who were unable to pay a five-shilling fine could be committed to stocks for six hours so the gaze and taunts of the community could humiliate the poor creatures into good behavior. In Massachusetts drunks were sometimes sentenced to wear a large red D on their clothing in the hope that communal exposure might induce temperance.[19]

Colonial America handled the law-breaker as an individual and kept the deviant in line through social rather than physical sanctions. There was no criminal class, and the urban proletariat and urban paupers, the main source of crime in later decades, were "insignificant groups in eighteenth century America."[20] However, immediately prior to the first American Revolution there was, according to Carl Bridenbaugh, "an alarming increase in robbery and violent crime."[21] The trend apparently continued after the Revolution: A. H. Hobbs reports that between 1791 and 1810 the total number of cases in Philadelphia courts increased from 357 to 810 a year, with property offenses doubling and personal crimes trebling.[22] By the 1820's, according to Gustavus Myers, New York City alone had 12,000 paupers, and by 1830 there were 75,000 persons throughout the United States imprisoned for debts of less than $20. While recognizing the near impossibility of valid comparisons, Beaumont and Tocqueville thought the crime rate in the United States was probably higher than the French rate in the 1830's. A criminal subculture emerged not only in the eastern seaboard cities but in the new towns along the Ohio valley, "where rings of horse thieves, bands of counterfeiters and arson racketeers operated . . . an ugly layer of vice, crime and lawlessness [coming mainly] from the aimless and uncertain life of floaters," in Richard C. Wade's words. The 1830's, writes Dolan, saw the first appearance of the "infested hell-holes," the "stench pots," in a word, the city, which later became the center of crime. The rise of crime, says Dolan, was "concomitant with the growth of the city."[23]

Buffalo in the 1830's could qualify as a hell-hole. Seven-tenths of the crime in the United States occurred along the Erie Canal, but Buffalo was indifferent to the problem. In 1832 when the city was incorporated the council refused to appropriate funds for a police officer. However, in 1835 the mayor appointed five watchmen to "perambulate the city . . . and endeavor to prevent riotous and disorderly conduct."[24] As late as 1845 the city had only one police captain and eight watchmen to police a population of nearly 30,000. A tumultuous place, the city seems to have had a high tolerance for violence. Fist fights occurred, even among the top people, who took pride in their physical prowess. Numerous (doubtless exaggerated) accounts tell of leading citizens beating up would-be robbers who accosted them in dark alleys. Riots were said to be ordinary occurrences, rather like "sporting events," as Roger Lane says with reference to Boston.[25] Hubbell reports a rather typical melee in 1832: a fight breaks out among the Irish dock-workers; then a crowd of 250 men and boys dash down Main Street to quell the disorder; the dockers unite in a solid front against the common enemy, and the two groups hurl rocks and insults at each other. "A fierce contest raged for over an hour," writes Hubbell "and frightful results were averted only through the argumentative influence and summary action of members of the city council."[26] In the 1830's the city council was the high tribunal of local government and represented the authority of the "city fathers," but in subsequent decades its influence waned, and the task of maintaining order fell to the police department.

In the 1830's Buffalo was still a self-policing community that relied on social sanctions to control, or neutralize, the disruptive elements.[27] The so-called police force was mainly engaged in riding herd on drunks and whores. *The Commercial Advertiser* explained in February 1837 that it has had to suspend the labors of its police reporter because of a "decrease in vagabondism." However, the city was now "inundated with loose characters who nightly prowl the streets seeking what they may devour," and it seemed again necessary to use the lash [of public exposure]." Presumably as a deterrent the names of arrestees were published: "Timothy Howard, a pimp, with three teams of prostitutes . . . his character is doubtless improved by their society," the editor added. The report continued:

> Jane Ross and Mary MacFarlane—two prostitutes—were
> sentenced to 15 days each for drunkenness and quarrelling
> [also booked] . . . a 14-year-old girl, drunk, here without
> friends or relatives. Is there not some society, or some in-
> dividual, who will step forward and snatch this young green
> brand from the burning? (*Buffalo Commercial Advertiser*,
> February 9, 1837).

Similar reports of characters brought to the watch-house recurred
throughout the year.

> January 3—Amasa Fuller, who described himself as for-
> merly a sheep stealer and now an itinerant Methodist
> preacher, was found incapable of taking care of himself
> and brought to the watch house, whence he was discharged
> on condition of pursuing his calling elsewhere for the
> future.
>
> January 9—John Gallagher—determined not to be idle while
> in jail, stole a watch, was discharged for the old offense,
> retaken and recommitted.
>
> January 14—A henpecked John Downes was brought to the
> watch house, charged with beating his wife, a gentle Cana-
> dian fair, of whom he appeared to have a most reverent
> horror.
>
> February 13—James, a fine Negro, was very drunk and
> abused his white wife Sarah—to prison . . . 15 days.
>
> May 2—Elizabeth Moody—found in the street drunk—sent
> to jail six days. Nancy Hayes—15 years of age—disorderly,
> drunk and a vagrant—30 days. Jane McGurty—drunk first
> time—discharged. Joseph Hall—found very drunk—6 days
> hard labor. J. H. Smith—drunk and mangy—fined $1. and
> costs. Denis Sutherland—drunk, first entrance . . . to watch
> house, admonished and discharged.

The *Commercial Advertiser* regarded "drunken, vicious women" as
"the worst deformation of the human race" and wondered if there
were not some means of "deterring women from thus degrading
themselves." The editor noted that the ball and chain gang had "ef-

fectually frightened the male loafers" and suggested that the females be set to picking wool, beating hemp, or other employment, which might be performed in a shed, "exposing them to the gaze of the public" (*Commercial Advertiser,* May 2, 1837). The crime news was written with a mixture of levity and vindictiveness, but seldom hysteria. The criminal was not yet seen as a member of the "dangerous class," and even the drunks had names. The authorities loved to preach and moralize. On St. Patrick's Day 1837 "a motley group of sons and daughters of Erin were collected from different wards in various states of hilarity from the libations they had made to their patron," and three juvenile delinquents were "severely admonished by the mayor and discharged" (*Commercial Advertiser,* March 18, 1837). The press tried to warn people to stay away from criminal haunts along the waterfront but to no avail. After a young man had been robbed of $80 saved from a year's work, the *Commercial Advertiser* (March 2, 1837) concluded that "villany assumes such Protean shapes as to allure new victims in the face of all warnings from experience of the past . . . innocent lads from the country are decoyed into some questionable resort, where their honest credulity renders them an easy prey to the sharper." Doubtless the elegant language was wasted on the potential victims, though the editor and his readers probably felt they were doing their bit as guardians of the public morals. Stiff penalties were meted out for vagrancy because the community abhorred idleness as the worst of sins: to live without visible means of support was a travesty of the spirit of capitalism. Six months in the work-house might not reform the vagrant, but it would teach him and others to stay out of Buffalo.

Generally, property crimes are punished more vigorously than offenses against persons. A 1837 court record shows two men received five years for counterfeiting; one, two years for grand larceny; and two got three months' hard labor for petty larceny (*Commercial Advertiser,* March 18, 1837). But the same year two men who during a drunken quarrel killed a third man by throwing him into boiling lye received only a brief prison sentence. In the 1830's felonies were usually handled by the county sheriff, but he only entered the law-enforcement process in response to citizen complaint. If no one came forward to ask for an investigation, even murder might be ignored. Waterfront killings were almost defined as good riddance to bad rubbish. Thomas Low Nichols, a radical humanist and editor of *The Buffalonian,* reported on March 7, 1838, the body of a William Donnelly missing since the night of December 31 had been discovered in the Canal, his skull broken. "We have no doubt that he was murdered. If that portion of the city (the waterfront) were sunk with its inhabitants," Nichols adds, "society would be no loser" (*The Buffalonian,* March 7, 1838).

On the other hand, murder which cannot be ignored, usually ended in public execution. In 1825, three brothers killed a peddler who tried to collect an old debt from them. They buried the peddler on their farm, then claimed he had given them power of attorney to collect his debts from other farmers. This obvious hoax aroused the suspicions of the community. An investigation followed, the body was discovered, the brothers duly tried and hanged.[28] The hanging drew a crowd of 30,000 people, many of whom had ridden all day in a wagon to witness the spectacle. Bands played slow and plaintive music; speeches were made, sermons preached, goodness approved, and evil denounced. Public execution was intended to provide instruction in the wages of sin. But an astute observer, Sidney Burr, noted that the next murder in the community was committed by a person who had witnessed the 1825 execution. Burr argued that crime is increased by the spectacle of the public execution because men thereby "become familiarized with blood and death."[29] About ten to fifteen executions occurred in Buffalo between 1825 and 1870.

By 1836 the watch-house had evolved into a city jail. Like 80 per cent of the other structures of the town the jail was built by Benjamin Rathbun, known as the John Jacob Astor of Buffalo. Benjamin, along with his brother Lyman and his nephew Allen, owned and operated the leading hotel, the main stage coach line, as well as a construction company employing over 2000 men in a time when few firms anywhere had more than a dozen workers. To sustain such a far-flung enterprise the Rathbuns resorted to the handy expedient of signing the names of eminent Buffalonians to their personal notes. The usual procedure was for Allen to forge the signature, then Lyman would take the "paper" to the bank, pick up $500 or $1000, and then repay it before the note fell due. The scheme worked well for five years; Buffalo gained needed construction and employment, and no one was a loser. The Rathbuns made signal contributions to the well-being and progress of Buffalo.[30] Benjamin was not a speculator but a builder, and where other local fortunes derived from outright theft of land from the Indians, Rathbun's came from hard work and organizational genius. Miriam Beard, the historian of business, calls Rathbun a "plain scoundrel" but concedes he made Buffalo into an "elegant town" through his ". . . many acts of swindling and forgery through which he carried on the improvements of the place."[31] Then in the crisis of 1837 the Rathbuns were caught short and could not pick up their forged notes. Similar notes turned up in New York, Boston, Cincinnati, for a total of $500,000—an enormous sum in an age when men worked for fifty cents a day. The Rathbun failure caused a crisis of confidence, and helped produce further panic throughout the country. Lyman opted out and skipped off to Texas, never to be heard of again (in 1932, 93 years later, a document was received by the Buffalo Historical Society describing his death in a gun battle in 1841). Allen, 19 years old at the time, was arrested in Ohio and intimidated into turning state's evidence. And Benjamin was left holding the bag. By a "gentlemen's agreement" he was induced to sign over all his property, valued at some $2,500,000, to a clique—or consortium—of six eminent Buffalonians in return for a promise of immunity from prosecution. The very same day Benjamin was arrested and thrown in the Buffalo jail, where he was kept for nine months and denied bail. Buffalo grand juries refused to indict him, and because local opinion was too favorable to him, his trial was finally held in the town of Batavia—30 miles away, a great distance in the time before railroads. Thomas Nichols covered the trial, and found it a "mockery of justice . . . with the jury packed, perjured and paid." But the court sentenced Rathbun to Auburn penitentiary for five years.

As Nichols dug into the case he became convinced that Rathbun was the victim of a "most foul and rank conspiracy." Motive was the measure of crime, Nichols said. "Rathbun's action was not a black-hearted fiend-like deed, that argued innate depravity, but merely an offense against certain laws which the rich have made for the protection of their property" (*The Buffalonian,* January 1, 1838). Though scarcely known today, Nichols has a good claim to being America's first muckraker. He described *The Buffalonian* as "an engine of moral progress" and with considerable force rammed the moral foundations of the local elite, printing what everyone knew to be fact: That Hiram Pratt, the president of the bank, the leading member of the Presbyterian Church, and the appointed mayor of the city, was a "perjured scoundrel," who acquired his fortune by trading whisky to the Indians in return for their land. Nichols charged that Pratt and five other eminent Buffalonians, including Millard Fillmore, got hold of Rathbun's property under false pretenses, double-crossed him, and sent him to prison. Pratt fumed, and Nichols headlined in his paper: "Hiram Pratt says the statements of *The Buffalonian* are outrageous. They are. The facts are outrageous." Libel charges were brought against Nichols, but local grand juries refused to indict him. One member of the clique collected a "gang of villains desperate enough to carry out his designs" and paid them $2000 to destroy the offices and press of *The Buffalonian.* They were foiled on the first attempt by Nichols and his friends, but Nichols realized that those who went that far would "stop at no rascality that would not peril their safety. Our safety is in their cowardice and our own high destiny" (*The Buffalonian,* May 12, 1838). Next, they physically assaulted Nichols, tried to kidnap him, and demolish his printing plant, whereupon he filed a suit against the clique. But later, by stacking a grand jury, the clique got Nichols indicted and sent to the Buffalo jail.

Assigned to a cell eight feet long and five feet wide, Nichols sent for his trunk and his books; his friends brought him cake and wine, cigars and flowers.[32] He consoled himself with the thought that Bunyan wrote *Pilgrim's Progress* in jail and continued to turn out copy for *The Buffalonian,* harassing poor Mr. Pratt, the principal "Divine," Dr. Love, and Mr. Foote, editor and owner of the leading paper, *The Commercial Advertiser.* Nichols penned epigrams on all the local elite:

EPIGRAM ON AN EDITOR

Corruption looked around for some fit tool,
Easily led, and yet not quite a fool;
Nature had left much malice and some soot—
The dark ingredient mixed, and formed a F—te

ON A JUDGE

Justice has fled, with streaming eyes
These words I heard her utter;
I've seen my representative
Lie, dead drunk, in a gutter.

ON A JAILOR

Monarch of misery, and fiend of fat
A hog his body furnished, and his soul a rat.

At the time the jail was filled with human debris: some eighty derelicts, murderers, psychotics, and drunks. "All the morning a vagrant belonging to the ball and chain gang has been having the most horrible fits," Nichols wrote. "He lies on the brick pavement and seems to be in the most dreadful agony; rolling over and over, grinding his teeth, biting his arms and foaming at the mouth. He is covered with filthy rags and disgusting vermin."[33]

Nichols turned the jail experience to his own advantage. He issued stock certificates for his newspaper with a picture of himself behind bars. Jail was no stigma to him, and his friends in the community held a benefit performance for him in the local theater, "crammed from pit to gallery." Afterwards the crowd marched to the jail, and he addressed them through the gratings. Then he went back to his cell and "supped on champagne and oysters, smuggled in for the occasion." The popular response he read as "the people's verdict." Released from the jail next day, after serving four months, he walked down Main Street and "ladies collected at the windows . . . some had even prepared wreaths to crown my freedom . . . there were banners, bands of music, demonstrations of popular feeling."[34] Here then was an almost revolutionary act: the jail-bird become a public hero, defying everything the respectable community held sacred. The authority of the elite had been shaken. Nichols had not been silenced.[35]

The rising threat of civil disorder in the 1840's and '50's stimulated demands for police protection in all the larger American cities. The citizen-cop, the watchman, could only be effective insofar as he was backed up by the community. In case of a disturbance the watchman was to raise the hue and cry and the citizens were to come forth and arrest or restrain the troublemaker. The system had worked in the medieval city. But by the eighteenth century it had broken down, even in England. By then, as Pringle mentions, the only people apt to answer the hue and cry were the friends of the felon.[36] So too in Boston by the beginning of the nineteenth century, watchmen were often assaulted and prisoners rescued by friends; "no peace officer dared to exercise his right to call upon the citizens for aid in making arrests."[37] By the 1840's, says Raymond Fosdick, American cities were living in a "state of terrorism . . . hardly a day passes but the thief or felon turns around and attacks the policeman."[38] The police could not control the situation, Fosdick continues, because "they inspire no respect, they create no fear."

It would be more accurate to say: since the police inspire no respect, it is necessary for them to create fear. After the passing of the watch-constable system, the law enforcement apparatus began to operate on what Hopkins calls the "war theory of crime control . . . actual fighting was the main job of the American police from the outset."[39] The policeman was supposed to be able to whip anyone on his beat: in the Buffalo Police Department of the 1870's, "more cases were settled out of court with fists than ever faced a jury" (*Buffalo Courier,* April 1, 1928). In the lore of the Buffalo Police Department stories abound of heroic battles between the cops and neighborhood toughs, who would even walk into the station to challenge the captain to a fistfight. From the 1840's to the 1880's there was a continuous battle between the toughs and the cops in every American city; Roger Lane says the balance of power shifted to the cops when they began to carry hand guns in the 1870's.[40] Thus police brutality became a hallowed tradition, an image deliberately projected for purposes of deterrence. By the 1870's American police forces had become paramilitary organizations, complete with uniforms, military ranks, and Prussian drills. The uniforms set the police off from the community but facilitated discipline and solidarity. The rationale of this new police-army was the sound oligarchical principle that an organized minority of ten can control an unorganized majority of a hundred. The police-army was designed for two main functions: riot control and guard-duty, i.e. protecting business property. Later the police developed into a cordon for segregating and containing the "dangerous class."

The Civil War aggravated pre-existing class antagonisms, brought prosperity to the prosperous, hardship to the penurious: profits soared, wages lagged. In Buffalo the 1862 draft riots erased all doubts about the need for an organized, paramilitary police force to control the unruly lower classes.[41] Crime seemed to increase before and during the war, but it was after the war that the crime rate took its great leap forward. It was then that Buffalo was "startled by a series of murders and incendiary fires that completely eclipsed all former crimes of a similar character, in the viscious and bold manner of execution."[42] From 1860 to 1867 arrests for arson increased from three to thirty a year, for assault and mayhem from 92 to 346 in 1865; 1194 in 1866, and 1555 in 1867. In 1854 yearly arrests numbered 2258; by 1874 that number had risen to 10,758. In 1866-7 incendiary fires were said to be almost nightly occurrences—a source of understandable panic. "After the conviction of . . . three wretches allegedly responsible for the fires, there was a general feeling of security among the people that had not been experienced for two years."[43] The new Buffalo police force played a key role in the apprehension of the incendiaries, but most of their work was less dramatic.

The waterfront, the tenderloin district, was the breeding spot of local crime and violence. The solid citizenry deplored the existence of such a phenomenon, but little could be done to eradicate it. The police force rarely entered the district, and never except in groups of three, with one cop walking ahead, and two behind for protection. Finally a partial solution was worked through "unofficial segregation . . . water front inhabitants were forbidden to appear beyond the boundaries of the area for any reason other than shopping . . . and had to show a purchase to avoid arrest."[44]

The police dealt with an almost exclusively anomic population. Two-thirds of those arrested were single males; probably most were transients, without roots in Buffalo or any other community. Judged by the occupational background not more than 2 per cent could have been upper or middle class, and not more than 15 to 20 per cent would have qualified as stable working-class, i.e. skilled craftsmen. Forty per cent were common laborers; 10 per cent were boatmen or sailors; 5 per cent had no occupation; 10 per cent were prostitutes. Like other economic activity, prostitution was passing from the free-enterprise to the corporate phase: where a Timothy Howard could operate with three "teams" in the 1830's, by the 1870's some ten top madams rented out whole battalions of whores, numbering 400 to 500 women, to the boats and barges as laundresses and cooks who doubled in sex.

While it was commonplace to attribute the post-Civil War crime wave to the Negro and the influx of foreign-born immigrants, Negroes constituted less than 1 per cent of those arrested in Buffalo, and fully 75 per cent of the arrested were native-born whites. The Irish did have a notably high arrest rate, however.

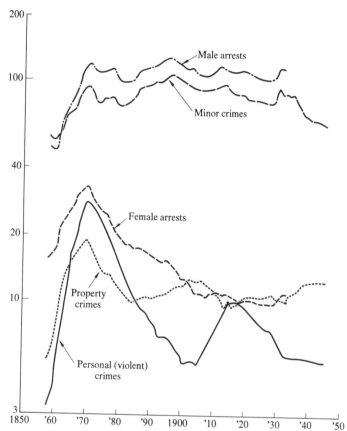

Figure 3. Relative[a] Changes in Yearly Crime Rates per 1000 Population Adjusted to 10-year Interval Averages—Buffalo, New York, 1856-1946.

[a] The degree of change in arrest rates, i.e. the *proportional* differences in rates from year to year rather than the *absolute* differences in arrest rates, is indicated by the semilogarithmic graph on which equal vertical distances represent equal ratios and not equal amounts (cf., Croxton and Cowden, *Applied General Statistics* [Englewood Cliffs, N.J.: Prentice-Hall, 1939], pp. 100-118.)

By 1876 the city police force, numbering 206 men, "drilled regularly in the schools of the soldier."[45] But when the troops were deployed against the railroad strikers of 1877, "they were greeted with shouts of laughter . . . it was easy to see the strikers were in no mood to be trifled with" (*Buffalo Morning Express,* July 21, 1877). Since they are drawn from the same community as the workers, American policemen have seldom been good strike-breakers; in fact, that inadequacy led to business demands for a national guard in the 1870's. Said the *Buffalo Express* (July 27, 1877): "Everyone . . . agreed the strikes showed the need for a standing army."

In Buffalo and throughout the country the crime rate increased drastically in the Civil War years (Figure 3). Partially, the increase was due to the growth of the police force: more cops, more arrests. Between 1830 and 1860 the population of Buffalo increased five-fold, the police force fiftyfold. The uniformed force came in 1866 with 105 men; by 1870 their number had doubled and by 1890 had grown by another 100 per cent, doubling again by 1910. But there is no clear correlation between the number of arrests and the number of policemen. After the mid-'70's the general arrest rate drops until the '90's, and both property and violent personal crimes decline as well. Then in the late '90's the rates begin to rise. Obviously,

Table 16. Growth of the Buffalo Police Establishment* 1830-1960

	Detectives	Patrolmen	Other	Total
1830				0
1840				3
1850				15
1860				30
1870	0	124	77	201
1880	8	128	70	206
1890	8	208	130	346
1900				
1910				732
1920	37	758	179	974
1930	69	803	271	1153
1940	69	766	304	1139
1950	70	834	282	1196
1960	115	717	487	1319

* Compiled from Annual Reports of the Buffalo Police Department.

Table 17. Male Arrests in Buffalo, 1946-1964 and 1860-1878a

			1946-1964			
Year	Mur-der_b	Assault	Burglary	Larceny (excl. auto theft)	Minor_c	Total Arrests_e
1946	20	1937	839	1748	9,005	14,584
1948	20	1901	1265	3688	10,513	16,443
1950	44	1806	1050	2309	11,631	16,355
1952	37	1728	1078	2381	9,432	14,181
1954	45	1483	1177	1882	8,168	13,082
1956	46	1431	1117	1790	7,651	12,278
1957d	9	1588	339	723	7,510	13,170
1960	15	2123	539	942	7,021-	14,267
1962	16	1540	543	1115	7,044	13,728
1964	19	1100	246	557	5,171	9,253

			1860-1878			
Year	Mur-der_b	Assault	Bur-glary	Lar-ceny	Minor_c	Total Arrests_e
1860	2	93	43	321	2149b	1997
1862	1	163	18	198	2530	2021
1864	5	296	29	324	2251	2078
1866	13	1115	99	843	4582	5665
1868	8	1348	94	721	5508	6522
1870	22	1868	112	863	4081	5924
1872	4	1859	164	?	5727	6563
1874	13	1808	158	964	6529	8804
1877d	8	1309	137	646	4136	6704
1878	?	1309	85	579	4433	6774

a. Data compiled from the Annual Reports of the Buffalo Police Department

b. Excludes negligent homicide

c. Includes only arrests for drunkenness, disorderly conduct and vagrancy

d. Where data for even numbered year not available nearest odd numbered year was used

e. Total includes arrests not listed in Table I and therefore exceeds the sum for each year in the 1946-64 period. (Major unlisted categories: rape, robbery, gambling, drugs, commercialized vice.) In the 1860-78 period totals are often less than the sum of the arrests shown for a given year because the minor crime category includes both male and female

f. Includes both male and female, the latter constituting some 15-30 per cent of the arrests

Male Population of Buffalo: Estimated as ½ Census Total: 1860 = 40,565; 1870 = 58,857; 1880 = 77,567; 1940 = 287,951; 1950 = 290,006; 1960 = 266,379 more is involved in the fluctuation of the crime rate than the mere presence of the police force. Interestingly, female arrests reached their hundred-year high mark in the 1870's and have since declined, contrary to the common belief that the "emancipation" of women "must" have led to greater feminine "criminality."[46] Also revealed is a baffling trend in violent crime (principally assaults): *(a) the rate reaches its peak in the early 1870's; (b) declines steadily until the turn of the century; (c) rises until 1918; and (d) recedes to the pre-Civil War level by 1940.* The pattern seems to be nation-wide, even world-wide.[47] The movement of property crime is more ambiguous but appears to be generally downward, at least until the 1950's. In Buffalo, the crime rate for the post-World War II period, say from 1946 to 1966, is lower than the rate for 1866 to 1878 (Table 17).

How can the configuration of crime—the peculiar rise and fall of the arrest rate—be explained? The sociologist immediately comes forth with the pat answer—urban-industrialism. Urban growth brings an anonymous environment, weakening the controls of the primary group, necessitating reliance on force and formal authority for the maintenance of social order. But in Buffalo, decades of rapid population growth do not necessarily have high crime rates. When the crime rate reached its zenith—1866-76—population increase was slight. In the years between 1830 and 1860 the population was increasing by more than 100 per cent per decade, and the crime rate seems to have been relatively low. Population was increasing between 1880 and 1900 when the crime rate was falling, and also increasing between 1910 and 1920 when the crime rate was rising.

The relationship between crime and industrialization is equally ambiguous. In the period of most intensive industrialization in Buffalo, 1877-1900, the crime rate was declining; the decade of 1910-20 was also a time of rapid industrial expansion and the crime rate was rising.

Similarly with economic conditions: efforts to correlate crime with the business cycle have generally failed. Dorothy Thomas, for example, writes that "it is impossible to assume either an inverse or direct [relationship] between crime in general and the business cycle."[48] Our data reveal no clear connection between crime and economic activity. The severe depression of the early 1870's coincided with a high crime rate, but in the equally severe depression of the 1930's the crime rate was falling. The relative prosperity of the 1880's saw a decline of the crime rate, but the prosperous years of 1914-18 brought a great increase in crime.

There is no clear relationship between crime and urbanism, industrialism and economic conditions—existential realities. Is it possible then that the fluctuation of the crime rate reflects some pulsation in what Durkheim called the "collective consciousness"?

In examining more than 134 years of Buffalo history the most striking correlation is that between war and crime. The arrest rate thrusts upward in the Civil War and World War I years and declines as the war fever subsides. Unfortunately, there are no records of crime in Buffalo during World War II, but other studies reveal a national increase in violent crime between 1941 and 1945, reversing a previous downtrend.[49] Noting the rising assault rate in New York City in 1942, Willbach concluded, "force is being used as an instrumentality even off the battle ground. Crimes of violence increase in war time."[50]

But war also aroused the policing spirit. Uniformed, paramilitary police forces were established in American cities in the 1860's. The movement for a uniformed police had been under way earlier but was facilitated by the frustration and excitement of war which, as Roger Lane puts it, "stimulated the dormant urge to battle sin at home."[51] The same spirit prevailed in Buffalo, of course. In World War I the citizens of Buffalo eagerly volunteered for police duty, "made many meritorious arrests," were encouraged to look for spies and believed they faced the "enemy" at home, just like the Americans in France.

War is the ultimate anomie: the substitution of naked force for the rule of law. Under the pretext of military necessity every civil right can be suspended. Men can be impressed into military service, denied freedom, deprived of property and life itself. The Civil War established an official lawlessness in America, which has slowly and sporadically grown since that time. It brought the force of an alien and distant government into the everyday life of the average man. Citizens were conscripted to fight in war, and the burden as always fell disproportionately on the poor. For $500 the rich could hire a stand-in to fight for the preservation of the Union. The war brought draft riots—of truly mammoth proportions in New York City, Boston, and Philadelphia—which in turn stimulated upper-class demands for police protection from the "dangerous" lower class. Fortunes were made during the war, as big business defrauded the government, which in turn defrauded the people. The practice continued afterward with the land grab by the railroads, mining syndicates, and land speculators. "In 1860 more than half the land in the nation was held in trust for the people by the government," writes Ferdinand Lundberg, "but by 1900 fully nine-tenths of it had been given away to corporate interests. . . . Every great fortune that rolled out of the nineteenth century was rooted in fraud."[52] Most of America's sixty ruling families in the twentieth century had their origin in Civil War graft. J. P. Morgan's first swindle was the purchase of condemned government-owned rifles at $3.00, which were then resold to the same government at $22.[53] Money was lent to the government during the war at 50 to 100 per cent interest per year; goods unfit for sale on the open market (e.g. five million pairs of shoes) were palmed off on the government at five times their market value. After the war 155,000,000 acres of the public domain was up for grabs by the railroads and a "phalanx of capitalists were scrambling forward to share in this carnival of plunder," as Myers put it, "and not one of them did the turn of a hand's work, for even the bribing of Congress was done by their paid agents."[54]

How did this massive corruption affect the local scene and the crime rate? The Civil War ended the "era of localism," according to Miriam Beard. In America the business class was just beginning to develop a sense of civic responsibility when the Civil War opened the continent for their spoliation. "Business men neglected the cities they had made," writes Miriam Beard. "They were not content with a local stage. . . . By their own triumph, the dominating business groups of the Northeast were shaken to the core; the small, compact, slow-moving patriciate of New York was especially overwhelmed by the tremendous economic transformations caused by putting the country on a war-basis."[55] Corruption spread from the white house to the court house. New York City in the 1870's, says Herbert Asbury, "entered upon an unparalleled era of wickedness . . . the police were unable to enforce even a semblance of respect for law."[56] Writing of New York in 1872, Edward Crapsey says:

> With its middle class in large part self-exiled, its laboring population being brutalized in tenements and its citizens of highest class indifferent to the commonwealth, New York drifted from bad to worse and became the prey of professional thieves, ruffians, and political jugglers. The municipal government shared in the vices of the people and New York became a city paralyzed in the hands of its rulers.[57]

Such situations were duplicated in all urban areas, and Buffalo was regarded as one of the most lawless cities in the country. Mark Twain, for a time subeditor of the *Buffalo Express,* described the city as ". . . a 'sink of iniquity' . . . possessing the 'vilest sailors' slum in the United States . . . ruled by a corrupt municipal government waxing fat not only from protection of the underworld but also from direct plunder of the public."[58] However, as the effects of the Civil War wore off and the social system began to stabilize in the mid-'70's, the crime rate dropped. Following the stabilization there was a period of rapid capital formation, creating jobs for the working class, business for the middle class, fortunes for the upper class. Between the mid-'70's and the mid-90's the capitalist system functioned reasonably well, and there was sufficient confidence in the legitimacy of established authority to ensure the minimum of social order.

By the 1890's sounds of a new kind of war were heard in the distance. Sporadic and localized outbursts of class conflict occurred throughout the nineteenth century—and recall the escapades of Thomas Nichols in Buffalo in 1838-9. The Jacksonian "status revolution" was a nonviolent class war. But by the '90's there were visions of an organized, armed collision between capital and labor. The press described the Homestead strike of 1892 in a military vocabulary. Consider the Associated Press story, "Battle at Homestead: 12 Hours Duration; 20 men killed—11 workers, 9 Pinkertons. . . . The [Pinkerton] Commander in Chief, like the barons of the Middle Ages, had a force which he could increase at pleasure and which was at the service of those who paid him. The Carnegie Company claimed not only the right to regulate their own business in their own way, but the right to fortify their own position. It also claimed the right to introduce an armed force and to have free passage for that force from its armored boats to its fortification, and the battle had grown out of that state of things" (*Buffalo Express,* July 7, 1892). Nationally, the Pinkerton army numbered 35,000 to 50,-000 (larger than the standing army of the United States in 1892), and the agency claimed it could concentrate 2000 troops anywhere within the United States in forty-eight hours. The Pinkertons were drilled and trained in military skills, though their main function was informing, "intelligence gathering." (In fact, the organization was the CIA of the class war of the 1890's, and contributed one word which is still alive in our vocabulary: "fink"—certain foreign workers pronounced the letter P as F—hence the term as a corruption of Pink.) The battle of Homestead quickly escalated beyond the control of the Pinkerton "special forces"—only 300 Pinks had been sent to subdue 5000 strikers. Some 8000 Pennsylvania national guardsmen were called in on July 11. Then the war spread to other areas, following the line of the railroad, reaching Buffalo in August 1892, when 8000 New York national guardsmen were called in to "pacify" some 700 striking railroad switchmen (*Buffalo Courier,* August 16, 1892).

In the 1890's capitalists talked more of class war than did the Socialists, who still expected to vote in utopia. The Buffalo elite saw

Bryan's capture of the Democratic party in 1896 as a signal of coming chaos, much as Southerners reacted to the nomination of Lincoln in 1860. Eminent Buffalonians resigned from the Democratic party when it endorsed Bryan. "When the honor of the Nation and the interests of all our people are at stake," said Mr. Hutchinson, a party leader, "the Democratic party should be on the side of patriotism and sound money . . . Mr. Bryan has declared a class war. He talks of the common people and the other kind. I thought we were all common people in this country. We are not all capitalists but we are all workers. Every working man is trying to be a capitalist. It is a creditable ambition. He wants to make himself independent of old age and sickness—to get his little home and leave something for his family."[59] Mr. Hutchinson, an uncommonly wealthy banker, saw in Bryan the symbol of rebeling western farmers, and even a possible threat to that most fundamental pillar of American capitalism: the protective tariff.

Worse than Bryan, urban radicals were disturbing the tranquility of the working class, scoffing at the every-man-a-capitalist mythology promoted by Mr. Hutchinson. Workers were beginning to refer to themselves as slaves, coming to recognize they had no stake in the existing system. In 1894 Chicago saw not merely the national guard but the U.S. Army called in to break the Pullman strike. The strike leader, Eugene V. Debs, was imprisoned for six months and thereby converted to socialism. A corrupt and cynical capitalism tried to resolve its contradictions with jails and bullets. Armories were being constructed in American cities as bases from which to fight domestic insurrection. Two of these new fortresses of class war were erected in Buffalo in 1897 and 1902, from which the national guard periodically sallied forth to break the heads of strikers.

Between 1900 and 1914 both middle and upper class lobbied for enlargement of the police establishment. There was a spreading clamor for control, which always accompanies the growth of the war spirit. Populists, progressives, socialists, and assorted reformers demanded controls on big business, which in turn demanded controls

Table 18. Suicide and Homicide per 100,000 in the United States, 1900-1940*

Year	Suicide	Homicide	Year	Suicide	Homicide
1900	10.2	1.2	1920	10.2	6.8
01	10.4	1.2	21	12.4	8.1
02	10.3	1.2	22	11.7	8.0
03	11.3	1.1	23	11.5	7.8
04	12.2	1.3	24	11.9	8.1
05	13.5	2.1	25	12.0	8.3
06	12.8	3.9	26	12.6	8.4
07	14.5	4.9	27	13.2	8.4
08	16.8	4.8	28	13.5	8.6
09	16.0	4.2	29	13.9	8.4
1910	15.3	4.6	1930	15.6	8.8
11	16.0	5.5	31	16.8	9.2
12	15.6	5.4	32	17.4	9.0
13	15.4	6.1	33	15.9	9.7
14	16.1	6.2	34	14.9	9.5
15	16.2	5.9	35	14.3	8.3
16	13.7	6.3	36	14.3	8.0
17	13.0	6.9	37	15.0	7.6
18	12.3	6.5	38	15.3	6.8
19	11.5	7.2	39	14.1	6.4
			1940	14.4	6.2

* Data from Forrest E. Linder and Robert D. Grave, *Vital Statistics Rates in United States, 1900-1940* (Washington: U.S. Government Printing Office, 1943), 280-81; 288-89.

on radicals and labor. Crusades for urban reform gathered momentum. More arrests were made in this period between 1900 and 1918, partially because of increased police activity growing out of incessant demands to clean up vice and corruption. But national statistics also indicate a steady, fourfold increase of the murder rate between 1900 and 1918 (Table 18). The "habit of violence" grows in the years prior to World War I, a growth facilitated by the mood of the 1914-18 years.

After 1919 the violent crime rate in Buffalo and other cities declined. Was the war spirit dissipated for the brief, though bleak, two decades between 1920 and 1940? Perhaps. All we can say with confidence is that the best statistical studies show a decline of violent crimes in the interwar decades.[60] The general drift of the violent crime rate seems to be downward into the 1960's. While we cannot ascertain any change in the Buffalo crime picture, national statistics show an increase in crime in the 1960's.

Since the turn of the century the police establishment has grown steadily and rapidly. In 1902 federal, local, and state government in America spent a total of $50 million a year for policing; by 1913 costs had risen to $92 million; by 1922 to $204 million; by 1957 to $1623 million—in constant 1929 dollars.[61] By 1967, the police bill had risen to $2500 million—in 1967, not 1929, dollars, thus a somewhat smaller increase than it would appear.[62] Some 420,000 people were employed in police work in 1957 as opposed to 40,000 in 1903. In 1965 American business and industry paid out over $500 million to private police agencies.[63] It is possible that as many people are employed in private as in public police work—in 1950 Sutherland reported that the city of Indianapolis had 742 public police and 788 private police.[64]

Does the growth of the police establishment mean a spreading distrust? Does it mean that Americans are no longer able to police themselves? Is it connected with the growth of the city, the coming of the megalopolis, and then the tyrannopolis? Tocqueville wrote in 1835:

> I look upon the size of certain American cities, and especially on the nature of their population, as a real danger which threatens the future security of the democratic republics of the New World; and I venture to predict that they will perish from this circumstance, unless the government succeeds in creating an armed force which, while it remains under the control of the majority of the nation, will be independent of the town population and able to repress its excesses.[65]

The prediction materialized, but more was involved than the mere size of the city. Buffalo as a city of 47,000 functioned with a law enforcement apparatus of 15 men in 1845; by 1870 the city had 200 policemen and a population of 113,000. In the 1870's the national guard was created as an auxiliary police force, an instrument of class war. The impetus for the creation of the guard was the labor riots of 1877, and by the 1890's with 115,000 men the guard was four times the size of the regular army.[66] From at least 1866 to 1920, the upper class lived in genuine dread of revolution, accompanied by vast contempt for the lower class—an unmistakable change since the 1830's. Urban police forces were developed to cordon off the dangerous classes. Their first mission was riot control; their second the protection of business property; the third, and almost incidental, the protection of life and limb of the ordinary citizen.

The police establishment grew up in response to war—internal war, class war—which has been aggravated and intensified by the nation's involvement in external war.

Whatever disturbs the integration of society increases the crime rate because it stimulates both criminal and police activity. War *seems* to be an integrative force—people unite to fight a common enemy—but ultimately it is disintegrative. War may be a response to anomie—but it is inevitably a source of anomie, of confusion of values. So we may find the real origin of anomie, not in urbanization or industrialization but in war. Tyrannopolis and necropolis grow out of the war cult which has been churning its way to the top of Western civilization since the middle of the last century. Violence initially directed at an outer enemy spills over into domestic life. No one has stated it better than Herbert Spencer: "Where activity in destroying enemies is chronic, destruction will become a source of pleasure . . . warriors so much applaud ferocity that to commit a murder is a glory."[67]

PART THREE

WAR

The meaning of words had no longer the same relation to things. . . . Reckless daring was held to be loyal courage; prudent delay was the excuse of a coward; moderation was the disguise of unmanly weakness. Frantic energy was the true quality of a man. . . . The lover of violence was always trusted, and his opponent suspected. . . . If an enemy when he was in the ascendant offered fair words, the opposite party received them not in a generous spirit, but by a jealous watchfulness of his actions. Revenge was dearer than self-preservation.

THUCYDIDES, *The Peloponnesian War,* 426 B.C.

9

.

Anomie and arms:
toward a sociology of war

> The machine of warriors, created by the wars that required
> it, creates the wars it requires.
>
> JOSEPH SCHUMPETER, *Imperialism and Social Classes*

By definition war is a clash of armies, not of men. As Malinowski
puts it: "War is an armed contest between two independent political
units, by means of *organized military force,* in pursuit of tribal or
national policy." Sporadic outbreaks of violence, small brawls within
a horde or between clans, Malinowski continues, are the "antecedent
not of war but of crime [and] civic disorder."[1]

But the institution of war seems almost universal—a survey of 306
"simple societies" revealed that only nine, and these at the lowest
level of development, were definitely without warfare.[2] Even among
primates, the germs of organized violence are discernible, and J. B.
Scott sees the prototype of human warfare in the tendency of monkeys, apes, and baboons to gang up when they attack outsiders.[3]
Primates organize for the collective defense of territory, and it is
easy to imagine human warfare emerging out of these early protective arrangements.

Society itself is a defense system. Collectively, the baboons are able to cope with single predators lethal to the isolated individual. The baboon's cry warns his comrades of impending danger, provides the stimulus for organized flight. Occasionally the dominant males of the troop unite in concerted action to repulse the attacker. Somewhere along the path of evolution the higher apes improvised weapons, and that act marks the beginning of man, according to Robert Ardrey: "Man did not father the weapon; instead the weapon fathered man."[4] Technology—tool-making, man's defining feature—originated in weapon-making. Oakley speculates that the first men, hunting in groups, learned to kill medium-sized mammals with hand weapons which were earlier improvised for defense.[5] Weapon-use was a collective, not an individual, enterprise: the discovery of stores of femur bones estimated to be older than man are presumably the remains of the first primate arsenal.[6] The origins of human society may lie in unification for common defense. Then came the organized offense—and at that imaginary moment warfare came into being. Of course nothing is really known, or even knowable, about the origins of war or human society, except as Socrates said about the creation of the world, it happened a very long time ago. War was a developed institution by the paleolithic period, and paintings in the caves of the Spanish Levant show "battle scenes of armed warriors deployed against one another."[7]

Organized armed force developed in response to the need for protection and provided the impetus for social consolidation. Through warfare the scattered bands of early men were forged into tribes, later into larger, more complex units: confederacies, states.

Tribal warfare varies in character and intensity from a playful encounter to lethal aggression. Even the peaceful Arapesh of New Guinea once practiced a mild and sensible form of warfare: usually the loss of a man was sufficient to justify the flight of the losing party. The victors often paid the defeated for their losses . . . a pig for a man.[8] Before Europeans came to North America the Plains Indians fought a kind of play-war, where the object of the fight was not to exterminate the foe but simply to "count coup," i.e. touch his body.[9]

At the other extreme from the Arapesh are the Mandurucu of Brazil, who are constantly at war; look upon themselves as fierce aggressors, and divide the world between "people" and "enemies." The "enemy" caused the Mandurucu to go to war, says Robert Murphy, "simply by existing, like game to be hunted." War relieved boredom, promoted social cohesion by providing the occasion to "unite and submerge factional differences in vigorous pursuit of a common purpose."[10]

Far from being naturally blood-thirsty, men have to be socialized to cherish the horrors of war. In early society warring is the chief occupation of every adult male and, says Maurice Davie, "the exigencies of primitive existence make [war] the most important factor in his life." Women are seldom warriors, but the life of the male is usually divided into three stages: boyhood, warriorhood, and old age, with the first stage largely a preparation for the second, while the old men serve as instructors of the boys in the art of war. Instruction involves the inculcation of a callousness to human suffering, e.g. war prisoners are often "killed or tortured for edification and improvement of the children . . . ten-year-olds are encouraged to stab the bodies repeatedly with spears so that they may become hardened to the sight of death and blood."[11] The rites of passage, initiating the boy into the adult status of warriorhood, are an endurance test and involve learning to bear excruciating physical pain. The warrior is socialized into a kind of masochistic-altruism, a willingness to sacrifice himself for the welfare of the group. Without this "military altruism" human society might not have survived. But with it came a disdain for individual life. Did the "institution" of suicide, which seems so antithetical to the biological law of self-preservation, have its origin in the "institution" of war?[12] Perhaps all violence has its real source in war. Murder is individuated war rather than war being collectivized murder. Psychological theory (Freud) sees the bonds of society as a defense against the impulses of murder, i.e. aggression.[13] But aggression itself is learned behavior derived from culture not biology. Despite a recent revival of social Darwinism, with pictures of nature "red in tooth and fang," most animals under normal conditions are rather nonviolent.[14] War creates aggression and not conversely.

But war also propels the process of social evolution. The effect of nearly continual war on early man, Maurice Davie says, was to "solidify the group, develop discipline, and concentrate authority." In the beginning all men were warriors, but eventually a special warrior class was differentiated and set "immeasurably above the non-warriors." Thus war gives rise to a class system, and then a coercive regime, which destroys "primitive democracy." Davie's words are worth quoting at length:

> . . . discipline and subordination are indispensable on the warpath . . . and can only be made efficient by subjection to a single command. Thus arises the war chief with his power. The constant necessity of meeting pressure from without intensifies the internal organization of society and increases the power of the political head. . . . Political integration involves class differentiation and the dissolution of the more primitive state of equality. War destroys tribal democracy. The first line of demarcation appears between the warrior and the non-warrior class, raising the former immeasurably above the latter. The chief of the warriors often becomes the king and the warriors themselves form a noble caste, beneath whom are the common people. With subjugation further class distinctions arise. The conquered people are enslaved; thus is produced the widest possible social cleavage—that between freemen and slaves. The slaves are put to work to support the upper classes, who regard war as their chief business. . . . [Then] comes the state, which originates in war and exists primarily as an enforced peace between conquerors and conquered. . . . The state stands forth as fundamentally a war-band charged with the duty of (1) preserving group safety and (2) of guaranteeing domestic peace by using threat and force so as to render submissive recalcitrant subjects. The so-called police power, which includes the war-power, is merely another name for sovereignty; by it is meant the power of the state to do anything needful for the safety and welfare of the nation. All other powers are simply implications arising from it. In

general it may be said that the claim to the use of force distinguishes the state from all other institutions.[15]

The state is formed in war—either through voluntary federation of tribes (the confederacy) or through subjugation of one tribe by another (the conquest-state). But in both cases, says Ralph Linton, war is the uniting agency which produces the state.[16] Confederacies usually originate as a defensive alliance, and the central authority merely co-ordinates the voluntary activities of the federated tribes. Confederacies derive their power from the consent of the governed and, since the component tribes are always jealous of their rights, tend to be "democratic in fact if not in theory." Although resistant to attack, confederacies are liable to internal disruption. *Serious* tribal warfare, says Linton, always involves the expulsion, extermination, or enslavement of the defeated people. The conquest state arises when the conquerors realize that the conquered are worth more as subjects than as slaves, for it is the essence of the conquest state that its "rulers exploit societies rather than individuals."[17] Exploitation takes the form of tribute or taxes, and the conquered must be controlled in such a way that they will neither lose the will and capacity for production nor be driven to desperation and revolt. "The threat of force must always be present, but the use of force must be reduced to a minimum."[18]

Conquerors divide in order to rule: mutual hatreds are fomented, and organizations which could provide the base for revolt are eliminated. The organized and conquering minority seeks to disorganize —render anomic—the subject majority. In the successful conquest-state, the state itself takes over the functions of the tribe and may be endowed with tribal sanctity, says Linton, "as the threat of force is replaced by encouragements to willing submission."[19] In sum: the military conquerors first use coercive power to gain domination and then attempt to build a consensus to sustain their authority.

The state then has its origin in war, and war creates the basis of its dissolution. Historically speaking, the state is a fragile form of social organization. "The state," says Max Weber, "is a relation of men dominating men, a relation supported by means of legitimate (i.e. considered to be legitimate) violence. If the state is to exist, the dominated must obey the authority claimed by the powers that be."[20] Because domination arouses antagonism, the state is always insecure, always threatened by internal disintegration. Though men pretend to revere the state, no state in history has been able to function without a military and police apparatus to enforce its sacred edicts. Inherently insecure, the state seeks to extend its dominion in order to protect its power. And generally, the more tenuous the internal cohesion of the state, the greater is its tendency to wage aggressive war against both external and internal enemies.

The function of war, writes R. E. Park, is to extend the area over which it is possible to maintain peace.[21] Every state expands "its" peace to the limits of its ability—thus the Pax Romana, the Pax Americana. But not only does state power move outward, it moves inward and downward. The state as supreme power seeks to destroy or castrate all opposing powers within its boundaries, i.e. all semi-autonomous communities, tribes, clans, guilds, churches, parties, associations.[22]

According to Robert Nisbet, not the conflict of classes but the conflict between state and community has been the moving force of modern history. Nisbet attributes the decline of community in the modern (post-medieval) world to the rise of the state as a "revolutionary" force.[23] Occasionally the state deliberately destroys autonomous communities perceived as rival centers of power; more often the state simply moves into the vacuum left by the decay of communities. State power is augmented in the effort to hold together a dissolving social system. States sometimes launch wars in an effort to restore cohesion and avert internal revolution; more often the military establishment simply grows in periods of internal disturbance and unintentionally creates the conditions which bring about war. Military tyranny, says Gaetano Mosca, has been the common rule of mankind, and "any serious disturbance of an established order of a non-military type is likely to result in a reversion to military dictatorship."[24] Harold Lasswell makes the same point: prolonged crisis promotes the militarization of society.[25] If the ruling group cannot sustain itself by popular support (consensus), it resorts to violence to coerce compliance with its demands. However, the process of militarization cannot go on indefinitely; a critical point is finally reached when either war or revolution (or both) become inevitable.

When the state is weakened by anomie, i.e. internal discord, the power of the military grows because a lack of cohesion invites attack by outsiders and undermines the authority of the ruling class, which then resorts to force, terror, and intimidation to maintain its position of dominance. Times of anomie are times of war. Sorokin claims that outbursts of violence always follow any breakdown of the social system: "internal and external disturbances—revolution and war—are but logical and factual consequences of . . . the disintegration of the crystallized system of [social] relationships."[26] Sorokin's thesis is supported by careful statistical work, which seems to show wars and revolutions occurring with greatest frequency and intensity in periods of sociocultural transition—e.g. between the fourteenth and sixteenth centuries when the medieval order was collapsing, and in the twentieth century when the modern world entered its time of troubles.

In sum: anomie promotes the militarization of society, leading to wars between states and an intensification of the "class war" within the state. Violence is increasingly utilized as an instrument of social control, i.e., for deterrence, and thus further undermines the consensus which is the real base of every social order. Societies and ruling classes have often destroyed themselves through war. John Ruskin called the Peloponnesian wars "the suicide of Greece," and Michael Rostovtzeff shows that constant warfare brought on by Roman warriors in the end destroyed Rome. The nobility of the late Middle Ages, devoured itself in the great feudal wars and left the power vacuum later filled by the bourgeoisie. The aristocracy was not overthrown; it collapsed, and then the new capitalist class stepped into the "command post" once occupied by the nobility. As a ruling class grows feeble and rigidifies, it loses the capacity for creative adaptation to changing conditions, and hence its basis for popular support.[27] Then it seeks to hold on by the resort to force and tries to restore cohesion through involvement in war. The ruling class resorts to war to avert revolution and thereby creates the disaster it seeks to avoid. Bourgeois society began to dismantle itself with World War I. The wind of war sown in 1914 became the whirlwind of revolution reaped thereafter, even unto our own day. "Every society divided into classes is condemned to commit suicide," Karl Liebknecht wrote in 1906, "whether it wants to or not [it] begets the Oedipus who will slay it one day."[28]

10

The bitter harvest of deterrence: anomie, revolution, and war in Europe, 1848-1918

> The older sense of established safety had vanished and the nineteenth century was swept by spasmodic war panics.
>
> ALFRED VAGTS, *A History of Militarism*

War and revolution, each cause and effect of the other, grow out of the common ground of anomie. As the social fabric dissolves, strife increases, and then the state resorts to violence to maintain order, to deter disobedience. Threatened by class war, the rulers initiate state war to restore cohesion by mobilizing against a common enemy. But the strains of protracted war may exacerbate pre-existing tensions and bring on the revolution it is designed to avert. Such was the case of Europe between 1848 and 1918. The threat of revolution, arising out of the decay of the legitimacy of the old order, stimulated the growth of the military-police apparatus. Then the growth of armed force became a source of fear and the incentive for further armament. The resulting arms race between 1870 and 1914 was made palatable to the public by an ideology of military deterrence, of peace through strength. "If you want peace, prepare for war." But the logic of war preparation leads inexorably to what Thorstein Veblen called the defensive-offense: "retaliation on presumptive enemies for prospective grievances."[1]

Opening with a democratic revolution, the nineteenth century ended in militarist counterrevolution, a development hardly noticed at the time. By 1913 men had convinced themselves man had grown too rational for war, even though peacetime governments spent half their budgets on arms. During Europe's "century of peace" (1815-1914), "the number of men under arms increased eight-fold, while the population increased four-fold."[2] Still, no one expected war in 1914, not even the warriors who were preparing for it. "Those who can read the signs of the times," wrote Robert MacIver in 1912, "will rejoice that there is being prepared for the nations the healing way of peace, unmenaced by the blind catastrophe of war."[3] Then World War I devoured forty million lives and left a civilization in shambles.

Why the growth of arms in the nineteenth century? From 1815 to 1870 armies were "raised and maintained as much for fighting domestic insurrections as foreign wars," says Michael Howard.[4] As Bismarck observed: "Troops are the only answer to democracy."[5] The professional armies of Europe became a police force and grew in power with every social upheaval. The dread of revolution gave rise to despotism. In France, even those who had made the earlier revolution of 1789 feared they had destroyed not only the machinery of government but "the moral authority necessary for any kind of rule."[6] By the 1830's it seemed the future offered only anarchy or military dictatorship, and the governing classes much preferred the latter. With the uprisings of 1848, the thrust of the democratic revolution of 1789 spent itself. As Marx said, "great historic facts recur twice: once as tragedy and again as farce."[7]

But the revolutions of 1848 did provide the rationale for further repression. France recoiled into a police state, with Napoleon III using a red scare to engineer a *coup d'état* in the name of law and order.[8] Elsewhere on the Continent the insurrections of 1848 provoked either renewed efforts at the forceful preservation of the status quo (as in Austria) or a headlong rush into militarism (as in Prussia).

By 1848 the Austrian empire had become "Europe's China," walled off from the rest of the Continent by a dynasty which curtailed intercourse with the outer world and endeavored to arrest all change within the empire. Even the steam locomotive was banned until 1848. Newspapers, books, and mail flowing into and out of the empire were subject to confiscation and censorship; a swarm of spies kept daily surveillance on Vienna intellectuals. Already on the verge of dissolution the empire was a motley collection of races, classes, and nationalities, living in isolation and hostility. "My peoples are strange to each other and that is all right," said Francis II, emperor in 1848. "From their antipathy will be born order, and from the mutual hatred, general peace."[9] Ethnic and class antagonisms were exploited to keep the people divided, leaving the Habsburg monarchy with its 500,000 man army as the strongest single force within the empire. For a brief springtime of revolution in 1848 students, intellectuals, merchants, and workers united to forcefully expel the Habsburgs from Vienna, and even the Germanic and Slavic populations co-operated in the attempted overthrow of the old regime. But by autumn of 1848 the army had crushed the revolution and forcefully reinstated the monarchy. Francis II was retired; Franz Joseph, an 18 year old, was enthroned to reign for 68 years as the emperor of 38,000,000 subjects. Elsewhere on the Continent—in France, in Italy, in Germany—autocrats were installed to preside over nations ever on the verge of explosion.

Class struggle as a political activity, says Priscilla Robertson, was more the result than the cause of the revolutions of 1848. Class hatred had persisted in Europe since the Middle Ages; the mass of the people were kept down "not only by laws but by customs, by studied arrogance, by pious sanctions." When the new ideas of democracy, liberalism, and nationalism "loosened the sanctions which had kept each man in his place, a lot more force was let loose than men realized they had within them." People were frightened by the brief taste of freedom which the revolutions of 1848 brought, and they soon discovered that "the effort of doing something for themselves was not as rewarding as letting somebody on top do it—especially when it came to the task of overcoming the violence of the lower classes."[10]

Those at the top found that the military establishment was the best instrument for keeping the bottom people in line. Noting that international unrest was the safest condition for a dynasty at home, Jacob Burckhardt pointed out in the 1860's: "As soon as it is a matter of cutting off a threatening revolution, they [the dynasts] themselves effect something which passes as the equivalent of revolution and concentrate all weapons in their own hands. . . . The result is the series of wars into which Europe has recently passed. The nations of Europe, oppressed by militarism, arc setting about visiting infinite affliction on each other, chiefly because of *internal* ferment."[11] Disturbances in the Prussian towns were increasing between 1840 and 1848 as a result, says Gordon Craig, of the social dislocations of industrialism.[12] Called in to restore order, the army invariably created further disorder. There were pitched battles between soldiers and workers, and "the employment of troops as police made the uniform an object of hatred."[13] Fraternizing with the people was forbidden, and garrisons were rotated to prevent social ties from forming between the troops and the town population. When revolution broke out in Paris in February 1848 and deposed King Louis Philippe, Frederick William IV and his military chieftains concluded that only armed force could prevent similar action in Berlin. A psychology of deterrence was operating. The police chief of Berlin wanted a military back-up to "overawe the lower classes," and the generals, arguing for the use of guns against an unarmed civilian population, said the masses "must be made to see they can accomplish nothing against the military."[14] Actually there had been no trouble in Berlin prior to the entry of troops on March 12. But then public meetings which previously had been "temperate, even jocular" turned hostile. The troops were jeered; they lashed back, fired on the crowds. Barricades then went up throughout Berlin, and the army decided it had to crush the insurrection. The barricade fighters—workers led by students—had only two guns, but the army did not know how to defend itself against bricks and other missiles hurled from housetops or how to fight an invisible enemy. The army was frustrated and on the verge of demoralization and break-up when the commander, without knowledge of the king, ordered a retreat from the city. This capitulation before the masses in 1848 was to rankle for years and stir the passion for revenge.

Out of the 1848 uprising came a constitution *granted* by the king and a feeble parliament or national assembly. Initially the lower house of the assembly was to be elected by universal manhood suffrage; later, property qualifications limited the electorate. Constituted mainly of the bourgeoisie, with some representatives from the aristocracy and the working class, the assembly had little real power, except for its authority to veto military appropriations. But for the first time in its history the Prussian army had to worry about its public reputation. When the assembly refused to appropriate funds for an army reorganization plan in the late 1850's, the army tried to provoke a revolution, hoping the parliamentary liberals would "go to the streets" to muster the people against the military. Then the army would have the pretext to close the assembly and revoke the constitution. Until the 1860's the military command had vetoed plans for foreign wars because the army should be "reserved as a safeguard against revolutionary agitation on the homefront."[15] In 1861 the army made elaborate plans to march on Berlin with 35,000 infantry, 16,000 cavalry and 100 field pieces. Berlin had a population of 300,-000, but the city was neither armed nor organized for defense. The army forced the king to close the assembly, but the liberals refused to go to the barricades. No doubt in this case the overwhelming might of the army did serve as a deterrent to revolution—to the great disappointment of the army itself. The army and the assembly remained deadlocked for two years, and in this constitutional crisis Bismarck came to power.

Bismarck's aim was simple, his strategy subtle. His plan was to seek foreign success so Prussians would forget their internal differences. Six months after taking office as chancellor, Bismarck involved Prussia in a war with Denmark, with Austria as an ally. After easy victory over Denmark (1864), Prussia turned on Austria (1866), and as Craig puts it, "the antagonists of the army surrendered to a wave of patriotism."[16] Thereafter the mood of all classes of German society changed. Bourgeois liberals swung to support of the crown and the army, and even the working class was "brought into the fold" through war. A Bavarian statesman writes of mingling with the crowds in May 1870 (two months before the Franco-Prussian War) watching a military parade: "No trace of the former animosity against the military which used to be noticeable among the lower classes. The commonest working man looked on the troops with the feeling that he belonged or had belonged to them."[17] After the Franco-Prussian War the enthusiasm for things military was even more pronounced. In the 1870's Treitschke told overflowing German lecture hall audiences that the army was "the sole political institution which binds citizen to citizen . . . not the German parliament but the German army [is] the real and effective bond of national union."[18]

After the 1870's the hostility of class war was redirected outward; the nations of Europe were beginning to unite to fight. And it was not sadism so much as solidarity which provided the appeal of war. The state, says Veblen, used war "to hold the personal allegiance of a body of subjects exposed to the disintegrating discipline, [i.e. the anomie] of modern life."[19] The trend was evident elsewhere, but most pronounced in Germany. "The experience of war," Veblen continues, "induces a warlike frame of mind, and the pursuit of war, being an exercise in the following of one's leader and execution of arbitrary orders, induces an animus of enthusiastic subservience and unquestioning obedience. . . . subservience has become a passionate aspiration with the subject population, where the habit of allegiance has attained that degree of automatism that the subject's ideal of liberty has come to be the permission to obey orders."[20]

For Germany the internal benefits of militarism outweighed the external gains of conquest. From her three brief wars between 1864 and 1871 she got a compliant labor force which enormously facilitated her economic growth. Every German citizen was required to serve two years active duty in the army, and five additional years as a reservist. Veblen attributed the later "innocuous desuetude" of German socialism to the "discipline of servility" learned in the army.[21] After 1870 Germany was internally the most peaceful country in Europe, and, according to Gunther Roth, had fewer strikes and popular disturbances than any other nation.[22] But France was also calm, despite, or perhaps because of, her bloody liquidation of the revolutionary Paris Commune, which had come briefly to power in the aftermath of her defeat at the hands of Prussia. More Frenchmen were killed in the suppression of the commune—about 30,000—by the French army than were lost to the German army in the war of 1870-71.[23] Had France not been able to externalize her aggression through preparation for future war against Germany she might have faced full-scale revolution at home. But the threat of Germany gave cohesion to French society, and sustained the authority of the French military establishment, even though it had been disastrously defeated in war. After 1871 France, like Germany, enlarged its standing army and instituted full peacetime military conscription. The anger of class war subsided as the prospect of state-war loomed, and a kind of tranquility settled upon the civilized world. Sorokin's statistical computations show the quarter-century of 1875-1900 as one of the most peaceful on record for western society, with the least internal and external disturbances since 825-50 A.D. This was the calm before the storm; Sorokin's statistical indicators flip to the other extreme after the turn of the century and show 1900-1925 to be the bloodiest time on record.[24]

During the apparent peace that followed 1870, governments everywhere enlarged their military apparatus. Between 1880 and 1914 arms budgets quadrupled and men in uniform increased threefold (see Table 19). Rulers assured the public they armed only for deter-

Table 19. Men under Arms—Army and Navy (in thousands)

	1884	1900	1908	1914
Britain	281	327	375	397
France	556	659	657	834
Russia	806	938	657	1253
Germany	458	629	653	864
Austria-Hungary	300	383	389	443
Italy			270	345
U. S. A.	37	126	128	165
Japan	43	273	256	301

From: Philip Noel-Baker, *The Arms Race* (New York: Oceana Publications, 1958), 40.

rence. The standing army was justified as a deterrent to war; so, too, were the navies of the world. The influential American Admiral Alfred Mahan enunciated the thesis accepted everywhere: "the main use of arms is not to wage war but prevent war." Arms brought peace, according to Mahan, because they "inspire mutual respect and caution."[25]

Actually, the growth of armaments aroused a recklessness, not caution; furthered fear, not respect. Richardson shows a positive mathematical correlation between arms and insecurity but offers no causal explanation for this strange anomaly.[26] Arms create fear; fear necessitates arms—a formula which describes but does not explain the process. For countless complex reasons—the dread of revolution, the desire for foreign conquest, the drive for pre-eminence among nations—governments were determined to expand their military power. But to get public support for the military enterprise rulers had to frighten the people with theoretic threats from rival states. In the 1850's, for instance, English politicians conjured up the spectre of an imminent invasion by the French fleet as grounds for enlarging the British navy, which was already twice as large as the French navy. The French naval menace was wholly imaginary; France had not the slightest intention of attacking England, and the English "decision makers" knew it. But the public was panicked into endorsement of a new ship-building program.[27] Even in autocratic Germany popular support for the war-machine was required, and a "Slav Peril" was fabricated as a chief reason for increasing German armaments. The Slav Peril had become to German artisans and peasants a very real and present danger, says Munro Smith, and "disposed the people to accept the official legend of a Russian attack as the justification for the German declaration of war in 1914."[28]

Fear functioned to maintain the military establishment. The European aristocracy, initially a warrior class, presented itself as a protector of the people. The Habsburgs, for instance, derived their legitimacy as the defender of Christians against the Turks. For centuries the nobility had held rule by striking fear into the hearts of the people—fear of hell, fear of the infidel, fear of the Jew and, above all, fear of the nobility itself kept the masses properly subservient. Not unlike blacks in the American south, Eastern European serfs were physically whipped by their masters and their women were systematically violated as a ritual of humiliation. By the end of the century the cities were overflowing with recently emancipated peasants. The old aristocracy had been a visible enemy—a human presence—but the new ruling class, the bourgeoisie, was too remote and amorphous to be a target of hate or a source of fear. People seemed to long for a *tangible* fear to banish their anxiety and many of them (e.g. Adolf Hitler) found that the foreign enemy of the nation suited that purpose precisely. Even social democrats finally let their fear of the foreigner overcome their class animosity in 1914 and supported the war effort they had once promised to sabotage.

Whenever fear subsides, the military establishment loses its *raison d'être*. In the years immediately prior to World War I militarists everywhere on the Continent felt threatened by the growth of socialist internationalism, with its concomitant doctrine of pacificism. If Germans and Frenchmen had nothing to fear from one another, as the socialists declared, the public would have no reason to serve in and pay for a million-man standing army. The social democrats were explicitly anti-military and in both France and Germany were becoming numerous enough to take over the destiny of the state. In the elections of 1912 German socialists won 35 per cent of the vote and a third of the seats in the Reichstag. Liberals and socialists were demanding greater control over the German army, and were threatening to veto the military budget. The same development was taking place in France. Despite continuous talk of war, there had been no significant clash of arms for forty-four years. The military saw itself growing obsolete, and understandably wanted war to prove itself a necessary and viable institution, and to recharge its credibility as a deterrent. German generals felt they had been made to look ridiculous by the Emperor's (William II) peaceable settlement of diplomatic crises in 1905 and 1911, and there had even been talk of deposing him if he again showed weakness in the conduct of foreign affairs.[29] The Kaiser, William, was not really the war-monger that allied propaganda later made him out to be, and Germany herself, as Caroline Playne wrote in 1925, was seldom really provocative. But, says Miss Playne, "the primary delusion of the preventive effective of appearing provocative was cherished by Germany more closely than by other nations . . . she became military largely because she cultivated the affectation of being military, and she did this quite foolishly, contrary to her nature, contrary to her interests."[30] Such is the consequence of the deterrence game. The Kaiser had to present an image of belligerence to hold his military machine together, and felt he had to make good his threats or else lose face— and perhaps power. Having backed down in other diplomatic confrontations, the Germans were determined to stand firm in the Austro-Serbian crisis of July 1914.

The war came in August 1914 primarily because the armies wanted war. The German high command saw the Austrian empire as "visibly crumbling" before the forces of South Slav irredentism, supposedly led by Serbia.[31] Allegedly Serbia had plotted the assassination of Archduke Ferdinand, the heir-apparent, as a challenge to the authority of the Habsburg monarchy, a gesture which, in the name of deterrence, called for retaliation. Serbia had to be chastened, and the Austrians, with German connivance and encouragement, launched a "punitive expedition" against her. The Austrians became convinced, says Edmund Taylor, that "revolution and the disintegration of the empire [were] inevitable if Serbia, once more remained unpunished."[32] Serbia, today part of Yugoslavia, had been agitating for the defection of other Slavic peoples within the Austrian empire, though the assassination of the archduke had not been an official act of the Serbian government. Serbia complied with all the demands of the Austrian ultimatum. Still the Austrians refused to desist, and "with the bellicose frivoltry of senile empires," as Barbara Tuchman puts it, declared war on Serbia.[33] War was seen as a means of "re-amalgamating" the Habsburg armies, of restoring the cohesion of the military establishment which was the only force holding the empire itself together. Successful war might revive the vanished glory of the Habsburgs, and even a defeat would be better than the certain disintegration already upon them. "If the monarchy is doomed to perish," 82-year old Franz Joseph said on the eve of signing the declaration of war, "let it at least go down decorously."[34] Actually, the war did revivify the Austrian army, and for nearly four years it fought heroically, with few desertions, despite horrendous casualties (2 million men killed, wounded or missing). Moreover, the war reintegrated the empire itself, and the nationalities which seemed to be on the edge of rebellion in 1914 loyally supported the Habsburgs until October 1918.

Wars are often launched by "doomed classes" who feel themselves slipping and gamble on disaster, which, after all, is preferable to decay. In Russia, the Romanovs exhibited the same psychology as the Habsburgs. The imminence of dissolution seemed to spur the will to war. Russia had experienced revolution in 1905—the largest uprising and the most brutal repression in Europe since the Paris commune. Immediately thereafter some progressive reforms were instituted, but by 1914 the forces of reaction were in clear ascendency, and strikes and social disorders were increasing. "Another year of peace" says Taylor, "might have brought new upheavals."[35] But with war there came "a deep surge of national feeling, uniting all classes . . . an unmistakable reconciliation between the Romanov dynasty and the Russian masses. War brought to light treasures of loyalty, of heroism, of social cooperation that had lain hidden for years under the corruption and barbarism of the decaying despotism."[36] This "treasure," this outburst of solidarity which occurred everywhere in Europe, was too much for the ruling classes to handle and swept the world into a catastrophe no one had foreseen. The war brought cohesion; then it had to be perpetuated to prevent disintegration.

Once the war machine was rolling, its direction could not be reversed. When Austria mobilized against Serbia, Russia came to the latter's defense with orders for general mobilization, which was perceived in Berlin as a move against Germany. Emperor William informed his cousin Czar Nicholas that general mobilization would be tantamount to a declaration of war against Germany, whereupon Nicholas ordered that plans for general mobilization be changed to *partial* mobilization, i.e., against Austria only. Nicholas was then told by his chief of staff that partial mobilization was impossible, orders calling up all the troops had already gone out and could not be rescinded. Germany therefore declared war on Russia. Germany expected France to move against her in defense of Russia, but on the last day (August 2) France agreed to remain neutral. William welcomed the French verdict, ordered champagne to celebrate the occasion and said to his chief of staff, von Moltke, now we can turn to the East. Moltke said that was impossible, the war plan called for an attack on France, and 48,000 trains were already moving toward Paris. To reverse the plan would mean that the entire German army would fall into chaos.[37] Moltke, like his Russian military counterpart, threatened to resign rather than rescind the mobilization orders and risk the disorganization of the army, and the emperors, William and Nicholas, capitulated to the generals. Mobilization had always been part of the deterrence system, a threat which could be withdrawn if the adversary made concessions. But the huge citizen armies of 1914 could not be turned on and off like a light switch; millions of men could not be called up one day and sent home the next without dislocating the economy and administrative apparatus and discrediting the national leadership. The mass armies, says Edward Crankshaw, were "no longer the obedient pawns of statesmen; they had taken on a life of their own."[38] The war was fought to preserve the army and only ended when revolution threatened to destroy it.

Prior to World War I neither statesmen nor generals understood the dynamics of the mass army and the mass society which it represented. In August 1914 Europe's rulers expected a re-run of the Franco-Prussian war, a brief encounter limited both in goals and means. Despite the arms race of the preceding thirty years, none of the armies were equipped for a long war. At first, the aims of the contestants were modest enough: each professed only defensive intentions, none deliberately set out to exterminate the other. The German chancellor, Bethmann-Hollweg, hoped that "in spite of the war, indeed through it," friendly relations with England and France would be established, and create "a grouping of Germany, England and France against the Russian colossus which threatens the civilization of Europe."[39] In August, the Germans even planned to negotiate a settlement after six weeks if victory had not by then been achieved. But after a month of heavy losses (500,000 men) the French were in no mood to bargain. France had entered the war to reclaim Alsace-Lorraine, redressing the defeat of 1870. But six months of war cost her a million men, more than the adult population of the stolen province she intended to steal back from the Germans. After such a calamity no French government could have talked peace and remained in power; the dead had to be avenged. Even had France been willing to negotiate, the Germans were then determined to keep the ground gained earlier. "For the sake of its very existence," writes Craig, "the army had to bring the German people territorial advantages which would drown the demands of its critics in shouts of enthusiasm and gratitude and would leave the monarchical system stronger than it had been in 1914."[40] German insistence on the retention of occupied territory precluded the restoration of the status quo ante; negotiation, said German conservatives, would mean the relinquishment of conquered lands, "bought with the blood of our sons."[41] Any kind of settlement between 1914 and 1916 would have been in the self-interest of all parties: a French surrender would have benefitted France more than her victory in 1918, and a German defeat in 1916 would have been a blessing to Germany and the rest of mankind.

By 1916 the struggle had turned into a war of attrition, a kind of simultaneous suicide. On February 21, the Germans attacked Verdun to compel the French to throw in every man they had. "If they do so," reasoned the chief of staff, Falkenhayn, "the forces of France will bleed to death . . . whether we reach our goal or not."[42] The Battle of Verdun lasted until July 1, with some 400,000 casualties on each side. "What was meant as a trap for France," writes William Woods, "became a trap for Germany."[43] Both contestants suffered equally and gained nothing, not even an education, for in the next six months the Allies recapitulated the mistakes of the Germans. From July to November 1916 the Allies took the offensive at the Battle of the Somme. The first day of the battle the British sustained 60,000 casualties. By November the killed, wounded and missing on both sides numbered over 900,000. Nearly two million lives were squandered in 1916, and seldom in history have so many died for so little.

By the end of 1916 the Clausewitzian idea that the purpose of war was to change the policy of the adversary was abandoned. The Germans appeared to accede to earlier Allied demands, but by then the Entente wanted unconditional surrender. The German peace offer of December 1916 may have been phony, as Fritz Fischer claims, but the Allies made no effort to test its authenticity. Pressed to define Allied war-aims the British said simply: "Germany's conduct demands penalties."[44] By 1917 the earlier patriotic glow had dimmed, and leaders of the Allies were growing apprehensive over the "apathetic silence," of the masses, which, says Leon Wolff, "concerned them as much as the enemy did. Everybody blamed the leaders. Nobody blamed the Germans."[45] By reconcentrating attention on the German menace, the repressed anger of the citizenry could be deflected from the British establishment. Thus in 1917 the British launched another unnecessary offensive in Flanders, while all they really needed to do was bide their time while the blockade starved the Germans into capitulation, as it did a year later. Instead of waiting for a German collapse, the British played the "brutal and bovine game of attrition," as Lloyd George later called it. Obligingly the Germans played the same game. After 1916 Germany's sole war aim, as Karl Kautsky says, was that of "involving her adversaries in her own ruin . . . and in her endeavour to burn down her neighbor's house she did not observe that she was setting fire to her own."[46] In the 1890's the Kaiser boasted that he would rather have the entire German people perish than give up an inch of ground won by his ancestors. By 1918 Germany seemed to be acting on that principle: "Among the people who were sacrificed to William's war policy," Kautsky noted, "the German nation heads the list."[47]

Not the damage inflicted on others but the suffering willingly accepted is the mystery in the conduct of nations and peoples in World War I. Every major power was astonishingly indifferent to its own losses, and the squandering of Russian lives by the Czarist regime knew no bounds. Russian soldiers with towsacks for shoes and armed with bayonets tied to sticks were sent in swarms against German machine-gunners. By the end of 1915 the army had suffered 4,000,-000 casualties; by 1917 some 9,000,000—76.3 per cent of the men mobilized. In March 1917 a Russian general reported: "Not only have the soldiers no desire to advance, but their will even to defend themselves has been so terribly shaken that it is a real menace to the issue of the war."[48] Then the army fell apart, the imperial regime collapsed, and the revolution followed, "the outcome of the work of the disintegrating forces set in motion by the war."[49]

While the leaders were prepared to sacrifice the total population of

Europe to the god of war, they drew back when the war-process threatened to destroy the war machine itself. There had been sullen silence but no substantial opposition to the war until the Russian revolution seemed to offer an alternative to the on-going massacre. In 1917 the French army veered toward insurrection, with "battalions, even regiments, breaking up in active mutiny, involving at least 100,000 men and probably many more."[50] For all its show of order and strength, an army is a fragile instrument. Military organization is based on deterrence, and if the soldier ceases to fear the punishment his superior can impose upon him, discipline breaks down. If a sizeable number refuses to obey orders, the army simply ceases to function. In 1917 French mutineers were singing the Internationale, calling for peace with their German comrades, and planning revolution on the Russian model. The French high command perceived the gravity of the situation and sought to correct the conditions which provoked the uprisings by going on the defensive in the war. In 1918 the German general staff faced the same problem. In late October, the Austrian army fell apart after a last defeat by the Italians, and the Austrians signed a separate peace on November 4. On the same day revolution broke out in Germany and spread rapidly over the country, and "the fleet mutinied when its leaders tried to send it out on a last death or glory ride against the British navy."[51] By November 8, "the red flag was already flying in all the principal cities, [and] soldiers behind the front were electing soldiers' councils Russian fashion."[52] When the Social Democrats threatened to join the revolution, and with civil war "not hours, but minutes away," the general staff forced the Kaiser to abdicate in order to save itself.[53] At the front whole divisions were dissolving, and the soldiers, refusing to obey their officers, were straggling off toward home. To forestall complete dispersion of the army, General Groener ordered it to march home under its own commanders, and the war was over.[54]

The immediate cause of the war was the arms race propelled and rationalized by the idea of deterrence—the word means to turn away through terror. But men are often attracted by the very thing which frightens them. Kierkegaard defines anxiety as a condition where we desire what we dread.

Anxiety, flowing out of anomie, had been rising throughout the nineteenth century. Alarm over the prospect of internal disruption led to expansion of the police-military apparatus. Preparation for state war reduced the threat of class war. But once mass armies were in being, they took on a life of their own. First the solidarity and then the suffering of World War I made disengagement from the struggle impossible. To justify its own losses each side insisted that the other be punished, and demanding total victory, both were driven into mutual defeat. "Governments and individuals conformed to the rhythm of the tragedy and swayed and staggered in helpless violence," wrote Winston Churchill in 1923, "slaughtering and squandering on ever-increasing scales, till injuries were wrought to the structure of human society which a century will not efface. . . . Victory was to be bought so dear as to be almost indistinguishable from defeat."[55]

11

War as suicide: anomie and secular sacrifice in World War I

> The spirit that accepted the war in 1914 was in truth suicidal. The exceeding complexity of life—as compared with life previously experienced—had produced an over-strained generation. . . . There was a feeling abroad that life without great excitement was no longer tenable; that explosive forces to the right and to the left had become too threatening, too dangerous to tolerate, too intractable to coordinate, impossible to subdue. Nations of men, fearing one another, glided into a suicidal attitude. Then they departed from the course of life and plunged into the adventure of death.
>
> CAROLINE PLAYNE, *Society at War 1914-1916.*

War is obviously murderous—and often suicidal. In the end the victor may lose as much as the vanquished. Who really won the Peloponnesian War, the Punic Wars? Even Germany's definitive military triumph over France in 1870-71 was "in a profound and unforeseeable sense, a disaster; for herself and for the entire world."[1] World War I, as the British Foreign Minister Sir Edward Grey remarked, was a victory only for war itself. And after Hiroshima the U.S. Air Force General "Hap" Arnold said that no one wins a modern war, like no one wins a fire.[2]

Since the 1890's perceptive observers have grasped the mutual destructiveness of war. In a work of startling and unheeded prophesy Ivan Block pointed out that war in the twentieth century would destroy the then existing political organization, and "any attempt to make war would result in suicide."[3] Yet the prospect of suicide had no deterrent power, and in some unfathomable way may have brought on the general disaster of World War I.

In 1938 Karl Menninger discerned the shadow of universal war looming up again and threatening to substitute "for all petty and individualistic and nationalistic self-destruction another convulsive effort at world suicide more violent even than that represented by 1914-18." War, says Menninger, grows out of the "suicidal bent of nations," and the spectacle of the "almost joyous preparation for mass suicide" then in progress filled him with awe.[4] As the holocaust of World War II finally burned itself out in 1945, Hannah Arendt saw that the "power accumulating machinery built by imperialism can only go on swallowing more and more territory, destroying more and more peoples, enslaving and involving more and more human beings —until finally it ends by devouring itself."[5] By the 1950's even military strategists recognized that the world was tied together in a suicide pact. Decisive superiority in the number of nuclear weapons, writes B. H. Liddell-Hart, "does not ensure victory but merely mutual destruction—and there are no degrees . . . in the matter of suicide. That defining word has to be constantly reiterated . . . The natural consequence of nuclear parity is nuclear nullity."[6] Rationalists comfort themselves with the thought that no "sane" man, or group, instigates a self-destructive war, forgetting the suicidal character of Dr. Strangelove, who would rather be dead than red.

Since Freud, a simple pleasure-pain interpretation of human conduct is no longer tenable. Men and women sometimes *seek* pain, suffering, even death, and states and collectivities often seem actuated by a similar drive toward self-annihilation. Self-destructive action is not always consciously suicidal. Even physical disease has an underlying self-destructive component, and accidental deaths are often unconscious suicides.[7] The chronic gambler is said to be a self-defeating person who unknowingly seeks to bring about his own ruin in order to confirm an image of himself as a "born loser." And often it seems that ruling classes and military castes unintentionally defeat themselves by the gamble of war. History abounds with suicidal military ventures: Napoleon's invasion of Russia in 1812, the South's firing on Fort Sumpter in 1861, Japanese warlords bombing Pearl Harbor in 1941, Hitler's attack on the Soviet Union in 1942. In a still deeper sense, Toynbee attributes the death of seventeen of the twenty-one known civilizations to the "suicidalness of militarism."[8]

War necessitates masochism. The warrior is socialized to endure pain, to risk danger, even to sacrifice his life—i.e. commit suicide—to protect the group. Throughout the ages military personnel have displayed an unusual propensity for self-destruction. No statistical measure is available for earlier periods, but Durkheim's data on the nineteenth century show the military rate of suicide to be anywhere from two to ten times the civilian rate.[9] In the U.S. Army between 1920 and 1940 the suicide rate hovered between 35 and 40 per 100,000 as opposed to a civilian rate for males of around 15 to 20. Englebrecht attributes the high military suicide rate to the habit of unreasoning obedience which creates an attitude of submission and passivity, "an impersonal contempt for life which destroys all sense of individuality and belief in the importance of life."[10]

Modern warfare requires a kind of "psychic suicide," an abnegation of private judgment for collective authority. Military technology has abolished individual daring and initiative and made persistent and stuporous discipline the required virtue of the fighting man. Ivan Block explains how in the early nineteenth century the bayonet had been the key to victory. Combatants advanced upon one another without flinching, exchanged volleys, rushed upon one another. Thus the outcome of the battle was quickly decided, and the weaker side usually escaped without difficulty. "The victors sent two or three volleys after the vanquished, and the battle was over."[11] However, by the end of the century conditions were quite different: the soldier had to pass through a "zone of murderous fire" before he could even use his bayonet. Simultaneously military organization had become more thorough and comprehensive. In the Franco-Prussian War, says Block, subordinate commanders even down to the level of captains had "an extraordinary liberty" to decide who, when and how to attack the opponent—an autonomy which would be disruptive to future armies. "Courage now is required no less than before," writes Block, "but the courage of restraint and self-sacrifice are no longer scenic heroism. War has taken on a character more mechanical than knightly. Personal initiative is required but not visible."[12]

Not only the outlines but the details of Block's forecast were confirmed in World War I. As George Stratton wrote in 1916, the war had turned out to be "the murder of the unknown by the unseen," and the fighter was more docile than aggressive. "The more perfect the machinery for governmental fighting, the more completely must the individual surrender his will . . . drill and discipline drives out instinctive pugnacity."[13] Not the anger to kill but the willingness to die became the decisive determinant of victory in twentieth century wars of attrition. Between 1914 and 1918 millions of men laid down their lives in a kind of sublime anesthesia.

Looking back on World War I a decade later, Gilbert Murray said, "It is not that men want to kill but they want to face peril. They want to put forth for one great moment the extreme effort of mind and body of which they are capable. They want to do it for others, for some great *unspecified* cause, so that if they live those whom they saved will adore them, and if they die multitudes will bless their memory."[14] But deeper questions still remain: why, for instance, were men so eager to die for the unspecified causes of 1914?

By 1914, says John Nef, war had become the moral equivalent of religion, providing men with a mission at the time when "all sense of purpose in connection with peace and ordinary living was being lost."[15] The absurdity of war was recognized but embraced none the less. Thus the elder von Moltke, architect of the German victory in the Franco-Prussian war, a learned man steeped in history (translator of Gibbon's *Decline and Fall of the Roman Empire*), could say that *any war even a victorious one* was a misfortune for all the nations concerned. But he added in the same breath: "everlasting peace is a dream and not even a beautiful dream . . . war is a link in God's ordering of the world."[16] Even though they usually failed in the practice of the art of war, the Germans perfected the metaphysics of war. War is endowed with "moral majesty," Treitschke said in the 1870's, because the soldier is willing to "sacrifice not only his life but his very self . . . for the sake of patriotism." Here is the sublimity of war; Trietschke continues: "it weaves a bond of love between man and man linking them together to face death and causing all class distinctions to disappear . . . to banish war from the world would be to mutilate human nature."[17] But the glorification of war is not uniquely German; the same song has its French and Russian, English and American rendition. The text and title of the speech nominating Theodore Roosevelt for President in 1904 could have been taken from von Moltke: "Peace is a Child's Dream." And the venerable Justice Oliver Wendell Holmes sounds like an American Treitschke when he speaks of war. Struggle for life is the order of the world, Holmes told a Harvard audience in 1895. Our noblest ideals are drawn from war. The soldier is one who chooses honor rather than life. The glory of the soldier derives from his sacrifice not his cause. The martyrdom of Confederate soldiers defending slavery is as noble, for Holmes, as the death of those who died to preserve the Union. War is horrible and dull when you are in it. It is only when time has passed, says Holmes, "that you realize its message is divine." God's message, as relayed by Holmes, once decoded, reads simply: since existence has no transcendent significance, it is noble to throw your life away. "I do not know what is true," Holmes says. "I do not know the meaning of the universe. But in the midst of doubt, in the collapse of creeds, there is one thing I do not doubt, that no man who lives in the same world with most of us can doubt, and that is that the faith is true and adorable which leads a soldier to throw away his life in obedience to a blindly accepted duty, in a cause which he little understands, in a plan of campaign of which he has no notion, under tactics of which he does not see the use."[18]

From the turn of the century onward, the passion for self-surrender grows with the general bewilderment, the anomie of a dissolving civilization.[19] Caroline Playne speaks of the rise of a "combative and disordered spirit" in the two decades preceding World War I; Nef detects the emergence of a "cult of violence." Violence is no longer deplored as an unfortunate fact of life but celebrated as a good in itself. Nietzsche admonishes his safe and comfortable readers to "live dangerously." A secure and bored population longs for excitement and distraction. In his brilliant study of Sorel, Irving Louis Horowitz gets to the heart of the matter: "Pacificism [becomes] a symbol of decadence while violence [becomes] the supreme symbol of virility."[20]

As violence is increasingly celebrated, it more commonly occurs. The frequency of individual acts of violence rises in the 1900-1914 period. Political assassination becomes more common.[21] The murder rate in both Europe and America begins to rise around 1900.[22] (See Chapter 9.) Still more revealing is the growth of self-destructive violence. Everywhere in Europe suicide rates increased during the nineteenth century, reaching their zenith in 1913. The British rate rose

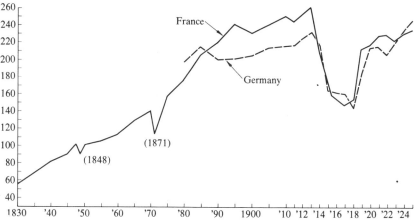

Figure 4. Suicide in France and Germany 19th and 20th Centuries*

* Data from M. Halbwachs, *Les Causes du Suicide* (Paris: Felix Alcan, 1930), 323, 369.

70 per cent between 1860 and 1911; the Scandinavian, German, and French rates followed the same pattern.[23] There are no reliable American suicide statistics prior to the twentieth century, but between 1900 and 1913 the U.S. rate rose about 50 per cent and then moved downward until 1930. Suicide rates always drop during war, as can be seen from M. Halbwachs's data (Figure 4).

But even more interesting is the sharp upsurge of the German and French rate between 1910 and 1913. And is it not strange that the suicide rates seem to reach their lowest point in 1918 when all the European nations have been exhausted by the war? Consider G. Fuellkrug's data on Germany:

Year	Suicide Rate (per million)[24]
1910	200
1911	208
1912	215
1913	220
1914	200
1915	160
1916	165
1917	150
1918	144
1919	180
1920	212
1921	194
1922	200
1923	207

If a high suicide rate indicates a collective discontentment, does a low rate mean the opposite? If so the German people, and statistics are the same for other Europeans, were never happier than in the misery of 1918—a not untenable proposition in the light of what is now known of masochism. Theodor Reik speaks of a social masochism, "overwhelming catastrophes affecting whole peoples . . . by a dark desire for suffering."[25] How many of his countrymen did Max Weber speak for when he said in the defeat of 1918, "I have never felt as I do in this hour of shame that it is a gift from heaven to be a German"?[26] And the sharp rise of the suicide rate before the war, between 1910 and 1914, does this point to a growing weariness with life, a growing readiness to plunge into the void?

As the suicide rates rose in the nineteenth century the birth rates declined. Do both phenomenon represent a repudiation of life? The

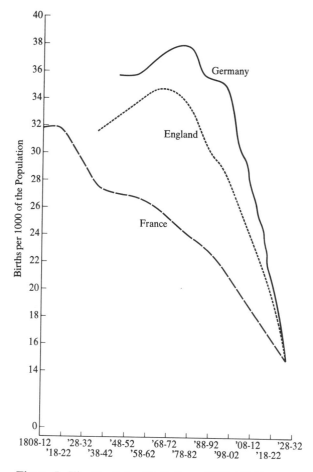

Figure 5. The Declining Birth Rate, 1808-1928*

* Data from: Warren Thompson, *Population Problems* (New York: McGraw-Hill, 1942), 153.

British social anthropologist Pitt-Rivers considers depopulation a form of suicide: "continuous decrease in fertility only occurs where a people are no longer interested in living . . . e.g. among . . . people whose social, religious, ideological framework has been smashed . . ."[27] With the growth of anomie, that is, the disintegration of the cultural framework of European civilization in the nineteenth century, the birth rate dropped, as shown in Figure 5. After some two centuries of continuous population growth in Europe and Europeanized areas of the world "the rate of increase . . . began to decline in 1870," as Quincy Wright reports.[28] Strangely, Wright does not comment on the inverse correlation between the dropping birth rate and the accelerating militarization of Europe from 1870 onward. The usual sociological interpretation attributes the declining birth rate to urban-industrialization. Yet in France, least urbanized, least industrial, of the major European countries, the rate dropped first and fastest. A deeper attitudinal variable seems to be in operation. Oswald Spengler says that the sterility of European civilization in the late nineteenth century cannot be understood in "mechanical" terms but represents a metaphysical turn toward death.[29]

World War I seems like the actualization of the metaphysical turn toward death which had taken place earlier. In the three years prior to the war the suicide rate climbed to the highest point ever recorded for Euro-American society. (See Figure 4.) In 1914 people were eager to "shed the burden of the brain," as Edward Crankshaw put it, and so everywhere sought escape from the tortures of self-preoccupation.[30] Men's minds seemed on edge in the last two or three years before the war in a way they had not been before, writes A. J. P. Taylor, "as though they had become unconsciously weary of peace and security. You can see it in things remote from international politics . . . [in] artistic movements like Futurism, militant suffragettes, working class trends toward syndicalism. Men wanted violence for its own sake; they welcomed war as a relief from materialism. European civilzation was, in fact, breaking down even before war destroyed it."[31]

August 1914 brought the exultation of self-surrender. Individualism is abolished; community restored. "We could feel in those hours [of August 1914]," wrote Max Scheler in his *Genius of the War:* "how a peculiar national fate touches the heart of every man—the smallest and the greatest. . . . The great course of world history and the innermost desires of the individual were suddenly tied together. Miraculously they became dependent on each other. No more were we what we had been so long: alone. The broken contract between individual, people, nation, world, and God was suddenly reestablished. The interchange of these forces was intensified more than it ever had been by any poetry, philosophy, prayer, or ritual."[32] In Munich, Adolf Hitler dropped to his knees and thanked God for this opportunity to fight for freedom. In Heidelberg, Max Weber said: "This war with all its ugliness is great and wonderful."[33] English and French intellectuals were equally ecstatic over the holy communion of war. Gilbert Murray spoke of the very high happiness which comes from having something before you, clearly seen, which you know you must do, and can do, and will spend your utmost strength and perhaps your life in doing. Very few people find this happiness in everyday life, "but in war ordinary men find it. This is the inward triumph which lies at the heart of the great tragedy."[34] In the last agitated days of peace a kind of suicidal serenity descended upon many European intellectuals. "The tension is now at its peak," the Austrian historian Redlick recorded in his diary on July 22, 1914, "but we in the know are quite calm." What he meant, says Crankshaw, was that war was certain, blessed release was at hand, and "in a few days neither he nor anybody else would ever have to think again . . . [and could] advance with glad cries into the great inane of violent action."[35]

The mood of joyful abandon was pervasive; the rush to war swept up the entire European population in a hysterical dance of death. The war converted anxiety into fear and called for great and noble courage. "When hostilities finally opened," writes Caroline Playne, "people felt that at last we get what we want! We can do and die! . . . no more negotiating . . . no more heeding, only rushing on, on, gloriously splendidly on, all traces kicked over, all bridles thrown away."[36] An ordinary German seaman recorded in his diary on hearing of the German declaration of war on Russia and France: "Our joy and excitement were boundless and lasted until late into the night." The only cloud in Seaman Stumpf's delight was the fear that England might not enter the war. When on the next day Germany declared war on England, Stumpf wrote: "All of us breathed a sigh of relief. The very thing for which we had so long waited and hoped, the thing we had *yearned for and feared* had come true."[32] People seemed to long for the ordeal of war as a means of experiencing elemental reality. Lloyd George spoke of the way all classes, high and low, were "shedding themselves of selfishness . . . and discovering the fundamental things that matter in life, which had been obscured from vision by the tropical growth of prosperity."[38] In August 1914 European people actively sought the danger of war.

The public response to recruitment accurately reveals the will to war. On August 1 only eight men enlisted in the British regular army at the Central London Recruiting Office. On August 4, after the declaration of war, there was "a seething mass waiting to be enrolled"; from distant corners of England men walked all night and slept in ditches in order to get to the nearest recruiting station; 200,000 reserves were called up and no absentees were reported.[39] In France the general staff had estimated that some 13 per cent of reserves would not show up, but in fact only 1.5 per cent of those called failed to report; 350,000 volunteered for army service, and even 3,000 deserters from the peacetime army returned to France to rejoin their regiments. "To die is nothing," said Georges Clemenceau, "we must conquer. And for that we shall need every arm [even] the weakest shall have his part in the struggle."[40] Even the weakest, the masses otherwise ignored, were called upon to serve—probably that accounts for the striking decline of the suicide rate noted everywhere in Europe in 1914. Isolated and foresaken men, candidates for self-slaughter in peacetime, are needed in war—needed to help kill other men.

Confronted with the threat of imminent invasion, the French response to the call to arms is an understandable defense of homeland. Both Britain and France were at least pseudo-democracies, which large numbers probably felt were worth defending. But even in the vile and hated autocracies of East and Central Europe the war was welcomed with the same enthusiasm. Some 15,000,000 Russian peasants willingly went off to fight for the Czar; in Vienna the urban masses rallied to the cause of the Habsburgs. "A city of two million, a country of nearly fifty million," wrote Stefan Zweig—

> . . . in that hour felt that they were participating in world history, in a moment which would never recur, and that each one was called upon to cast his infinitesimal self into the glowing mass, there to be purified of all selfishness. All differences of class, ranks, and language were flooded over at that moment by the rushing feeling of fraternity. Strangers spoke to one another in the streets, people who had avoided each other for years shook hands, everywhere one saw excited faces. . . . The petty mail clerk, who ordinarily sorted letters early and late . . . from Monday until Saturday without interruption; the clerk, the cobbler, had suddenly achieved a romantic possibility in life: he could become a hero, and everyone who wore a uniform was already being cheered by the women, and greeted beforehand with this romantic appellation by those who had to remain behind. They acknowledged the unknown power which had lifted them out of their everyday existence. Even mothers with their grief, and women with their fears, were ashamed to manifest their quite natural emotions in the face of this first transformation. But it is quite possible that a deeper, more secret power was at work in this frenzy. So deeply, so quickly did the tide break over humanity that, foaming over the surface, it churned up the depths, the subconscious primitive instincts of the human animal—that which Freud so meaningfully calls "the revulsion from culture," the desire to break out of the conventional bourgeois world of codes and statutes, and to permit the primitive instincts of the blood to rage at will. It is also possible that these powers of darkness had their share in the wild frenzy into which everything was thrown—self-sacrifice and alchohol, the spirit

of adventure and the spirit of pure faith, the old magic of
flags and patriotic slogans, that mysterious frenzy of the
millions which can hardly be described in words, by which,
for the moment, gave a wild and almost rapturous impetus
to the greatest crime of our time.[41]

Even Zweig, opposed to war in theory, found that there was something "majestic, rapturous and even seductive" in the outbreak of
mass enthusiasm which he could escape only with difficulty.

By coincidence Leon Trotsky happened to be in Vienna in August
1914. Almost alone among European intellectuals, Trotsky had foreseen the coming of the war, and anticipated its transformation into a
long and suicidal battle of attrition, while everyone else, on both
sides, expected the troops to be home before the leaves turned in
autumn 1914. Trotsky had covered the Balkan wars of 1912-13 as a
newspaper reporter. In Belgrade in 1912 he watched, "as if it were
a phantom," a regiment going to war in uniforms of protective color-
ing and bark sandals, and men wearing a sprig of green in their caps.
The sandals on their feet and the little sprig of green in their caps, in
combination with the full fighting outfit, gave the soldier "the look of
men doomed for sacrifice."[42] And the sacrifice, or the risk of it, was
accepted willingly. As pointless as the war might be, it offered the
prospect of escape from the even more intolerable boredom and de-
mentia of daily life. Reflecting on the exaltation of the Vienna crowds
in August 1914, Trotsky later wrote, "the people whose lives, day in
and day out, pass in a monotony of hopelessness are many: they are
the mainstay of modern society. The alarm of mobilization breaks
into their lives like a promise; the familiar and long-hated is overthrown, and the new and unusual reigns in its place. Changes still
more incredible are in store for them in the future. For better or
worse? For the better, of course—what can seem worse . . . than
'normal' conditions?"[43]

In November 1914 Trotsky was writing of the boundless chaos
enveloping Europe, with silence from the masses of workers, de-
ceived and betrayed by the Social Democrats. In 1917 it was Trotsky

who pronounced the most fitting epitaph for the war: "this unparalleled self-annihilation of mankind."[44]

Yet Trotsky with all his genius does not get to the root of the war. The day Trotsky left Vienna for Zurich, with Austrian state police fast on his heels, Bertrand Russell walked the streets of London incredulous at the crowds cheering for war. Like Trotsky, Russell kept his cool, managed to transcend his patriotic impulses, though he was forever shaken by the realization that "the anticipation of carnage was delightful to something like 90 per cent of the people . . . I had supposed that most people liked money better than almost anything else, but I discovered they liked destruction even better."[45]

What is this will to destruction, which seems so antithetical to the self-interest of the person and very laws of nature? What men sought to destroy in 1914 were the individuated routines of peace upon which the private self is built. Nietzsche, 14 years dead in an insane asylum, a madman's madman, described in 1883 what happened in 1914.

The will to destruction, says Nietzsche, is "the will of a still deeper instinct—of the instinct of self-destruction, of the will to Non-Entity."[46] Nietzsche opens his last and greatest work with the modest note that he is going to relate the history of the next two centuries describing what must necessarily happen: "The triumph of Nihilism."

Nihilism is a synonym for anomie. Those the sociologist calls deviant, Nietzsche designates as the "botched and bungled" who are "the insane (also artists), the criminals, the anarchists . . . not the oppressed classes, but the outcasts of the community of all classes hitherto."[47] Once religion, morality, had protected the "botched and bungled" against nihilism, but now—Nietzsche is writing in the 1880's —they no longer have any consolation and thus "they destroy in order to be destroyed . . . compelling the powerful to become their hangmen."[48] No one is really excluded from Nietzsche's category of the "botched and bungled," even the most "noble members of a people" who are overwhelmed by a secret desire to kill themselves when war comes: "They throw themselves with delight against the new danger of death, because in the sacrifice for the fatherland they believe they have found at last the permission they have been seeking, the permission to evade their human purpose. War is for them a short-cut to suicide, it enables them to commit suicide with a good conscience."[49] Nietzsche embodied the fundamental contradictions of European civilization on the eve of World War I: nihilism and the will to power, each feeding on the other.

War is the will to power in its pristine form. The essence of war is the act of annihilation, which turns men into nihilists. Self and other are so entwined—woven out of a single garment of destiny, as Martin Luther King put it—that willful damage to the other always entails symbolic or psychological damage to the self. Devaluation of the other, necessitated by the act of killing, results also in a devaluation of the self. If the self is without value, then everything is meaningless, and nihilism follows inevitably. What then is Nihilism? Nietzsche sets forth the answer as a catechism.

> Nihilism is . . . the belief that everything deserves to perish. The conviction of nihilism [is] . . . that life is absurd in the light of the highest values already discovered.
> What does the nihilist do? . . . One actually puts one's shoulder to the plough; one destroys.
> What is the "deed" of nihilism? . . . the deed of nihilism is suicide.
> I believe life is absurd; I believe everything deserves to perish; I seek to destroy all life, to lead the living to suicide.[50]

Thus men were led off to war in 1914; thus they returned in 1918.

If the nations of Europe were not suicidal at the outset of the war, they appeared to become so after suffering astronomical casualties, irretrievable losses. For everyone who lived through World War I, death was an omnipresent reality, and those not actually caught in the fighting had to think-war, think-death.

Of course death is always part of life. Still the normal death from age, disease, accident can be blamed on nature, defined as unavoidable and thus accepted. Usually even war can be attributed to forces beyond the control of ordinary men—to the machinations of kings and militarists—and confronted as an *imposed* disaster. But World War I was uniquely traumatic because in the beginning "everyone" approved the massacre and the victims felt they themselves had *willed* the calamity which engulfed them.

Normal death is excused as an act of fate or God. But when men die at the hands of other men punishment of the offender is demanded. Punishment will not resurrect the deceased, but it does designate the agent responsible for his demise, relieving the doubt and guilt of the rest of the community. Writing of Truman Capote's *In Cold Blood,* a study of the multiple murder of a Kansas farm family, Conrad Knickerbacker describes how the killing was incomprehensible until the culprits were apprehended. Members of the community who had known each other for years came to suspect and distrust "not terrible strangers, but themselves. . . . Neighborliness evaporated. The natural order seemed suspended. Chaos poised to rush in."[51] But once the offenders were publicly identified through official punishment the town breathed easy again and the semi-trust of normal life returned. So too with the multiple murder of World War I which shook the moral foundations of every national community in the western world. Punishment of the "enemy" located the blame for the disruption outside the community and thus deflected guilt from self to other. At the peace conference in 1919 the victors were more interested in putting the stigma of guilt on the Germans than in creating the conditions for future security. The famous war guilt clause of the Treaty of Versailles opens with the sentence: "The Allied and Associated Governments affirm and Germany accepts the responsibility of Germany and her allies for causing *all* the loss and damage to which the Allied and Associated Governments and their nationals have been subjected as a consequence of the war *imposed* upon them by the aggression of Germany and her allies."[52] Allied leaders had to blame Germany for the war in order to disguise their own complicity in the deed.

War is supposed to have an aim other than sheer destruction. But after the first few months of catastrophic losses in World War I each belligerent seemed to be fighting only to punish the other, and the very thought of peace became a betrayal of the dead who must be avenged. Each sacrifice demanded further slaughter:

> We are the Dead. Short days ago
> We lived, felt dawn, saw sunset glow,
>   Loved and were loved, and now we lie
>   In Flander's fields.
> Take up our quarrel with the foe:
> To you from falling hands we throw
>   The torch; be yours to hold it high
>   If ye break faith with us who die
> We shall not sleep, though poppies grow
>   In Flanders field.[53]

In the inter-war years, 1918-39, it almost seemed as if Europe, and especially Germany, had acquired a collective death wish from the agony of 1914-18. The war experience forged an identification with the dead which generated a will to die and a thirst for further war. "The days, the weeks, the years out here shall come back again," says Paul in *All Quiet on the Western Front,* "and our dead comrades shall then stand up again and march with us, our heads shall be clear, we shall have a purpose, and so we shall march, our dead comrades beside us, the years at the Front behind us:—against whom, against whom?"[54]

12

War as suicide: Nazism, the death-wish institutionalized

> Death is the final goal of the scientifically drilled nation. The task of the leaders becomes easy when the followers are ready to die.
>
> KONRAD HEIDEN, *Der Fuehrer: Hitler's Rise to Power.*

The act of annihilation turns men into nihilists. Instead of shocking men into sanity, the catastrophic losses of World War I only kindled a blind fury which led on to mutual ruin. "Everything happened as if at a certain point violence became self-supporting," writes Raymond Aron. "In war, as with fissionable materials, there is a critical mass. Since 1914, Europe has been shaken by wars in 'chain reaction.' "[1] Nazism is the connecting link in the chain, the creature of the First, the creator of the Second, World War. Systematically liquidating both external and internal "enemies," Nazism was total war escalated to its suicidal consummation.

Fascism was a cult of death. Franco's Falangists had the motto, *Vive el Muerto* (Long Live Death!), and the Nazi movement was built on thanatolatry, a term Leo Alexander coined to designate an "idolatrous delight in death." Within the elite S.S. destructive urges, initially turned outward on the "enemy" finally turned inward as fratricidal strife. S. S. men were often killed by their comrades; the murderous impulse became suicidal. Concentration camps says Alexander served as a training and proving ground to develop in the S. S. man "the extreme readiness to kill as well as an exultant gladness over dying."[2]

Education for death began early in the life of the Nazi. By the age of 12 the young boy was learning that death for the Fuehrer was more glorious than life itself and took an oath: "I consecrate my life to Hitler: I am ready to sacrifice my life for Hitler. I am ready to die for Hitler, the savior, the Fuehrer.[3] And the high school senior is told he may have to die for Hitler before he is twenty, "but is that not a wonderful privilege . . . to die for the savior of Germany?"[4] Note the emphasis is on the masochistic rather than the sadistic side of the coin of destruction. The aggressive impulses are subdued; the masses are taught to willingly accept death, not to inflict it on others. Self-sacrifice becomes the highest heroism, as Peter Nathan explains: "The fear of not being manly enough leads to a glorification of death. The fear of fear gives rise to courage. The terror of showing oneself a coward makes a man rise to heights of self-sacrifice. . . . Heroism and self sacrifice in battle are the denial of fear and cowardice . . . a masculine denial. They mean 'I am a man.' It thus comes to be that the height of masculinity is to be killed. The greatest joy which a young man can hope for is to die for his fatherland, and the only justification for the existence of women is that they should produce men to die."[5]

Nazism was an attack on the life process itself. On the thinnest pretext women were sterilized—even to eradicate color blindness. "We must not have soldiers who are color blind," Ziemer was told. "It is transmitted only by women."[6] In the concentration camps men's testicles were crushed, "with the girl typists and secretaries of the Gestapo prison looking on."[7] Though justified as a means of extracting a confession, or even to further science, the real function of the torture was instruction of the torturer. For instance, 25 or 30 victims would be placed in a special van with an observation window on the side. Air would be withdrawn from the van, and the "experimental subjects" would die of lung hemorrhage as the "observers" watched at the window.[8] Were the on-lookers trying to overcome their own fear, convince themselves death has no sting? Was the experience an innoculation against human compassion? In 1935 the Nazi minister of public health published a work proclaiming that "love of one's fellow man had to disappear, especially in regard to inferior and asocial elements . . . in order to secure the continuance of a racially pure people free from hereditary taint for all eternity."[9]

The brutality of Nazism was designed to create a community of hate. "Through work and industry a people has never grown free," Hitler declared in the 1920's, "but only through hatred."[10] Hitler's uncanny hold on Germany came from his power to give voice to the smoldering hatred of the masses in a time of anomie. From the beginning Hitler, like millions of others, was at war with civilization itself. "Yes, we are barbarians!" he announced in 1933. "We want to be barbarians! It is an Honourable title. We shall rejuvenate the world. This world [western civilization] is near its end."[11]

Hitler's hatred of civilization dates back to his early manhood in Vienna. When he came to Vienna at the age of 19 he was "not wholly twisted or evil," says William Jenks—but six years on the skids generated a psychopathic rage. After years of frustration and humiliation, Hitler left Vienna in 1913 passionately yearning for "the hour of doom of this Babylonian realm." No hero, leader or dictator of the first half of the century, writes Jenks, "was ever so marked and molded by a modern city as was Hitler."[12]

At the turn of the century Vienna was the most cosmopolitan and anomic of the great European cities: a polyglot of "races" and religions where, in Hitler's words, "dazzling riches and loathsome poverty alternated sharply."[13] The population had increased 259 per cent since 1860, of the 1,674,957 residents only 46.6 were natives, and statistically there were 51 persons per house in Vienna, as compared with 31 in Berlin, 30 in Paris, 8 in London.[14] Tens of thousands of men slept in the parks, lived in the gutters of the Danube canals, and

Hitler was among them. In 1924 he wrote of his revulsion for the big city which "first avidly sucked men in and then so cruelly crushed them."

> I, too, had been tossed around by life in the metropolis. . . . in my own skin I could feel the effects of this fate and taste them with my soul. One more thing I saw: the rapid change from work to unemployment and vice versa, plus the resultant fluctuation of income, ends by destroying in many all feeling for thrift, or any understanding for a prudent ordering of their lives.[15]

Hitler's life partakes of the anomie of the metropolis. His days are spent aimlessly walking the streets, reading newspapers in cafes, listening to Parliamentary debates from the visitors gallery, arguing with the Social Democrats on street corners. Occasionally he drops in at the museums. He feasts his sado-masochism on Wagner—later he claimed to have attended more than forty performances of *Tristran und Isolde* alone. He lives in flophouses, putters at odd jobs—shovels snow, beats carpets, carries bags at the railway stations. He paints a few watercolors which he peddles on the sidewalks. In the winter of 1908 he was literally "without a shirt and underdrawers," an authentic bum sleeping in shelters for homeless men. He was without friends or family, and was detested by the other derelicts. Gradually he discovered that the world's misery had its roots in "Marxism and Jewry." Vienna had brought him "face to face with inscrutable destiny" and laid the "granite foundation" . . . of his *Weltanschauung*. He has gone through his "greatest spiritual upheaval," a struggle for identity, but he emerged psychologically victorious: "I had ceased to be a weak-kneed cosmopolitan and became an anti-Semite."[16]

If Vienna was the "push" of Hitler's life, World War I was the "pull." The loneliness and chaos of the city was supplanted by the comradeship and structure of the army. Thirty years later as supreme commander on the Eastern front, he recalled how he "passionately loved soldiering" in World War I.[17] His conduct as well as his words testify to a suicidal courage in 42 months of active duty as an infantryman and a dispatch runner. He won five decorations for valor, was wounded in 1916 and hospitalized for two months, was temporarily blinded by gas and hospitalized again in 1918.[18] In a letter written to his former Munich landlord in 1914, Hitler describes his experience in the Battle of Ypres:

> . . . we went through a withering fire. One man after another collapsed ahead of us. Our major came up, fearless and calmly smoking, with his adjutant, Lieutenant Piloty. The major took in the situation at a glance and ordered us to assemble to right and left of the highway for an assault. We had no more officers, hardly any non-coms. . . . [we] ran back to get reinforcements. When I came back the second time with a troop of scattered Wurttembergers, the major lay on the ground with his breast torn open. A heap of corpses lay around him.
>
> By this time there was only one officer left, his adjutant. We were boiling with fury. "Herr Lieutenant, lead us at them!" we all shouted. . . . Four times we went forward and were forced to retreat; of my whole detachment only one man was left aside from myself, and finally he too fell. A shot tore off the whole left sleeve of my tunic, but by a miracle I remained untouched.
>
> For three days we fought like this, and on the third day the Britishers were finally licked. . . . *In four days* our regiment of thirty-five hundred men had melted away to six hundred. There were only thirty officers left in the whole regiment. Four companies had to be dissolved. But we were all proud of having licked the Britishers. Since then we have been in the front lines the whole time.
>
> I am now carrying dispatches for the staff. With regard to dirt, conditions are a little better here, but it is also more dangerous. In Wytschaete alone, on the day of the first attack, three of us eight were shot off, and one badly wounded. We four survivors and the wounded man were cited for distinction. And this saved our lives. For while the list of those proposed for the 'Cross' was being discussed, four company commanders came into the tent, or dugout.

Due to lack of space, the four of us had to step out. We hadn't been outside for five minutes when a grenade struck the tent, gravely wounded Lieutenant-Colonel Engelhardt and killed or wounded all the rest of the staff. It was the most terrible moment of my life. We worshipped Lieutenant-Colonel Engelhardt.

I am sorry, I have to close now. . . . Day after day we are under the heaviest artillery fire from eight in the morning to five in the afternoon. In time, that shatters even the strongest nerves. . . . We want an all-out fight, at any cost, and we hope that those of us who have the good fortune to see their homeland again will find it purer and more purified from foreignism.[19]

Having survived this "immersion in death," as Robert Jay Lifton would call it, Hitler felt he owed his own life to a chain of miracles and enjoyed the special protection of Providence.[20] The confrontation with death and danger seems to have an addicting power: throughout the war Hitler kept putting himself in a position to be killed, as if testing Fate or playing Russian roulette, no doubt an exhilarating experience for the survivor. It's not that Hitler wants to kill himself—he does not care much for either life or death—but, like the attempted suicides in James Weiss' study, he is engaged in a gamble with death, trying to ascertain if Fate really is on his side.[21] That was the secret of his success in the disordered world of postwar Germany and finally the cause of his downfall. He was a gambler who won all but the last hand.

When peace broke out in 1918, Hitler wept. Incomparable irony: the Vienna tramp cries about the fall of the Hohenzollerns. For Hitler miserable days follow: "All was lost . . . hatred grew in me, hatred for those responsible for this deed."[22] Who brought about the German defeat? Not the monarchy, not even the Entente, but the invisible foe, the Jew-Bolsheviks who betrayed the country in the November revolution. Since he now knew what was wrong with the world, he set out to change it, to wage war on evil. For four years he had seen human life sacrificed at command and the principle that the end justified the means raised to the highest morality. "He never got over that," writes Otto Tolischus, "and the morality of war became the guiding morality of his life."[23]

With the armistice, chaos had come again, many times compounded. The collapse of the regime left the average German disoriented, "like a man deprived of his old and now comfortable straight-jacket."[24] Hitler is the embodiment of anomie; back in Munich in 1919 he found himself "numbered among the nameless . . . one of the millions whom chance permits to live or summons out of existence without even their closest neighbors condescending to take any notice of it."[25] Then he joined the German Workers Party (its seventh member), found his calling, discovered he could speak.

Among the "botched and bungled"—to use Nietzsche's phrase—Hitler's words found a resonance. Two of the initial six members of the German Workers Party were Captain Ernst Roehm and Dietrich Eckart. Roehm was a scar-faced professional soldier—the upper part of his nose had been shot away in 1914—and a homosexual. Eckart, the spiritual founder of National Socialism, was a journalist and poet, a one-time Vienna vagrant who had taken to morphine, been confined to a mental hospital, and in 1923 died an alcoholic. Another of the "spiritual fathers" of Nazism, the right-wing intellectual and critic August Moeller, died a suicide.[26] Later there was Goering, a drug addict; Goebbels, a cripple; Himmler, with an acute psychosomatic stomach disorder; Hess wounded; Ley, an alcoholic; Borman, an ex-convict. And all the Nazi leadership had undergone "the traumas of the trenches."[27]

Nazism was a kind of *participatory tyranny*. Not the official party program but the opportunity to indulge in sadism attracted members to the movement. Hitler's strategy—says William Shirer—was to provide the masses with a few simple ideas, some pageantry and color, "and acts of violence and terror, which if successful, would attract adherents (were not most Germans drawn to the strong?) and give them a sense of power over the weak."[28] In the beginning ex-servicemen were assigned to meetings to silence hecklers, then they were

organized into strong arm squads, and finally outfitted in brown uniforms as storm troopers (S.A.). "Not content to keep order at Nazi
meetings," Shirer continues, "[the S.A.] soon took to breaking up
those of other parties."

The S.A. became an army for waging internal war, against the
Communists, the Social Democrats, the parties of the center and
finally the Weimar Republic itself. By 1930 this private army of the
party numbered 100,000, larger than General Groener's *Reichswehr,*
the regular army of the German Republic. By 1932 the S.A. had
400,000 members and reached 2.5 million by 1934. Given the discord of Germany in the 1920's, the growth of the S.A. is not hard to
understand. Like the soldier, the storm trooper had a uniform, a public identity, a name, and a mission. He faced danger, largely self-
created, which gave drama to his life. He had comradeship, and lived
among men as equals. In the 1930's Theodore Abel collected some
600 autobiographies of ordinary Nazis and S.A. men, throughout
which runs the common theme of war as a means of banishing
anomie. "When I joined the Party [one wrote] my life once again
came to have significance. . . . Our meetings now held a very special attraction; we were once again 'among men' as we had been at
the front." Another says: "The philosophy of the movement endowed
my hitherto aimless life with a meaning and a purpose." The ordinary
Nazi in Abel's autobiographies comes through as less sinister and
perverse than the leadership of the party, and inspired by comradeship rather than malice. "What fellowship there was among the men
who had left their wives, families and parents, preferring the sacred
sign of the swastika to their means of livelihood. They mocked Hell,
Death and the Devil in their faith in a just cause. What joy and honor
to be allowed to fight side by side with such comrades." Then there
is the always baffling altruism of the warrior: "The war had taught
us one lesson [writes another of Abel's informants] the great community of the front. All class differences . . . disappeared under its
spell. Out there it was what a person *was,* not what he seemed to be,
that counted. There was only a people, no individuals. Common suf-

fering and a common peril had welded us together and hardened us; that was why we were able to defy a world for four years. . . . Out there we actually lived the inscription of the tomb of the great Swiss, Pestalozzi, 'Everything for others, nothing for oneself.' "[29]

Neither the left nor the center was able to harness the fury and the "altruism" which carried the Nazi's to power.[30] Up to 1933 the left retained its working class support and the center remained stationary, but neither had much to offer to the *declassé* of all classes—the alienated population. By the 1930's there was a new mass of young people (4,600,000 new German voters), born since 1910 and come of age in a time of extensive unemployment and dislocation. Family life was disorganized by the upheaval of war and economic crisis: "the youth could get no view of life, no traditional class conceptions," writes Heiden, "[and] in the cynicism of this youth, and not in the rage of the 'dispossessed petty bourgeois' [the origins of Nazism are to be found]. No one will seriously try to explain the philosophy and behavior of an SS man by the fact that the SS man is a baker or stationer."[31] The left promised but could not deliver a rational utopia, which beneath the rhetoric was not vastly different from the ideal of bourgeois capitalism—the promise of improvement of the conditions of material welfare. But the Nazis offered the anomic population the mysticism of war. As one of Abel's subjects wrote: "There was no point of contact with the men in power [in the 1920's]. For they had banished the glorious old black-and-white-and-red banner and substituted a flag in its place that meant nothing to the front fighters. What became of the memory of the dead? Their blood called to high heaven for vengeance! Then came a light in the darkness. A movement for freedom was founded in Munich. In 1923 we heard the name of Adolf Hitler for the first time. Who was the man? He was a simple front soldier, an Austrian who had fought and bled under the German flag. What did he want? The thoughts raced through my brain. Truth, honor, faith, discipline. Unity of all people of German blood. . . ."[32] And for the young, who had not experienced World War I directly, there was the internal war to create cohesion and comraderie. "We were united by the terrorism raging around us every hour of every day. It was natural for everyone to take the part of his comrade, and the fellowship thus cultivated was in itself a great experience. Yet the ideal we defended rose above our fellowship."[33]

In the beginning Nazism was a revolutionary movement, an attack on the establishment. Abel's typical Nazi was strongly dissatisfied with the republican regime in Germany but had no specific anti-Semitic bias. But once Hitler *was* the regime, opposition to the existing order, obviously, had to be terminated and the storm-troopers tamed. For the first 15 months after his appointment as chancellor, Hitler let the S.A. run loose. Initially the S.A. had "proved its heroism" in street brawling as a kind of auxillary police force. Then they began to roam the streets alone in search of enemies of the state, made raids, imprisoned men in S.A. bunkers, the private jails of each S.A. unit. "The movement could no longer offer the attraction of . . . the street brawl . . . of Nazi meetings before the seizure of power," writes Hans Gisevius. "Nevertheless the battle continued; the difference was the beatings were handed out for the purpose of feeling the reality of power."[34] The S.A. leader was a virtual demi-god, and his efficiency was judged by the numbers in his bunker and the brutality with which he conducted the prisoners "education." Eugene Kogon describes how S.A. collected its political enemies— Communists and alleged Communists—"in army barracks, abandoned factories, remote depots, ancient castles, where it gleefully proceeded to inflict all manner of tortures on its victims."[35] In 1933 there were some fifty of those torture chambers mainly around Berlin. But this uncontrolled policing activity of the S.A. was beginning to hurt the prestige of the new Nazi government, and since the regular prisons were already overflowing, the Gestapo created concentration camps in order to normalize the situation. Soon the free-enterprise brutality of the S.A. was transformed into the corporate terror of the S.S.

Hitler found himself unable to control the violence he had unleashed. Created to seize power, the S.A. was a threat to anyone in power—including Hitler. As he analyzed the S.A.:

"This group of destructive elements is formed of those revolutionaries whose former relation to the state was shattered by the events of 1918; they became uprooted and
thereby lost altogether all sympathy with any ordered human society. They became revolutionaries who favored revolution for its own sake and desired to see revolution established as a permanent condition . . . during last week
[Hitler continues] I discovered the diary . . . of a man
who in 1918 was thrown into the path of resistance to the
law and now lives in a world to which law in itself seems to
be a provocation to resistance. It is an alarming document—
an unbroken tale of conspiracy and continual plotting. It
gives one insight into the mentality of men who, without
realizing it, have found in nihilism their ultimate confession
of faith. Incapable of any true cooperation, with a desire to
attack all order, filled with hatred against any authority,
their unrest and disquietude can find satisfaction only in
some conspiratorial activity of the mind, in perpetually plotting the disintegration of whatever the set up of the moment
happens to be. . . . This group of pathological enemies of
the state is dangerous.[36]

So, in the customary way of the tyrant, Hitler liquidated his enemies
as an object-lesson in deterrence. In the blood purge of July 1934
the S.S. shot Roehm and 80 other S.A. leaders and in addition
around 100 people who were on the government black lists, including
Hitler's immediate predecessor as chancellor, General von Schleicher;
and a former minister of defense, General Bredow; Gregor Strasser,
an early Nazi leader; a former prime minister of Bavaria, the head
of the Catholic Action movement in Berlin; and a number of other
middle level politicians. Apparently the S.S. on its own enlarged the
black list. Some 200 people were openly, publicly murdered—but no
one protested. General Blomberg speaking for Hitler's cabinet praised
the action for having averted civil war. The army high command remained silent, even though two of its own had been slain. President
von Hindenburg approved the action. The S.S. men who carried out
the deed were publicly praised and promoted. Two weeks later, Hit-

ler spoke to the Reichstag explaining that Roehm's activity constituted a mutiny:

"The nation must know [Hitler said] that its existence . . . will
be threatened by no one without punishment! And for all future time
everyone must know that if he raises his hand to attack the State, certain death will be his portion. [Hitler admitted the action was illegal]
but at that hour I was responsible for the fate of the German nation,
and I was therefore the supreme judge of the German people."[37]
After the speech Goering jumped up shouting that the voice of the
German people cried out as one: "We will always approve of what
our Fuehrer does"—and thunderous applause followed. Goering always insisted his own measures would not be crippled by judicial
thinking, "I don't have to worry about justice; my mission is only to
destroy and exterminate, nothing more."[38] By July 1934 "Our
Fuehrer" and his S.A. gangs had already destroyed the organizational
base for any opposition to the regime. Communists, Socialists, even
the center and right wing parties were suppressed. The trade unions
were broken. Elections were suspended and the Reichstag made into
a rubber stamp. Then the S.A. was eliminated.

By fall 1934 the Nazi regime rested on two institutional pillars:
the S.S. and the Army, each devoted to the dispensation of violence.
Formed under Heinrich Himmler in 1929 as an agency within the
S.A. to serve as Hitler's bodyguard, the S.S. grew from 280 men to
5,000,000 men by 1945.[39] This vast police apparatus employed the
energies of millions of men, ranging in social status from the doormen
of apartment houses and concentration camp guards to physicians
who tortured prisoners in the name of science. The Gestapo—the
intelligence arm of the S.S.—became a state within a state (once a
person was in the hands of the Gestapo he was debarred from any
appeal to the law).

The purpose of the Gestapo was to create a "legend of terror"—in
Crankshaw's phrase—to render the population more subservient to
Nazi domination. Thousands of ordinary citizens were made honorary
members of the Gestapo, and every means was used to get people to

inform on one another. The Gestapo employed some 100,000 paid informers and received the services of countless "free informers." Children informed on parents; husbands on wives—thus many ordinary Germans could enjoy a vicarious participation in the tyranny which ruled over them. The Nazi system took root in the local community where the gossipy woman would warn her neighbors what would happen if they failed to display the Swastika, and unintentionally spread the atmosphere of terror. Allen reports the case of a doctor in the small (10,000 population) town of Thalburg who went to a party and, after one drink too many, sought to entertain people by imitating Hitler's way of speaking. "The next morning his hostess reported him to Nazi headquarters. Word of this spread quickly, and soon Thalburgers saw that it was better not to go to parties at all. "Social life was cut down enormously [one Thalburger recalls] you couldn't trust anyone any more." In the end, social life was reduced to its most elementary level—evenings of beer and cards, small gatherings in private homes: "What was the value of getting together with others to talk if you had to be careful about what you said?" But Thalburg, like other German towns, had voted the Nazis into power (by 63 per cent), and in May, 1933, some 5,000 of the citizens marched in a parade to the city square where socialist papers and pamphlets were burned, along with some 500 volumes (one quarter of the holdings) of the public library including Remarque's *All Quiet on the Western Front*. The local Nazi speaker urged citizens to contribute their own books to the bonfire and told the German youth to learn how to hate foreigners: "clinch your fists and think: . . . revenge is mine."[40] By burning books the arsonist makes himself the superior of the author.

The informing system of the S.S. created the feeling that no one could trust anyone in his immediate environment—associates, friends, even family—consequently, by a strange alchemy, he came to trust even more the distant leaders of the state. Initially, the Gestapo reported only on Nazi party members; in 1938 a new law gave it surveillance over the entire Reich, and in the end over all of occupied

Europe. The Gestapo selected and delivered the victims to concentration camps, another part of the S.S. bureaucracy. The camps were the terminal point in the terror—"deterrent"—system which was Nazi Germany.

Himmler was the creative genius behind the S.S. Hitler had the extravagant savagery of the warrior, while Himmler displayed the pedantic cruelty of a master-cop. Himmler institutionalized Hitler's charisma. The S.S. was an educational system for building the new Nazi man, with Himmler as a sinister parody of the German schoolteacher. Himmler loved to lecture people and was "always trying to extend his knowledge"—says his doctor, Felix Kersten—"one could not imagine him without a book or a document in his hand."[41] Himmler saw his S.S. as having two functions: to train the new ruling class and to eliminate all opposition to the regime. He made himself an object of universal hatred in order to engender universal fear. By the mid-1930's resistance to the regime had died out.

> Had the Gestapo in its arrests, proceeded purely on the basis of opposition, the camps should have become deserted. But the subsidiary purposes—the deterrent effect on the population, the exploitation of slave labor, the maintenance of training and experimental facilities for the S.S.—came more and more to the fore in keeping the camps filled. . . . In the end the camps grew to such monstrous proportion that the regime was no longer equal to the task it had set for itself. The S.S. and all its camps drifted toward the abyss in a state of virtual paralysis.[42]

Like any bureaucracy the S.S. had a built-in dynamism for expansion and needed new clients in order to justify and continue its own existence.

Had Germany not turned outward in 1938, the S.S. and the Army would have devoured one another. These two organizations had lived in bitter though tacit contention since 1933. The Waffen S.S.—an armed paramilitary unit—was a threat to the army's monopoly on the means of violence, and the Gestapo was used to keep the generals subservient to Hitler's will. At the top level the Gestapo framed Field Marshal Fritsch, the chief of staff, on a phony homosexual charge and brought about his dismissal. At lower levels S.S. men arrested soldiers in bars, claiming they had police power over all Germans. Fights, even massive brawls, between S.S. men and army personnel were common.[43]

By 1938 the Nazi war machine was rolling and like a bicycle had to remain in motion or topple over. The bloodless victory of Munich in 1938 left the Nazis frustrated: plans for total war had to be momentarily shelved and S.S. schemes for the total liquidation of the Czechs were set aside. (The S.S. had to wait for the invasion of Poland to practice its skills.) But at Munich it was clear to the Italian foreign minister Count Ciano that the Germans would fight, even if given much more than they asked, because they were "possessed by the demon of destruction."[44]

With diabolical honesty Hitler cut through the venerable Clausewitzian hypocrisy which pretends war is an instrument of policy. For Hitler war was not a means to peace but proof of power. He craved the daring and danger of war—how else could he validate his divinity? And when he could no longer control the world like a god through the magic of his voice, through the utterance of commands, then at least he could bring it down in ruins—that too was power.

From the outset the Nazis prepared for war—and no one objected. Between March 1933 and October 1934 the army was enlarged from 100,000 to 300,000 men, and an enormously expanded "defense" budget eradicated unemployment. "Belief in a coming war had become a permanent aspect of Nazi rule," writes Allen.[45] Still, when the real war came in 1939 the German people were taken by surprise. There was no jubilation as in 1914—a resigned population simply marched like lemmings into a sea of fire.

On the eve of his invasion of Poland Hitler feared some "dirty dog" (*Schweinhund*) would pull another Munich and deprive him of the chance to fight. Hitler told a conference of his military chiefs on August 22, 1939:

The time has come to fight a war. For us it is easy to make the decision. We have nothing to lose; we can only gain. . . . No one knows how long I shall live. Therefore a showdown which it would not be safe to put off for four to five years, has an opportunity. . . . The destruction of Poland has priority. . . . I shall give a propagandist reason for starting the war—never mind whether it is plausible or not. In starting and waging a war it is not right that matters, but victory.

Close your hearts to pity! Act brutally! Eighty million people must obtain what is their right. . . . The stronger man is right. Be harsh and remorseless! Be steeled against all signs of compassion. . . . Whoever has pondered over this world order knows that its meaning lies in the success of the best by means of force.[46]

After subduing Poland, Hitler looked for new worlds to conquer and found the Soviet Union. Operation Barbarossa, the German code name for the war on Russia, was to be a new kind of war, even for the Nazis. The struggle was one of ideologies and racial differences, Hitler told his general staff in March 1941, and will be conducted with unprecedented, unmerciful and unrelenting harshness. After deciding to strike down the Soviet Union, Hitler wrote Mussolini: "I again feel spiritually free."[47]

The Nazis read history but repeated it anyway. Hitler's assault on Russia began on the same day as did Napoleon's 1812 invasion— June 22—and his armies moved down the same road Napoleon had taken to Moscow, into the same calamity. A third of the German army was wiped out in the Russian campaign, not by the Russian winter, easily mastered by the Germans in World War I, but by the Red Army. Like Napoleon, Hitler had early successes, and by the autumn he believed that Russia was finished. "I declare today," he told the German people on October 3, 1941, "and I declare it without reservation that the enemy in the East has been struck down and will never rise again."[48] Hitler had convinced his generals, "We have only to kick in the door [of the Soviet Union] and the whole rotten structure will come crashing down." General von Kleist later reported that "hopes for victory were largely built on the prospect that invasion would produce a political upheaval in Russia."[49] But as Alexander Dallin's detailed study reveals, the Germans made no effort to organize an opposition government, to win over dissident elements, or even to utilize land and resources taken in the first successful months of the war. Under the slogan "freedom from Bolshevism," Hitler offered the Russian people nothing but extermination or enslavement, because "his peculiar dialectic posited an inexorable conflict between Teuton and Slav, superior and inferior."[50]

Strife had become an end in itself, and the only aim of Nazi policy was to maximize the number of divisive elements in the Eastern space. The whole Russian campaign, says Dallin, was a foolhardy gamble that made no provision for failure. Yet Hitler's life since 1914 had been a gamble, and since he almost always won, he had reason to think of himself as an instrument of divine will. "The self-anointed superman begins to believe in himself," writes Dallin, "and like Faust over-reaches himself. It was Hitler's faith in his invincibility that proved to be his doom. Yet of a more modest, more partial faith he was incapable."[51]

Foreseeing his own doom, Hitler did not hesitate to take the rest of Germany down with him. Hitler was a patriot, eager to kill, willing to die, for his country. As the Russian campaign matured into a disaster, the general staff advised a strategic retreat, but Hitler forbade any further withdrawals and thereby needlessly sacrificed hundreds of thousands of German soldiers. After the surrender at Stalingrad, Hitler was furious because the German commander, Paulus, had not committed suicide. "Paulus should have shot himself," Hitler raged, "just as the old commanders who threw themselves on their swords when they saw that the cause was lost. . . . What is life? Life is the Nation. The individual must die anyway. Beyond the life of the individual is the Nation."[52]

By 1945 Hitler had decided the German nation did not deserve to survive. Although defeat was certain, instead of capitulating Hitler ordered the destruction of German industrial installations. Albert

Speer concluded Hitler was "deliberately attempting to let the people perish with himself. He no longer [sic] knew any moral boundaries, was a man to whom the end of his own life meant the end of everything."[53] On March 18 Speer informed Hitler that the war was lost economically and militarily. To save even the German nation, some material basis must be preserved, Speer argued. In response, Hitler said, "If the war is to be lost, the nation also will perish. This fate is inevitable. There is no need to consider the basis even of a most primitive existence any longer. On the contrary it is better to destroy even that, and to destroy it ourselves. The nation has proved itself weak, and the future belongs solely to the stronger Eastern nation. Besides, those who remain after the battle are of little value, for the good have fallen."[54] That same day, Trevor-Roper reports, Hitler and Borman issued new orders of destruction: the fight was to be continued without consideration of the German people.

During the last years of the war thousands of outstanding Germans were murdered by the Nazis, "with the express purpose of preventing them serving a non-Nazi, post-war Germany," according to Terrance Prittie. "The murders were carried out in a mist of *Goetterdaemmerungsgeist*—a crazy compound of spirit of revenge, a sense of unpardonable guilt, and unregenerate, suicidal readiness to collaborate in the extinction of the German race."[55] In this last purge, the result of the July 20, 1944 plot to kill Hitler, some 7,000 arrests were made and 5,000 of Hitler's opponents were killed by Himmler's S.S.

In the end even Himmler displayed a compassion never manifest in any of Hitler's actions. Himmler had orders to blow up the concentration camps as the Allied armies approached, but Kersten, his doctor, persuaded him not to do it. Kersten also prevailed upon Himmler to circumvent Hitler's order to blow up The Hague. "The Hague is a Germanic city," Himmler declared, "It will not be destroyed. Certainly the Dutch have not deserved this favour. . . . Ach. Herr Kersten, we have made serious mistakes. If I could have a fresh start, I would do many things differently now. But it is too late. We wanted greatness and security for Germany and we leave behind us a pile of ruins, a falling world. . . . [I] always wanted what was best, but very often I had to act against my real convictions. Believe me, Kersten, that went very much against the grain. . . . But the Fuehrer decreed that it should be so. . . . *As a loyal soldier I had to obey, for no state can survive without obedience and discipline.*"[56] (Italics mine.)

Himmler is only a soldier, an obedient servant, the "Field Marshal" in the Nazi war against the civilian population. His assignment called for the elimination of "negative beings," i.e. Jews, Slavs, Gypsies, even Germans, should they be Jehovah's Witnesses or Social Democrats. He grits his teeth and does his job. He forces himself to watch executions in order to steel the resolve of his men; once, in fact, he almost cracked, cried out that he couldn't take it. His excruciating stomach cramps, which would sometimes last for four or five days and often left him unconscious, were an expression of the deep division in the man, as if the body were rebelling at the dictates of the mind. Who, after all, really likes killing? But someone has to do the dirty work: "Extermination is exactly the same as de-lousing [said Himmler] and getting rid of lice is not a question of ideology. It is a matter of cleanliness. We shall soon be de-loused."[57] Then the new day will dawn, the crooked shall be made straight, and a racially pure German Reich instituted. The utopian end vindicated the barbarous means. The S.S. must struggle to bring this new world into being; only then can Germany have peace and freedom. The task is hard, but the reward is glory. At a speech to his S.S. generals in Poland in 1943, Himmler says, "Most of *you* must know what it means when a hundred corpses are lying side by side, or five hundred or a thousand. To have stuck it out and at the same time (apart from exceptions caused by human weakness) to have remained decent fellows, that is what has made us so hard. This is a page of glory in our history which has never been written and will never be written."[58] Ah! The Polish campaign, the Russian campaign . . . those were the days of glory for the S.S! Like an old veteran recounting the "horrors" of Verdun, Himmler addressed an S.S. contingent stationed in France. Yes, he knew they found police work distasteful; forcible deportations were difficult, unnerving—

> Exactly the same thing happened in Poland in weather forty degrees below zero, where we had to haul away thousands, tens of thousands, hundreds of thousands, where we had to have the toughness—you should hear this but also forget it again immediately—to shoot thousands of leading Poles, otherwise revenge would have been taken on us later . . . all duties where the proud soldier says: "My God, why do I have to do that, this ridiculous job here!"—*It is much easier to go into combat with a company than to suppress an obstructive population of low cultural level,* or to carry out executions, or to haul away people, or to evict crying and hysterical women [Carrying arms is easy]. . . . It is much more difficult in other positions . . . in this silent compulsion work, this silent activity.[59]

What made the liquidation of peoples so difficult? Is it that conscience makes cowards of us all—even Himmler and the S.S.?

Himmler had a bizarre devotion to Hitler. Hitler's word was law to Himmler, says Kersten, "supreme above all the ideals and directives he issued himself; when Hitler had spoken, [Himmler's] own convictions were at once laid aside." When it was clear that Germany was beginning to lose the war, Kersten gently sounded Himmler on the question of disassociating from Hitler. Himmler would not countenance the thought, whereupon Kersten asked him half-facetiously, "Would you hang yourself if Hitler ordered it?" "Yes, certainly. At once," Himmler replied. "For if the Fuehrer ordered anything like that he has his reasons. And it's not for me as an obedient soldier to question those reasons."[60]

Nazism is the logical fulfillment of the war system. Hitler conjured up the hatred of a common enemy to overcome the anomie of Weimar Germany. "If I want to weld the people into unity," he said in 1928, "I must first form a new front, facing a common enemy. Then each man will know that we must be one, because this enemy is the enemy of us all."[61] At the front in 1914-18 there was no class division, no bourgeois and proletarian platoons, only the company. To create that cohesion at home, it was necessary to battle in the meeting halls and in the streets. "Germany will not be saved by men who fall victim to universal world love," Hitler declared, "but by those who direct universal hatred to themselves."[62]

Hate is more the derivative than the cause of war; men hate because they fight and not conversely. Prior to 1914 Europeans thought of themselves as belonging to a single community of western civilization; in fact, George Thompson calls World War I a Civil War. Virulent national hate came after the fact of killing, as an accompaniment of the will to punishment engendered by the war itself. Massive carnage aroused hostility which was played upon and utilized to sustain civilian support for the war. Allegedly Ernest Lissauer penned his "Hymn of Hate" to buttress the fighting spirit of the Germans:

> Hate by water and hate by land
> Hate of the head and hate of the hand
> Hate of the hammer and hate of the crown
> Hate of seventy millions, choking down.
> We love as one, we hate as one
> We have one foe, and only one
> ENGLAND[63]

The American ambassador to Berlin in 1917 noted how "hate is cultivated in Germany as a noble passion."[64] Whether German's hate-quotient was higher than that of France or England or the United States is difficult to ascertain. Confused and weary with war, the ordinary German was prone to laugh cynically about the Kaiser's tirades against "perfidious Albion," the treacherous British shopkeeper. The Englishman, after all, was a distant demon, too remote to stir up the righteousness of indignation.

Anger acts as an antidote to despair, and in the wreckage of war in 1918 Germans were looking for someone to hate. "He who is unable to hate is no man," wrote Oswald Spengler.[65] Later the S.A. leader Ernst Roehm was to attribute Germany's troubles to the fact that she had "forgotten how to hate. Virile hate has been replaced by feminine lamentation."[66] Hitler's charisma derived from his ingenious capacity to provoke and articulate the hatred of the common man. Himmler rationalized the passion out of Nazi hate, transformed brutality into a scientific system of deterrence, i.e. terror. And with the terror came distrust and the final debilitation of German society itself.

The Nazis set out to make themselves hated and succeeded; sought enemies and found them; and thus for a time held together a tottering social structure. But Hitler's 1000 year Reich lasted only 12 years and was ultimately devoured by the enmity which it deliberately unleashed. Nazi hate of Jews and intellectuals depleted the cultural and scientific community, to the ultimate damage of the German war machine. Nazi hate of the foreigner precluded the formation of a stable regime in occupied countries and prevented the consolidation of German hegemony over Europe. By frightening and enraging the rest of the world, they were left with no alternative but self annihilation. And finally Nazi terror fostered that "incredible passivity" which Joost Meerlōo saw as a "mass suicidal drive" inducing millions of Germans into an unprotesting doom.[67]

13

War, social cohesion, and anomie: reflections on the power of danger

> War is the province of danger, therefore courage is the first quality of the warrior.
>
> KARL VON CLAUSEWITZ, *On War*, 1823

> . . . by the reign of wrath,
> Our lives are driven downward.
>
> ROBERT DUNCAN, American poet, 1968

War creates cohesion—and dissension. Opposition to a common enemy provides a unifying purpose, and dispels internal discord. War with the outgroup brings peace to the ingroup, says William Graham Sumner.[1] But war may also aggravate pre-existing tensions and rupture the fabric of society. Is war, then, a source of integration or anomie?

War necessitates cooperation and concerted action. Under threat of attack, men join together for mutual protection. Human society may well have originated as a defense community, as Chapter 9 suggests. In her study of warfare in Melanesia, Camilla Wedgewood writes: "Common danger, until it becomes so excessive as to create panic, has always and among all peoples, the power to submerge individual antagonism and unite men."[2] Primitive warfare, where de-

199

struction is usually minimal and political and economic objectives absent, often has no other aim except to sustain solidarity. In the remote Pacific islands the population of only a few hundred people typically divides into two warring groups, instead of forming a single peaceful group, because each unit needs the opposition of the other to preserve its own integration.[3] Similarly in advanced societies each state seems to require a rival state to hold itself together, and the rulers often seek war to prevent class dissension. "Foreign war as a remedy for internal tension, revolution or insurrection," writes Quincy Wright, "has been an accepted principle of government since the days of the Roman Republic."[4] In Rome, extensive revolutionary violence occurred only after the removal of Carthage as a uniting common enemy.[5] In the Middle Ages, the Papacy deliberately launched the Crusades as a cure for the private feudal wars of the time; the arms of Christians were turned on the infidel to maintain peace at home. The principle was still in operation in 1914 when the dynasties of Europe attacked each other to stave off their own dissolution (See Chapter 10). And for millions of Europeans the ordeal of war seemed to give new meaning to life. "War sends the current of purpose and activity flowing down to the lowest level of the herd," said Randolph Bourne as he watched the United States prepare for World War I, "the nation moves lumberingly, but with ever accelerated speed and integration toward the great end, 'the peacefulness of being at war.' "[6]

The "peacefulness of war" puzzles the rational mind, but certain men seem to flourish on war. The danger of war transforms anxiety into fear, providing a focus for cohesion. Men can unite around their fears but by definition anxiety can not be shared (See Chapters 3, 4). The frequency of anxiety disorders seems to subside during war. British psychiatrists found their practice lagging in World War II; on the continent mental hospitals were emptied, and even the incidence of physical diseases declined.[7] Suicide rates consistently and substantially drop during war (see Figure 4). Jack Douglas thinks the abatement of suicide may be a statistical illusion caused by the neglect of the record keepers; in the emergency of war governments would hardly give top priority to gathering suicide data.[8] But while the suicide rate decreases for all *men* of all ages and for civilians as well as military personnel, the rate for *women* rises. If the alteration of the suicide rate only reflected the inadequacy of statistics, the pattern would be similar for men and women. But the male rate declines about 30 per cent while the female rate rises some 5 per cent, as shown by our limited study of Tulsa, Oklahoma, in World War II and Fuellkrug's exhaustive analysis of Europe in World War I.[9] There is no compelling reason to doubt the statistical correlation between war and suicide. Durkheim's explanation of the reduction of suicide in war still seems valid: "Great social disturbances and great popular wars . . . concentrate activity toward a single end, and at least temporarily cause a stronger integration of society . . . as men are forced to close ranks and confront the common danger, the individual thinks less of himself and more of the common cause."[10]

War provides distraction for the self-preoccupied. In secular society where each man is supposed to live for himself alone, the war demand for altruism comes as a blessing in disguise. By merging the "I" with the "We" the person becomes for a time larger than himself, finds his life by losing it (see Chapter 11). War legitimates the "escape from freedom," releases the person from the moral obligation to plan for his private welfare. The mores of peacetime, designed to produce safety, comfort and predictable routine, are cast aside, and quite opposite values are enthroned. "War is the province of physical exertion and suffering," says Clausewitz, "war is the province of chance . . . [and] daring."[11] For the anomic, whose life is otherwise dull and aimless, war brings purpose and relief from boredom. Perceptions of the ever elusive connection between anomie and war are at least as old as Homer, who, according to Aristotle, denounced the "tribeless, lawless, heartless one—the natural outcast—as forthwith a lover of war."[12]

The love of war runs deep. In vesting the war-making powers in

Congress, the founders of the American Republic intended to pave the way for universal peace. Yet Congress, as bellicose as any monarch, has enthusiastically endorsed every American war, as the following data show:

Congressional Vote for Declarations of War[13]

	House	Senate
War of 1812	79-49	19-13
Mexican War (1846)	174-14	40-2
Spanish-American War (1898)	311-6	67-21
World War I (1917)	375-50	86-6
World War II (1941)	388-1	82-0

War creates national purpose and occurs most often in times of deepening anomie. After independence the former colonies, reconstituted as states, were always on the verge of dispersion and needed war to unify as a nation: hence the War of 1812. As rivalry between north and south was beginning to split the country the Mexican war of 1846 momentarily restored cohesion. By 1898 sectional strife was ending but class conflict was mounting; unable to cope with its internal crisis, the nation unified by turning outward as an imperialist power. The Spanish-American war mobilized a latent solidarity in the American people; the war, said Charles Horton Cooley at the time, "was bringing about a fresh sense of community throughout the country and so renewing and consolidating the collective life of the nation."[14] World War I re-integrated a nation on the edge of class war (see Chapters 6, 7); World War II revived a nation for ten years prostrate with economic depression. Even the advent of the Cold War, dated at President Truman's decision to intervene in Greece in 1948, was described as a "time when American democracy worked with unexampled efficiency and inspiration to produce national agreement . . . a great time to be alive."[15] War has been the only agency that can "discipline and integrate" the human community, observes William James, regretfully.[16] Before 1914 war was commonly celebrated as "the health of the state" because it activated dormant energies and moved society to a higher plane of organization.

But organization for war has disorganizing consequences: established moralities decay with a "reversion to the tribal morality which commands solidarity," in the words of Willard Waller.[17] Thus the Spanish-American War breathed new life into the doctrine of white supremacy. American imperialism abroad was rationalized and justified by an ideology of Anglo-Saxon superiority, which simultaneously legitimated a new oppression of blacks, orientals and immigrants within the country. Partially as a result of the tribal spirit of anglo-mania fostered by victory over Spain and nurtured by the consequent subjugation of the darker peoples of America's newly acquired empire, the nation acquiesced in the Southern policy of segregation and voter disfranchisement which finally nullified political rights blacks had won during Reconstruction.[18] After 1898 the Southern attitude increasingly became the national attitude on race. Between 1900 and 1920 discrimination against blacks and foreigners increased; racial restrictions on immigration were imposed. Significantly, the Ku Klux Klan, founded in 1866 but dead by 1880, came back to life in 1915 and grew to five million members by 1925.[19] Antagonisms stimulated by war are often vented against aliens and so called racial inferiors. World War I brought attacks on ethnic Germans who were American citizens; World War II saw a massive and systematic assault on Americans of Japanese ancestry.[20] Racial disturbances in America between 1900 and 1967 cluster in war periods, as data in Table 20 indicate.

Does the external violence of war generate the internal violence of crime? Herbert Spencer argued that feelings of hostility provoked by perpetual conflict abroad must inevitably come into play at home in lawless attacks on people and property.[21] Spencer thought crime declined in England as international contention subsided during the first half of the nineteenth century. After 1870 the English crime rate continued downward but the German rate rose, as Robinson's study reveals.[22] Both countries were rapidly industrializing, but Germany

Table 20. Correlation Between War and Racial Disturbance in the
United States, 1900-1967*

Years	Number of Disturbances
1900-1904	0
1905-1909	2
1910-1914	0
1915-1919	22
1920-1924	4
1925-1929	1
1930-1934	0
1935-1939	1
1940-1944	18
1945-1949	0
1950-1954	0
1955-1959	0
1960-1964	11
1965-1967	150

* Data from Warren Schaich, The Relationship Between War and Riots: A
Conceptual Approach (Buffalo: Unpublished M.A. Thesis, State University of
New York, 1968), 10. Disturbances do not include lynchings or brief clashes
between crowds, but only riots resulting in severe personal injury, loss of life,
and arrests for property damage.

was becoming a militant society, while England was still moving in
the direction of peaceful development.

Did a new quality of strife enter American life when the country
started on the road to war and imperialism in 1898? Spain was easily
defeated, but then the army had to pacify the Philippines, a three-
year police action resulting in 100,000 Filippino casualties. Between
1897 and 1902 the United States army quadrupled in size (to
around 100,000). The philosophy of militarism was beginning to
permeate the social structure, "exercising an influence on American
life in the first years of the twentieth century that was without precedent in American history."[23] William Graham Sumner said the United
States had, in fact, been conquered by Spain, by the Spanish idea of
military imperialism, and with it would come a growth of domestic
antagonism.[24] Indicating the escalation of internal conflict, crimes of
violence grow more frequent: the national murder rate doubled be-

tween 1900 and 1910, then doubled again by 1920, while assaults show an even steeper rise, as pointed out in Chapter 8.

When war produces vast social upheaval, an increase in crime is to be expected. But except for the Civil War, the United States has never known the full catastrophe of war—the devastation of the land, the burning of cities, the starvation of civilians, the slaughter of millions. Still violent crimes increased in the 1917-18 period and again

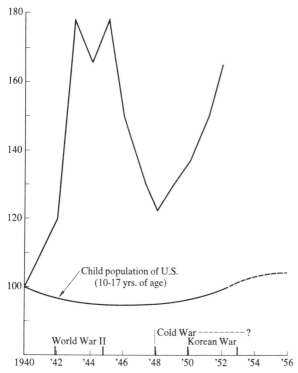

Figure 6. Juvenile Court Delinquency Cases Reported to the Children's Bureau, 1940-1952

From Edwin H. Sutherland, *Principles of Criminology* (Philadelphia: J. B. Lippincott, 1955), 207.

in 1940-45. Not the experience but the *idea* of war determines the "behavior" of the crime rate. War brings about a change in what Durkheim called the "collective consciousness," and produces an atmosphere of belligerence which is translated into criminal violence. Consider juvenile delinquency: the incidence of juvenile court cases rose 80 per cent during World War II, then dropped sharply for three years, but began to climb again in 1948, as shown in Figure 6. E. H. Sutherland attributes the wartime upsurge in delinquency to "changes in the family and local community institutions. Parents join the army, engage in war industries . . . and neglect the supervision of children."[25] However, no dramatic alteration of family and community occurred in 1948, nor even in 1950 with the Korean war. But the onset of the Cold War in 1948 brought a collective mood of acrimony which may have been registered in the juvenile delinquency rate.

Of course, crime and delinquency statistics may only reflect an intensification of police activity, but that too is war-related. "The

Table 21. Index of Crime in the United States, 1960-67
Rate per 100,000

	Murder	Rape	Robbery	Aggravated Assault	Burglary	Larceny
1960	5.0	9.4	59.9	84.7	500.5	282.3
1961	4.7	9.2	58.1	84.4	510.6	288.9
1962	4.5	9.3	59.4	87.3	256.4	308.4
1963	4.5	9.2	61.5	91.0	566.9	344.0
1964	4.8	11.0	67.9	104.5	623.8	382.6
1965	5.1	11.9	71.3	109.5	651.0	408
1966	5.6	12.9	80.3	118.4	708.3	456.8
1967	6.1	13.7	102.1	128.0	811.5	529.2
1968	6.9	16.5	147.3	147.1	981.5	684.1

Data from *Uniform Crime Reports,* 1967, p. 61, and 1968, p. 96. Note data is given as crimes known to the police. Crimes known to the police seem to run almost twice as high as the arrest rate which the FBI gives for 1960 as follows: Murder = 5.5; Rape = 7.4; Robbery = 35.9; Assault = 64.0; Burglary = 134.8; Larceny = 254.7. (See *Ibid.,* p. 91.)

raison d'être of the policeman and the criminal law," writes Jerome Skolnik, "arises ultimately and most clearly from the threat of violence and the possibility of danger to the community."[26] When agitated by thoughts of a common external peril, men see more danger within the community. War heightens the awareness of danger, which evokes the policing spirit (see Chapters VII, VIII). Every American war has been accompanied by an enlargement of the police establishment.

Is the increase of crime and police activity in the 1960's connected with the widening war in Southeast Asia? For the years 1960, 1961 and 1962 the crime rate stabilizes, and then rises from 1963 through 1968, as shown in Table 21. FBI data show residential robberies ris-

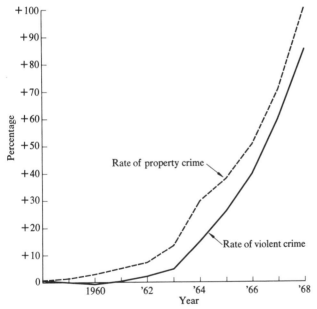

Figure 7. The Increase of Crime in the 1960's*

* Data from "Crime in the United States," *Uniform Crime Reports of the F.B.I.* (Washington: U.S. Government Printing Office, 1969), p. 2.

ing by 100 per cent, bank robberies by 300 per cent during the decade; both personal and property crimes show their greatest leap between 1965 and 1968, as Figure 7 indicates. Materially the years 1960-65 were not vastly different from 1965-70—e.g., the unemployment rate remained fairly stationary over the decade. But the climate of opinion changed from a kind of tentative hope (1960-63) to growing despair and anger; the war in Vietnam seems to be the primary variable in this change of mood. By the end of the decade banks were not only being robbed with greater frequency but for the first time in American history burned as a political act.[27]

Not solidarity but dissension has come out of the Vietnam war. The war in Southeast Asia undermined the authority of established institutions (the courts, the universities, the military services) and thus prepared the ground for revolution. As Martin Luther King said in 1966, "The bombs we drop abroad explode at home."

In times of peace war looks like a rational, ordered enterprise, serving as an instrument of cohesion as well as of policy. But once under way, the wrath of war unleashes passions no longer obedient to the commands of reason, and order gives way to anomie. "Realize, while there is time, the inscrutable nature of war," said Thucydides, "and how when protracted it generally ends in becoming a mere matter of chance, over which none of us can have any control, the event being equally unknown and equally hazardous to us all."[28]

14

Anomie and force: the case of Rome

History can be used like "an algebra book with the answers in the back."[1]
The story of Rome is completed; the outcome of her effort to rule the world
through force is already known. But re-examination of the career of Rome
can illuminate the abstract relationship between consensus and coercion,
between anomie and violence. And just as algebra is the foundation of higher
mathematics so history is the basis of a science of society. "Every sociology
worthy of the name," writes C. Wright Mills, "is historical sociology."[2]

Rome is a vast algebra book and also a bible. From Rome's thousand
year life each subsequent age extracts a moral to suit its own purposes.
Writing at the high noon of the Enlightenment, Gibbon attributed the fall
of Rome to the triumph of Christian superstition. Jeffersonians read the
lesson of Rome as a warning of the dangers of the destruction of the independent farmer. In the 1890s Samuel Dill could find the anomic mood of
the *fin de siècle* in the age of Nero. Rostovzeff, uprooted by the Russian
Revolution, saw the death blow to Rome in the revolt of the masses – a theme
popularized by Ortega y Gasset in the 1930s. During World War II Camus
used the Emperor Caligula to personify Hitler. More recently, Stringfellow
Barr's *Mask of Jove* points to the peril inherent in our own military-industrial
complex. There are many ways to work an algebra problem.

Rome is the history of class struggle. Spartacus, who led a slave revolt
in 73 B.C., is still the hero of revolutionaries. The German Left Socialists
who held power for two months in 1918-19 called themselves Spartacists.
Overthrown by the army, the leaders, Rosa Luxemburg and Karl Liebknecht,
were murdered; most of their followers eventually died in Hitler's concentration camps. Between 73 and 71 B.C. the Roman Spartacus assembled

Reprinted with permission from *Catalyst*, Spring 1969.

an armed force of 120,000 men which defeated many Roman armies. Finally cornered, Spartacus and his men "fought with desperate ferocity until all but 6,000 perished, and these were crucified along the whole road from Capua to Rome"–about 60 miles.[3] Crucifixion was used as a deterrent: through terror the Romans maintained public order but destroyed the basis of all positive allegiance to the social system. However, the idea of Spartacus was not destroyed and even today in America there is a small group of Trotskyists who go by his name.

Rome is the history of war. Today there are intellectuals on the right who find in Cato the Elder (234–149 B.C.) an embodiment of their aspirations. A columnist in William Buckley's *National Review* writes under the pen name Cato, and a "Catonic strategy" has been advocated for winning the Cold War by a complete destruction of the Soviet Union.[4] An 83-year-old Senator, Cato was convinced Rome would never be safe until Carthage was annihilated. Cato prevailed over the milder "Scipionic" policy of "detente," and Carthage was destroyed but Rome never recovered. "The destruction of Carthage," writes Tenney Frank, "was the first avowed concession to the feeling which had been growing for half a century that Rome was the destined ruler of the world, and might therefore be a law unto herself." Thereafter the possibility of forming a federation of equals, of peaceful arbitration of difference and of "healthy emulation between states passed away from the ancient world."[5]

The symbol Spartacus and the symbol Cato are key terms in the algebra of Rome: they signify the perversion of the basic ideal of justice upon which the Republic was founded and announce what Rome is to become. Naked force becomes the sole instrument of social control, and "those who once were brothers were turned into cunning or savage beasts."[6] Seldom has power corrupted so absolutely.

In the beginning Rome was an asylum for the outcast. Though it need not be taken literally, the legend that Romulus, founder of the city, was a feral child suckled by a wolf provides an interesting key to Rome's self-conception, to her initial humility.[7] According to Lewis Morgan, drawing on Livy, Romulus invited all persons from surrounding tribes, "slave as well as free to share with his tribe the advantages and destiny of the new city."[8] The situation of the city between the Latins, Sabines and Etruscans, writes Fustel de Coulanges, "condemned it to perpetual war, and war required that there should be a numerous population. The kings, therefore, had welcomed and invited all foreigners, without regard to their origins."[9]

From the beginning the population of Rome was divided into two distinct classes, the patricians and the plebeians. While both were personally free and served in the army, and were organized in *gentes, curiae* and tribes, only the former held powers of the government.[10] The plebeians were the uprooted — adventurers, outcasts and drifters, those who always flock to the cities. By the time of Servius Tullius (576 B.C.) the plebeians were about as numerous as the patricians. Through the army the plebeians were integrated into the political system of the city. The constitution of Servius transferred power from the *comitia curiata*, based on the gentes, to the *comitia centuriata* — the army. Every member of the army became a citizen, though the army itself, like the population, was divided into five classes based on property-ownership. Each class had a different voting power — vote was by group rather than individual — but the vote was meaningful as an indication of consensus, knowledge necessary for the wise waging of war. The army assembly elected the chief magistrates of the city as well as the officers who led them in battle. In the early Republic citizens were soldiers, soldiers citizens. "The primary organization of the people into an army with the military spirit it fostered," writes Morgan, "created the cohesive force which held the republic together, and afterwards the empire."[11]

Rome transformed the warrior into a soldier. In Homeric Greece, battles were usually fought only by leaders: the common soldier seems merely to "afford the leader with a modicum of moral support and an enthusiastic audience."[12] But by the beginning of the Roman Republic the decisive factor in military strategy was the common soldier — "not as an individual; rather as one of many, almost as an automaton in a machine — a battering machine."[13] Organizational competence rather than individual military genius enabled Rome to become master of the ancient world. The backbone of the Roman army was the non-commissioned officers — disciplined, methodical, and, as Polybius puts it,

> not so much venturesome and daredevil, as natural leaders of a steady
> and sedate spirit . . . not men who will initiate attacks and open
> the battle, but men who will hold their ground when worsted and
> hardpressed and be ready to die at their posts.[14]

The soldier has good reason to stand his ground: those who fled were, if caught, sure to be tortured and beheaded. Thus the soldier faced the choice between a risk and a certainty. Army discipline was based on deterrence, on the terror of punishment. Legions disgraced in battle were decimated — i.e., every tenth man was chosen at random for execution as an example to sustain the wavering courage of their comrades.

But in the early republic there were positive incentives for military loyalty and courage. The citizen-conscript army was after all fighting for the fatherland and the preservation of a way of life. The entire population benefitted from the early wars — the plebeians won their political rights as well as economic rewards through war. Between 400 and 290 B.C. the territory of Italy under Roman rule doubled, and five acres of land was given to every citizen thus creating "a race of peasant proprietors."[15]

Although there were distinctions of rank based on heredity as well as wealth, every citizen had some stake in the society. Even the domestic slavery of the time was almost humane, when contrasted to the brutalities of slavery in the first century. With seldom more than one or two slaves per farmstead, the slave lived with the family and shared in its social and religious life. This was the age when Cincinnatus, the very embodiment of noble simplicity, could be recalled from working his three acre farm, to be supreme commander of the Roman army in a time of military set-back.

Appointed dictator by the Senate, Cincinnatus ordered all business in the city stopped and all men of military age to the parade ground, "the Field of Mars," each to bring with him five days bread ration and a dozen stakes. Cincinnatus' force then set out to support the beleaguered regular army; the enemy was defeated, a stern though merciful peace was negotiated.[16] Then Cincinnatus returned to his plow—the story resembles the career of General Grant who unfortunately did not return to his grocery store.

When Rome was a simple agricultural society with a limited territory and no part of it far from the city, senators and knights on the one side and the people on the other knew each other well. "They were neighbors at home and they served together in the army as officers and men; they had common interests, interests of national welfare, in the elective assembly."[17]

Though stratified the population was integrated into a single community. The popular assemblies gave voice to the grievances of the people, enabling early Rome to resolve her internal differences without resort to violence. Although later overshadowed by the professional army and often merely a tool in the hands of the plutocracy or the demagogue, the popular assembly did adopt "liberal and statesman-like agrarian and colonial laws when it was controlled by the rural element of the citizen-body."[18] By 290 B.C. the legal distinction between patrician and plebeian had been formally abolished, and in the assembly all men's votes were equal. The assembly had attained full legislative power and could, theoretically, override the counsel of the senate (always either an hereditary or appointive body), and, says Frank, "Rome was fast becoming almost a pure democracy."[19]

But the Roman thrust toward democracy was permanently aborted by the Punic Wars. Forged in the crucible of war, the Roman Republic was finally devoured by the "furies" unleashed by her sixty year struggle with Carthage. In the 4th century B.C. Rome emerged as the leader of the Latin confederation and unified peninsular Italy under her hegemony. Though the dominant military power of Italy, Roman success did not rest on armed might alone. She turned her defeated enemies into allies, and eventually conferred upon them full membership in the commonwealth. She extracted neither monetary nor symbolic tribute from her subordinate Latin allies; allowed them to retain their own local government, although Rome kept sole authority in making foreign policy. The central idea of Roman statesmanship, writes Frank, "was that a 'prudent liberality' should bind the conquered and the conqueror for the sake of their mutual interest. . . . A more revolutionary policy history can hardly display.[20]

The generosity of early Rome is often obscured by the brutality of late Rome. Initially Rome had an unusually liberal policy of emancipating slaves and giving them the privileges of citizenship, a privilege the Greeks refused to their freedmen; special courts of equity were created to protect the rights of foreigners in Rome; the *mos maiorum* – the mores – did not recognize the right of aggression or conquest as a just cause of war, unlike the Greeks who justified the subjugation of barbarians on grounds of national superiority. "A sense of fair play and a respect for legal orderliness," writes Frank, "permeates the whole history of [the Roman] people."[21] Just as her domestic generosity drew applicants for citizenship from all over Italy so her foreign policy attracted allies.

In politics friends are often more dangerous than enemies. Rome was sucked into the First Punic War when the Sicilian city of Messana defected from Carthage, who possessed over half the island, and sought an alliance with Rome, and a protecting guard of Roman troops. The loss of the city was unacceptable to Carthage, so the two great powers fought for 14 years, and Rome found herself in possession of Sicily. Then Carthaginian garrisons in Sardinia mutinied, and offered the island to Rome. The "gift" was refused and in fact at this time – 241 B.C. – Rome offered to help Carthage. Hostile to any insurrection, Rome invariably sought to maintain the status quo. Carthage attempted to crush the Sardinian uprising but the regular army sent to the island for that purpose joined the mutineers. The insurgents fell into a quarrel and were driven out by the natives. The fugitives then placed themselves at the service of Rome, asking the senate to take over their claim to the island. Rome realized that Sardinia, "under discordant native rule, would not long maintain its independence if Carthage chose to reconquer it, and she accordingly accepted the offer and took possession."[22] Carthage protested that she had prior claims; in the ensuing quarrel Rome declared war, and Carthage capitulated. So Rome found herself with two unwanted pieces of real estate – Sicily and Sardinia – as well as the permanent vengeful enmity of Carthage. "It is safe to say that the idea of universal power never occurred to any Roman before the Punic war," writes Frank, "a series of accidents led the nation unwittingly from one contest to another until, to her own surprise, Rome was mistress of the Mediterranean world."[23]

The first Punic war gave rise to the second. Seeking to redress the humiliation of earlier defeat, Carthage pushed out into Spain. Rome sought defensive alliance with the independent city of Saguntum and drew a defence line at the river Ebro. Hannibal, the son of the ruling Barcid family which had "lost" the first Punic war to Rome, was the leader of the Carthaginian forces which attacked Saguntum and moved to invade Italy from the north. Seeking to divide Rome from her allies he counted on the defection of the Gallic tribes of the north which had recently been at war with Rome and promised the southern Italian allies absolute autonomy under Punic protection. Hannibal did not intend to make Italy a dependency of Carthage nor did he envisage the destruction of Rome. Hannibal's aim was neither "extermination nor conquest . . . [but] simply to administer a thorough humiliation that would wipe out the disgrace of former defeats."[24]

But the war escalated, became for Rome a struggle for survival, and left the life of the commonwealth "deranged . . . in all its aspects."[25] At the outset the war unified the Roman commonwealth; but as it progressed class antagonism magnified. In the ancient world, writes Toynbee, "class conflict was always simmering below the surface . . . and any major international conflict was apt to turn into a class conflict as well."[26] In most of the city states of the Latin confederation "the rich saw their interest in a Roman victory, while the poor saw theirs in a Carthaginian victory."[27] Like Napoleon devoid of a revolutionary ideology, Hannibal posed as the "liberator from the Roman yoke."[28] Though most of the cities remained loyal to Rome, (those which defected were decimated as an example to the others), class dissension weakened the morale of the Roman armies. Even though fighting on their own soil and outnumbering Hannibal's forces by two to one, the Roman legions were trounced time and again. Hannibal won the decisive battle of Cannae with 50,000 men against Roman forces totalling over 100,000.

Morale of the Roman citizen-soldier was dissipated by long separation from home. Though accustomed to physical hardship, "the prolonged unbroken absences . . . were an unfamiliar tribulation for the peasant-soldiers."[29] The long absence usually meant bankruptcy for the family farm and it meant that the man could no longer function as "cultivator of the Italian soil and father of an Italian family."[30] Among legions which had served six or eight years away from home there were even mutinies, almost unheard of earlier. The ineffectiveness of the conscript citizen army led to the development of the volunteer mercenary army toward the end of the Hannibalic war, a significant change as Toynbee explains

> The conscript's loyalty was to their fatherland; the volunteers to their leader. The volunteers looked to their leader to make their fortunes for them . . . the inducement that led them to risk their lives. When the leader was killed the army deserted. . . . In the old Roman army of peasant conscripts the only requirement of a commander was that he should be a member of a noble *gens* who did not lack the characteristic virtues of his class. In the new Roman army the essential requirement in a commander was that he should be a 'charismatic' leader . . . [and] like a lion tamer, the commander of an army of deracines could not afford to switch off the current of his 'personal magnetism,' even for a moment.[31]

In the century after the second Punic war the charismatic military leader gradually moved into ascendancy in Roman political life. The existential base of the old army and the old society had been destroyed by the war. An estimated half of the population of Italy was either killed or driven into exile but worse than the loss of life, says Toynbee, was the "deracination" of the Italian peasantry. The small farmer had been eliminated by the war; in his place came the plantation worked by hordes of slaves to turn a profit for the land-owner. Thus there arose a new Roman commercial and industrial class "whose fortune had been made by the wars that had been the Italian peasantry's ruin."[32]

Since slaves were now aggregated in large numbers, uprisings began to occur. In Greece slavery was on its way out—by 135 B.C. the average number of slaves per slave-owning family was not more than three—but in Italy and Sicily by the second century slavery had "rankled into an enormity."[33] In 198 B.C. and 185 B.C. insurrections were easily put down but by 135–32 there were regular Roman military operations against "organized armies of insurgent slaves."[34] A band of 400 slaves captured the Sicilian city of Enna and were joined by the local urban slaves; they established a government, built an efficient army of 60,000 and captured other Sicilian cities. The slave city-state of Ennus lasted four years. Betrayed by treachery from within, the city was taken by the Roman army. The slave-king's bodyguard of 1,000 men committed suicide, and order was forcefully restored, until the year *ca*. 104 when another slave kingdom called Athenio was formed. The slaves of Athenio defeated four successive Roman armies. Finally overwhelmed the last 1,000 survivors of Athenio's army capitulated. They were shipped to the amphitheatre at Rome and to provide a public spectacle were fed to the wild beasts. According to Toynbee, "Sicily was devastated in the Slave War far more cruelly than in the Romano-Carthaginian War."[35]

As the slave population grew and the small farmer was driven from the land the urban proletariat expanded. During the Punic war large numbers of the rural population had fled to the cities seeking protection from Hannibal's forces; after the war they remained in the cities and were joined by others. Since the proletarian was propertyless he was not eligible to serve in the army, and because most of the work was by then done by slaves he was chronically unemployed. At the top of the social pyramid was the small senatorial class—the governing class, or aristocracy, and the equestrians—the "knights" or capitalists. The Roman capitalists acquired their fortune by performing services for the state, not through diligent work like the mythical "protestant-ethic" capitalist of modern society. The Roman capitalist grew fat on government contracts, tax-gathering, and fleecing the poor as moneylenders. A new social structure had come into being with Punic wars, and "slowly the old settled ways of full faith and confidence in established custom, in *mos maiorum*, began to break up and dissolve."[36]

The old moral order could not insure justice under a new existential reality. The senatorial oligarchy, holding tenaciously to its power and wealth, was unable or unwilling to implement the reforms which might have assured its continuity as a ruling class. Alarmed by the slave revolts, and the destruction of the small farmer, which meant the depletion of Rome's military man-power, Tiberius Gracchus attempted to institute a land reform program. Laws were passed aimed at breaking up the large estates and resettling part of the urban population on the land. The answer of the land-owning oligarchy was to have Tiberius clubbed to death. Ten years later Gaius, the brother of Tiberius, attempted to carry on his program of reform, and he too was assassinated, along with several thousand of his followers. The slaughter of the Gracchi, writes Cowell, "marks a turning point in Roman political life, no violence or political murder had ever occurred on such a scale before."[37] The slaughter unleashed an era of internal violence. For the first time, men in public life began to carry daggers and surround themselves with bodyguards as a kind of private police force. From the assassination of Tiberius in 133 B.C. to the ascension of Augustus in 31 B.C. lawless violence grew by what it fed on—the Roman Republic.

The Roman revolution was not a mass movement but a struggle between factions of the oligarchy, between the conservatives (*optimates*) and the populists (*populares*), and the private armies which they raised. For all the famed discipline of the Roman army—or perhaps because of it—the ultimate loyalty of the soldier was personal rather than institutional, an allegiance given to the supreme commander rather than to the abstract principle of the state. The first major step toward the replacement of the citizen-conscript army was taken by Marius. Opening recruitment to all classes, even the propertyless urban population, Marius armed his men at state expense. To encourage volunteers he announced that legionnaires would be paid off in land and established the precedent of allotting lands to the solidiery, which became a major incentive for further territorial conquest.[38] Then came Sulla, followed shortly by Pompey, Crassus and finally Julius Caesar, all of whom rode to dictatorship on the shoulders of their private, publicly financed armies. After Caesar's assassination there followed 15 more years of civil war. Mark Anthony and Octavius—later Augustus—inherited Caesar's army and following. Anthony fell, and Octavius went on to defeat the forces of Cassius and Brutus, the last armed representatives of the senatorial oligarchy, at the Battle of Actium in 31 B.C. Octavius was declared emperor but the life had gone out of the Republic long before. "Marius and Sulla," writes Syme, "overthrew *libertas* by force of arms and established *dominatio*. Pompeius was no better. After that, only a contest for supreme power."[39] In 55 B.C. Cicero was already lamenting "the decline and virtual extinction of our institutions . . . there were no principles by which to steer."[40] After decades of internal strife between rival factions, armies, urban mobs, armed bands of thugs (private body guards) neither life nor property was secure, and property had always been the more sacred of the two.[41] "The rule of law had perished long ago," writes Syme, "with might substituted for right. Worn and broken by civil war and disorder, the Roman people were ready to surrender the ruinous privilege of freedom and submit to strict government as in the beginning of time. So order came to Rome."[42]

Though cloaked in republican pretenses, the order of imperial Rome rested squarely on force, which was destined to generate future turmoil but no further revolutions. No system of government, Mommsen wrote in the 19th century, had so completely lost the idea of legitimacy as that which Augustus established. Sulla came to power with an army of 10,000; Julius Caesar with 50,000; Augustus with 400,000. Of the latter, 275,000 were pensioned off, the others were retained as a permanent standing army. After Augustus the Emperor ruled at the pleasure of the army, illustrating the principle outlined by MacIver

> The standing army is first created as an instrument of the will of the oligarchy . . . but the personal character of military command and the withdrawal of the army from the normal life of the community render this instrument serviceable to the ambition, not of the oligarchical class as a whole, but of the military leaders . . . [so that] the fate of the state may thus depend on the answer to the question, whom does the army obey?[43]

In the early Republic officials, even military leaders were elected; after Augustus every major office-holder is *de facto* an appointee of the Emperor. Government is increasingly militarized "through the infiltration of soldiers into the staffs of higher civil magistrates."[44] Within the military system a secret service develops (by the 2nd century A.D.) with "extensive spying . . . prominent generals and senators as well as lowly Christians . . . no class high or low could escape. In addition to investigating and arresting, the S.S. was commissioned to carry out political assassinations."[45] Within this "militarized bureaucracy" as Rostovzeff calls it, there were "countless thousands of policemen . . . all of them the personal military agents of the emperor." Their duty, Rostovzeff explains, was to watch the people closely, arrest those considered dangerous to the emperor and "to quell any troubles and strikes that might arise from taxation and compulsory work."[46]

With the passing of the Republic government grows remote and alien. The popular assemblies lapsed into "utter insignificance."[47] Public business in the senate was once conducted openly; after Augustus secrecy prevails. Under Julius Caesar the protocols of the Senate meetings were published (later said to be Europe's first newspaper), "a practice ended by Augustus and never resumed." Julius Caesar tolerated "the most venomous attacks against himself"; a century later written or spoken criticism of the emperor was punishable by death – "the first death penalty for literary treason was meted out in A.D. 21."[48]

Although the office of emperor was supreme its occupant was never safe. Not open organized opposition in the Senate but conspiracy within the army and the imperial entourage was the omnipresent threat.[49] Of the seventy emperors between 27 B.C. and A.D. 476, twenty were murdered, seven committed suicide; of the first fifteen after Augustus nine died violent deaths. Even two corporals once conspired to usurp the usurper's "crown."

Understandable attempts to detect and suppress conspiracy led to an understandable spread of distrust. Social life was "de-politicalized." Politics was a tabooed subject of conversation at the dinner parties of the aristocracy because "the least loose word, perhaps even the recital of a dream, might be carried to high places . . . and doom an innocent fellow guest to a sudden and atrocious death."[50] But avoidance of social activities could also arouse suspicion: a prominent Roman who lived quietly at home would "immediately be suspected of disaffection by the Emperor's clique."[51] Tiberius and Claudius even attempted to close the inns and taverns, "because of the morbid fear that any gathering of Romans would lead to a conspiracy against the government."[52] The Emperor Trajan refused his permission for the creation of a volunteer fire department as politically dangerous. Every club had to be approved by the Senate and as a rule licenses were only granted to the most innocuous ones – "friendly or burial societies. . . . This strict limitation of clubs completely shut a whole range of possible interest and usefulness."[53]

When politics dies culture decays. Serious involvement in art or philosophy, history or science is potentially subversive to the totalitarian state. After Augustus the educated leisure class in Rome turned to safe and trivial amusements, to an apolitical indulgence in illicit sexuality, gluttony and drunkenness. The intellectual life of the time is "an arid desert of cultivated impotence."[54] Cut off from meaningful participation in public life, the upper class is peopled by "jaded souls . . . tortured by an aimless restlessness."[55] Continuously bored, the wealthy ceaselessly search for excitement. "A thirst arises for novelties, unfamiliar pleasures, nameless sensations," writes Durkheim, describing the symptoms of anomie, "all of which lose their savor once known."[56] The mood permeates the top strata of imperial Rome, and Nero, described by Tacitus as a "lover of the impossible," is the very embodiment of anomie.

To treat the soul sickness of the upper class Seneca devised a therapy strikingly analogous to psychoanalysis. Seneca's spiritual patient must be "encouraged to make a full confession of the diseases of his soul." Through daily self examination self-knowledge is acquired, "dispelling the ignorance which is the source of the soul's disorder." Change of location — the geographic cure — is no help, since we take our vices with us. But consolation can be found in the inner life because "the mind can create its own world . . . each man is miserable just as he thinks himself." Seneca's soul-doctor, the practical philosopher, does his best work "by private counsel, adapted to the special needs of the spiritual patient."[57] Man must find the springs of his happiness in himself, but he cannot live for himself alone: "man is born for social union, which is cemented by concord, kindness and he who shows anger, selfishness, perfidy or cruelty to his fellows strikes at the roots of social life."[58] Long before psychiatry discovered the process of projection, Seneca saw that the faults which irritate us in another are often lurking in ourselves. "Forgive if you wish for forgiveness; conquer evil with good; do good even to those who have wrought you evil."[59] The final aim of therapy is to "unmask the objects of [our] dread."[60] Once the source of anxiety is discovered, serenity is possible.

For the Roman the objects of dread were both real and imaginary. Seneca, as Nero's prime minister, spent years in daily, even hourly, danger of death and like other noble Romans — Brutus, Cassius, Cato the Younger, Cicero,

Petronius, Nero himself—died a suicide. The Romans had an unusual propensity for suicide but the famous cases we know about correspond to Durkheim's altruistic rather than the anomic pattern; suicide was a means of averting torture and disgrace when the battle was lost.[61] Imperial Rome was a culture of dread and the lawless unpredictable terror was reenacted in the family of the slave-supported upper class. "Every great house is a miniature of the Empire under Caligula or Nero," writes Samuel Dill, "a nursery of pretenders capable of the same enormities."[62] The paterfamilias had absolute authority over his wife, his sons, grandsons, unmarried daughters and the wives of his sons and grandsons, "even the right to inflict the death penalty."[63] Paternal tyranny was tempered by affection in dealing with family members, but the slave had no claim on the love of the master. Not only whipping and confinement but the executions of slaves are provoked by the slightest misdeeds. Cato the Elder casually boasts of whipping his slaves for minor infractions, though compassionately he chains his rural slaves only during the winter months. The runaway slave was usually tortured to death, as "an exemplary to terrify any of his fellow slaves."[64] According to Westermann under the empire there were definite prohibitions on the right of punishment vested in the paterfamilias.[65] Still in a case in A.D. 61 where a slave had murdered a Roman prefect, the latter's whole household of 400 slaves were condemned to die, and the Senate, despite popular opposition, upheld the decision.[66]

As a social status, slavery represents almost total anomie. The slave could neither marry nor own property, and as "a permanent captive in a foreign land all former ties of race, kinship, locality, tribe, family or village community were snapped once and for all."[67] The farm slave of the 5th century B.C. had been part of the family; hence there was a "positive" control over him, but with the alienated slave of the first century, "fear of punishment was the only sanction of his conduct."[68] Understandably the slave is seen as "a liar and a thief . . . destitute of conscience." Slaves in first century Rome numbered some three to four hundred thousand, about one third of the city's population.

The slave system victimized both slave and master.[69] "The master of a horde of slaves," writes Fowler, "had half his moral sense paralyzed, because he had no feeling of responsibility for so many of those with whom he came in contact every day and hour." The erosion of the sense of justice in dealing with fellow citizens was due in large measure, Fowler continues, "to the constant exercise of arbitrary power at home, to the habit of looking upon the men who ministered to his luxurious ease as absolutely without claim upon his self respect or benevolence." The sexual licientiousness and exploitation of ancient Rome is partially attributable to the peculiar institution of slavery, and the reckless disregard of human life so characteristic of Rome in its late phase is a clear derivative of slavery and "of the unconscious cultivation, from childhood onwards of the despotic temper."[70] But deeper still, is the alienation from self, the crisis of identity produced by the dependence of the master on the slave. Dill relates the tale of the Roman noble taking his seat in his sedan and requiring the assurance of his slave that he was really seated.[71] Observing a rich man carried by slaves, while one slave was charged with reminding him in advance of the name of acquaintances who might be approaching, Pliny commented

> We walk with the feet of others, we recognize our acquaintances with the eyes of others, rely on others' memory to make our salutations, and put into the hands of othes our very lives; the precious things of nature, which support life, we have quite lost. We have nothing else of our own save our luxuries.[72]

Barr notes that in response to the loss of identity, many men and many women tried to regain identity, "not by seeking the self-knowledge Socrates urged, but by striving to force others to identify and respect them."[73] Rome herself was a monstrous parasite living off the labor of others. Her wealth derived, not from her own efforts in agriculture, commerce or industry, "but from indemnities paid by conquered peoples . . . and the booty brought home by victorious generals."[74]

While the upper class was corrupted by conquest and luxury and the slave brutalized by exploitation, the "free" proletariat (*plebs urbana*) was left to rot in idleness, physically sustained by a meager wheat dole and diverted by grotesque spectator sports. In 55 B.C. 320,000, a third to a half the city's total population was "on welfare," i.e., receiving free wheat from the state, but "housing" remained in the hands of private enterprise; the free population rented rooms in four story tenements owned by "slum-lords." In these "rabbit warrens" rooms could be used only for eating and sleeping and most of the day and night people "prowled about, either idling or getting such employment as they could, legitimate or otherwise."[75] Under such conditions, Fowler observes, "there could of course have been no idea of home, nor of that simple and sacred family which had once been the ethical basis of Roman society."[76] The Roman "lumpen-proletarian" could hustle a few dollars at odd jobs (dock hands, porters) and during the Republic made pocket money by selling his vote in the assembly. There were a small number of free artisans — bakers, weavers, fullers, dyers, shoemakers, doctors, teachers, painters — organized in guilds, (*collegia*) but Rome never developed an industrial working class. When the Roman could not work as a farmer or warrior he was simply unemployed. Even for the employed, the workday was short — only six hours — and one out of every three days was a public holiday."[77]

The holiday spectacle was more than mere amusement: it was an integral part of the framework of terror which contained the urban population. In sheer magnitude Roman "spectator sports" were unsurpassed until the 20th century. Crowds of a quarter of a million attended the chariot races — larger than the number at the Indianapolis auto-races today. Although extremely dangerous the chariot races "lacked the international brutality" of the gladiatorial "games"; consequently the former were never as appealing as the latter.[78] The games were "the rage of all classes," says Dill, and by the third century A.D. as many as 175 days of the year were devoted to them, with 10,000 to 20,000 gladiators, criminals, war-captives and "subversives" in a single season sent to their death before cheering crowds of 80,000.[79] The games lasted from morning until nightfall, and though they were initially privately financed by wealthy politicians seeking favor with the populace, from 105 B.C. onward they were organized and paid for by the state. Often defended as a school for courage, the games actually fostered "a cowardly delight in the sufferings of others."[80] Mattingly continues: "It is hard to exaggerate the demoralizing effect [of the gladiatorial shows]. . . . The sight of other men bleeding and dying does not make a man brave himself."[81] Whether consciously or unconsciously intended the effect of the game was to engender, not valor, but cowardice. The games were used as a ritual of intimidation, thus rendering the population subservient to the ruling powers. The amphitheatre became an arena for mass executions. In 104 B.C. 1,000 slave insurgents were fed to the lions; in 80 B.C. the dictator Sulla put to death 6,000 of his political opponents and compelled the Senate to observe the spectacle as an object-lesson in the dangers of dissent.

The Romans invented the strategy of deterrence. "They knew how to undermine by terror the very souls of their adversaries."[82] In the beginning the "adversary" was the external military rival but after the establishment of empire the "enemy within" became the culprit to be deterred. To maintain a steadily disintegrating social order the emperors had themselves declared gods—the ultimate in the process of sacralization—and Rome began to deify herself. Hence, as Sorokin notes, "violation of the law was regarded as a religious crime." The punishment of criminals—heretics—grows harsher as

> There now develops, instead of a simple and comparatively mild system of penalty of the Republican period a very complicated, very severe, often barbarian system of penalties. The death penalty, which almost disappeared in the Republican period, now is reestablished and often assumes the most qualified forms (burning, crucifixion, etc.) . . . In addition, quite frequent becomes hard labor, imprisonment in state mines, banishment, exile, fines and a vast system of torturing and painful bodily punishment.[83]

As the mores—the *mos maiorum*—deteriorated, as the society descended into anomie, the threat of official violence was increasingly used to compel compliance to the letter of the law which further undermined committment to the spirit of the law.

Anomie is the touchstone of Roman history from Augustus onward. There was a minimal peace (i.e., an absence of major wars and open revolution), a rising level of material comfort, and times of relative tranquility like the 2nd century A.D. which Gibbon thought one of the happiest periods in human history. But beneath the splendor of imperial Rome was that "profound malaise common to aging nations," as Jacob Burckhardt said, which not even the best of emperors nor the wisest of policies could cope with or correct.[83]

By the third century A.D. anomie has become manifest everywhere. "Chaos and misery reigned through the empire," writes Rostovzeff.[85] Civil strife provoked and made possible onslaughts of neighboring enemies, weakened the empire's powers of resistance and forced the emperors in dealing with the population to have constant recourse to the method of "terror and compulsion, which gradually developed into a more or less logically organized system of administration."[86] There was no systematic or totalitarian plan in the policy of the emperors, Rostovzeff continues, but only a gradual yielding to the aspirations of the army as a means of preserving the empire itself. The emperors of the third century were not ambitious men, seeking power for its own sake.

> If the policy gradually produced a slave state with a small ruling minority headed by an autocratic monarch, who was commander of an army of mercenaries . . . it was not because such was the ideal of the emperors but because it was the easiest way of keeping the state going and preventing a final breakdown.[87]

Toward the end of the Empire, men seem to Rostovzeff to have "utterly lost their balance . . . the peasant hated the landowners and the official; the city proletariat hated the city bourgeoisie, the army was hated by everybody."[88] Rostovzeff thought that the resentment of the lower classes, the main stay of the army by the third century, found expression in the attack of the army on the upper class. More recent research shows the army as thoroughly democratic in orientation, attacking rich and poor alike.[89]

Of course the "hate" which Rostovzeff speaks of is unmeasurable, and the Romans had long ceased to waste any love on one another. But there are tangible measures of growing disorganization: roads unsafe; public buildings deteriorating; population declining; banditry increasing; the disappearance of Latin as the official language and its replacement by native dialects; the final decay of art and high culture. Figures in the painting and sculpture of the time, writes Burckhart, "show in part a natural ugliness and in part somethings diseased, scrofulous, bloated or sunken."[90] Studious natural historians were of the opinion that "the cosmos itself was going into general decline . . . rivers [were said to have] grown sluggish and mountains [to lose] their height.[91] City populations passed deeper into destitution and debauchery. By the 4th century free wine supplemented the wheat dole and anyone with money to spend "passed whole nights in the taverns . . . gambling companionship was the only bond which still held people together."[92]

Dis-urbanization begins. From the 5th to the 3rd century B.C. men fled an insecure country-side for the protection of the city; from the 3rd to the 5th century A.D. the movement was reversed. To escape the persecutions of Diocletian (A.D. 284–305), many Christians fled to the barbarians for refuge and found it."[93] During the third century the army had expanded to some 400,000 and "Diocletian increased it to at least 500,000."[94] Both military and legal means were employed in the effort to halt the flight from the cities and the empire, but without success. Along the frontiers men fled from civilization and lived in the wilderness. "Caves along the Rhone valley, unoccupied since the Stone Age," MacMullen writes, "received in the mid-third century a population of fugitives some of whom never sought out their homes again."[95] Some of the defectors joined religious communities; others passed into the ranks of the brigands, and occasionally later joined religious orders: "In the fourth century we meet with monks made over, or abbots reclaimed and elected, from a life of brigandage, and the leaders of [several fierce bands] eventually received veneration as saints."[96] Robber bands had always existed. What was new to the third century was the growing number of recruits to the outlaw-life, without which "brigandage could never have challenged the massed authority of Roman laws and armies."[97] As MacMullen puts it:

> A widespread sympathy felt, or half-felt, for the lives and deeds of outlaws testifies to a loosening loyalty within civilized society, where to be poor, to be rejected, to scrape a living irregularly in the company of others clinging like one self to the edge of the respectable world; to envy and then to hate the man of property, and to admire the style of his plunderers; to consort with them, then shield them, and at last join them, were the successive steps leading beyond the boundaries of the law.[98]

There was a steady erosion of the authority of the central administration, which now rested solely on force: from the reign of Diocletian onward the Emperor's palace was called the *castra* — the camp — and the entire Imperial government was known as the *militia*.[99] The army grows in numbers, declines in effectiveness, finally becomes "counter-productive." Sent to the provinces to restore order, the army created further disorder. What confronted the head of state, MacMullen writes, was "a sense — how widespread among his subjects or how deeply felt and destructive we cannot say — that someone who broke the law might be an ally, and officers who enforced it enemies."[100]

Every effort to arrest the decay merely accelerated the dissolution of Roman society. To curtail the loss of labor power men were "frozen" in their jobs with virtually every occupation "from waterman on the Tiber to the Senator made hereditary."[101] Class is turned into caste; laws forbade intermarriage between trades, e.g. the son of a sailor could not marry the daughter of a baker. Frontier guardsman was made an hereditary status, but those who did not care for the job simply merged into the barbarian population. There was wholesale desertion from the army, and "slaves have to be called to arms."[102] Rome's organizational finesse deserted her altogether: laws binding men to their trade simply drove away unwilling workers, or made for fantastic "goldbricking."[103] For instance "hereditary" ship captains and crews responsible for bringing grain to the city would take months to traverse a route normally requiring weeks. "While the city was on the verge of famine, or when supplies were urgently needed for the army in Gaul," writes Dill, "the captains often lingered in port on any pretext, or made circuitous voyage in pursuit of their own profit."[104] New laws were passed — "going off like fire crackers in the gathering dusk of disorder."[105] But devoid of a supporting consensus, of moral authority, the laws were not only useless, but detrimental, aggravating the alienation which they were designed to rectify.

With the population thus demoralized the empire could no longer defend itself. "Human nature is having its revenge in wholesale flight from cruel servitude," writes Samuel Dill, "and the disinherited are carrying brigandage even up to the gates of Rome."[106] In 453 the city was sacked by Vandals under Alaric, which was the first time in nearly a millenium Rome had been invaded by a foreign enemy. Although Alaric held Rome for only a week the flight from the city gained momentum thereafter. The rich had begun their departure earlier, retiring to their rural villas, which in time became a castle and a feudal estate. Around the castle grows a colony of clients and patrons, artisans, slaves, small proprietors, bailiffs, idlers and formerly detached individuals and these "clusters of men mark the transition to the medieval and Byzantine world."[107] In the last years of the Empire there was no organized collision of classes, of poor against rich. The rural as well as the urban population formed "vertical rather than horizontal relationships." The weak allied with the strong, the powerful noble who through influence, bribery and armed force as well could protect them from "the still more ruinous demands of the imperial government." The formal collapse of the centralized authority of the Western Roman empire is dated at A.D. 476; afterwards the decentralized anarchy of feudalism prevails, transformed later into the anarchy of nation-states.

Haywood questions even the idea that Rome fell, saying "change is not necessarily decay."[108] But the most incontrovertible evidence of Rome's decline is demographic. The population of Western Europe in the 2nd century A.D. was an estimated forty million; by the 8th century it had dwindled to ten million, perhaps fewer, and no city of the time, except Rome had more than a few hundred inhabitants. And Rome itself, which at its peak had contained over a million, after the 7th century numbered scarcely 20,000 souls.[109] The fall of Rome, writes Samuel Dill, is a "tragedy in the truest sense, such as history has seldom exhibited, in which, by an inexorable fate, the claims of fancied omnipotence ended in humiliating paralysis."[110] A tragedy yes, but one mankind can rejoice in. *Richard III* is a tragedy but his demise brings us nothing but relief.

Several conclusions can be drawn from the Roman experience.

First, Rome's initial power grew out of her spirit and policy of prudent generosity, which attracted citizens and allies, enabling her to become the dominant city-state of the Italian Peninsula and eventually the Mediterranean basin.

Second, an almost inadvertent expansion led to an unintended collision with Carthage and the long struggle of the Punic Wars which (1) destroyed the independent small farmer and introduced the slave-worked plantation, and the citizen-conscript army, necessitating eventually a professional army; and (2) created an upper class whose wealth and position rested on conquest and an impoverished and anomic proletariat.

Third, after a brief effort to build a "league of nations" with the Hellenic states where Rome would only be the first among equals, she resorted to naked force to extend her dominion and maintain her accidentally acquired empire.

Fourth, simultaneously force came to dominate the internal life of Rome. Political violence was first introduced in the assassination of the Gracchi for attempting to implement land reform laws duly passed by the assembly and the senate. Class struggle between the conservatives (*Optimates*) and populists (*Populares*) followed until the volunteer professional army with its charismatic leaders—first Marius, then Sulla, followed by Pompey and Caesar—usurped the authority of "democratic" institutions, destroyed the Republic, and left supreme power in the hands of a single emperor, whose fate depended on the dubious and erratic loyalty of the military establishment.

Fifth, the insecurity of the emperor led to a constant preoccupation with conspiracy—a continuous "witch hunt," which de-politicalized social life, spread distrust, and sabotaged allegiance to Rome.

Sixth, because there was no principle of legitimacy and cohesion and no opportunity for participation in political life, terror was increasingly used to control the population. Direct violence kept the slave population in tow; the indirect and vicarious violence of the gladiatorial games engendered cowardice and subservience in the free population. Slaves and proletarians constituted 90 percent of the population; the small upper class lived a functionless and parasitical existence which left it aimless, demoralized, and cruel.

Seventh, unable to "legitimate" the violence which it unleashed, the Roman Establishment was finally undermined by massive defection and desertion. Unable to maintain order despite overwhelming physical force, the Roman Empire collapsed and died an unmourned death.

Finally, as to the Pax Romana, curiously praised in our own times, Tacitus wrote its epitaph: "To plunder, butcher, steal, these things they misname empire; they made a desolation and they call it peace."[111]

On Durkheim, Suicide, and Anomie: Correspondence Between Isabel Cary-Lundberg and Elwin H. Powell

To the Editor:

In the April 1958 (pp. 131–139) issue of the *Review*, a workmanlike study by Elwin H. Powell is entitled "Occupation, Status, and Suicide: Toward a Redefinition of Anomie." This raises the decisive problem of definition, for which Mr. Powell gives Durkheim as his source; he writes: "When the ends of action become contradictory, unaccessible or insignificant, a condition of anomie arises. Characterized by a general loss of orientation and accompanied by feelings of 'emptiness' and apathy, anomie can be simply conceived as meaninglessness" (p. 132). In a footnote (11), Mr. Powell explains that "Anomie is both a social condition and a psychic state. It is sometimes referred to as a 'social and emotional void' or 'separation-anxiety' (de Grazia). Merton on the other hand stresses the idea of normlessness. The term meaninglessness can serve as a common denominator for these different perspectives" (p. 132).

Our first question to Mr. Powell: *can it?*

Durkheim's major concern in *Le Suicide*[1] is with a society as a collectivity, with the state of its *ordre collectif* and of its *conscience collective*. To describe Europe's collective consciousness pre-1900, Durkheim used the term *malaise*.[2] A sickness, not economic but moral, he said, afflicts France and the West because all previously existing *cadres* have either broken down or been worn away by time. The family unit, its members dispersed and divorced, no longer exercises its old cohesive powers. Religion, through no fault of Science, is tossed aside by men who simply will not bow to

Reprinted with permission from *American Sociological Review*, April 1959.

the limits it places on conduct. The gravitational pull of political parties grows ever weaker, while the mutually binding and integrating demands on workers in the old *corporations des métiers* are binding no more.

Under these conditions, said Durkheim, a society begins to distintegrate. The sole survivor as enforcer of law and order is *l'Etat* which, clumsy, slow, inefficient, is eluded at every turn by a scattered and diffused "dust" of people. Thus: social disorganization; discarded and discredited norms; a flat unwillingness to accept in any form a checkrein on pleasures, appetites, production, or prosperity: this constellation of signs Durkheim translated into Greek. To the negative prefix *a*, he added the plural of laws, *nomous*, and turned the "no-laws" of *anomous* into French as *l'Anomie*. That is why Durkheim's first mention of the term occurs as "the state of unbridledness" (to put it awkwardly), or, in French, "L'état de dérèglement ou d'*anomie*. . . ."[3]

In de-controlled societies "suffering" from anomie, he said, large numbers of men are driven to suicide by frustration at the collapse of exaggerated hopes, by exasperation at the failure of excessive ambitions, by rage over being balked in any pursuit, and by fury at another standing in the way of success or happiness: hence homicide precedes suicide.[4] Durkheim found anomie in a "chronic state" in the commercial and industrial world;[5] but, he added, economic anomy is not alone. Equally suicidogenic, and "more chronic," is domestic anomie, "the state of anomie produced by divorce" (*l'état d'anomie conjugale*).[6]

Anomie, definitively defined as "a state" of disorder, disruption in the social collectivity, needs no "common denominator" and can by no scientific canon "be simply conceived as meaninglessness." However, Mr. Powell continues: "Anomie is a crucial factor in the etiology of suicide. Thus suicide rates can serve as empirical data for testing a general theory of action; . . . Behind the diverse manifestations of the act of self-destruction, however, there is a common sociological ground—anomie" (pp. 132–133).

Our second question to Mr. Powell: *can there be?* Not, surely, unless one is prepared to jettison Durkheim's entire thesis. "Behind the diverse manifestations of the act of self-destruction," Durkheim maintained, *there is no common ground*. There are, on the contrary, three possible grounds—egoism, altruism, and anomie—occasionally in combination. "It is not a mere metaphor," he recapitulates, "to say of each human society that it has a greater or lesser aptitude for suicide; . . . Each social group has a *penchant collectif* for this act. . . . It is made up of the currents of egoism, altruism or anomy running through the society under consideration."[7] When Durkheim had set forth his "third type," he wrote: "Anomy, therefore, is a regular and specific factor in suicides in our modern societies; one of the springs from which the annual contingent feeds. So we have a new type to distinguish from the others. . . ."[8]

When Mr. Powell turns toward a "redefinition" of anomie, he arrives at an arresting formation, totally alien to the original *anomie*, which he applies to the top Professional-Managerial category of occupations (Type I) in the following words: "Living by the unexamined directives of the culture the person has the sense of being totally controlled by forces outside himself. Hence he feels that he is not really living at all. The boredom of 'not living' grows into a general loss of spontaneity that culminates in the inner deadness which precedes the physical death of the suicide" (p. 139). With this statement, either Mr. Powell is creating a new type of suicide unknown to Durkheim and irreconcilable with *l'anomie*;[9] or he has stumbled onto a new fact of great scientific value.

In Type I, he writes: "the self is almost completely enveloped in the success ideology and presents the paradox of what may be called *institutionalized anomie*. . . ." Now two such opposite social configurations could never, in Durkheim's thought, be wedged into one terminological conveyance.[10] Not only are the italicized terms mutually contradictory, but the notion of success as "enveloping" is sheer iconoclasm — *unless* something in the social order has changed. Something has.

For Durkheim and his era the dominant form of business enterprise was the sole proprietorship; and the employing proprietor was credited with contributing a larger quota of suicides than his workmen.[11] In the United States as a whole, however, the individual proprietorship has all but been displaced by the industrial corporation and the industrial union, both heavily weighted against individual action, decisions, responsibility, and individuality as such, in the interest of collective action, group decisions, group benefits, and behavioral conformity. In consequence, Mr. Powell seems to be reporting a fundamental alteration in the American *conscience collective* as reflected in the rates of executive suicides. It is just possible that these ought now to be considered with those of the military *élite* corps,[12] in the category of *le suicide altruiste*. For of this Durkheim wrote: "If, as we have just seen, excessive individuation leads to (egoistic) suicide, insufficient individuation has the same effects. When man has become detached from society, he encounters less resistance to suicide in himself, and he does so likewise when social integration is too strong."[13]

Mr. Powell, we believe, has inadvertently come up with the new fact that *institutionalized business and industry* have shifted suicides of "organization men" from the anomic-individualistic category to an emergent altruistic-organizational category. We therefore strenuously disagree with his [statement]: "As opposite poles of a continuum, two forms of anomie can be discerned: the one results from the self's dissociation from, the other from its envelopment by, the conceptual system of the culture. Both render the individual impotent . . ." (p. 139).

Impotence is extraneous to anomie, as defined. Anomie by its very nature can never be enveloping. Therefore, *if "envelopment" is the generator of these suicides*, then they must be of another type—the very conclusion with which one of Mr. Powell's statements leaves us: "The occupation tends to create both by selection and by the nature of the role itself either a dissociated or an enveloped—'self-less'—personality." Anomic suicide cannot be both.

We solicit Mr. Powell's re-examination of his primary source. His findings do not require him to "re-define" *l'anomie*. On the contrary, they require Durkheim's type of refined analysis and penetrating insight, (1) to distinguish the data for egoistic, altruistic, and anomic suicides; and, if our assumption is correct, (2) to evolve a fresh approach to the "success ideology" which will endow its Twentieth-century frame of reference, the [modern] corporation,[14] with the requisite *esprit de corps* to account for managerial-type altruistic suicides.

Isabel Cary-Lundberg
New York, New York

Rejoinder to Dr. Cary-Lundberg

To the Editor:

While in general agreement with Dr. Cary-Lundberg, we must take issue with her conclusion that a re-reading of Durkheim obviates the necessity for a redefinition of anomie. Noting that Durkheim was chiefly concerned with society as a collectivity, Dr. Cary-Lundberg rejects the attempt to treat anomie as *both* a state of mind and a social condition. This is consistent with the anti-psychological orientation of Durkheim. For Dr. Cary-Lundberg, "Anomie, definitively defined as a 'state' of disorder, disruption in the social collectivity, needs no common denominator. . . ."

But so understood the idea of anomie loses much of its significance for the study of social pathology in general and suicide in particular. For it is not the external fact of "de-regulation" but the internal experience of chaos which is instrumental in the process of self-destruction. Thus some larger concept is necessary to suggest the way in which social forces (either disorder or its opposite) are translated into individual despair. For this purpose we adopted as a synonym for anomie the term *meaninglessness* — an awkward word which nevertheless depicts the suicidal frame of mind and at the same time points to the objective conditions of its origin.

Meaning is *social, not societal.* Following George H. Mead, it can be said that meaning is an emergent generated in the social act. When the self is powerless to act — that is, impotent — meaninglessness (i.e., anomie) follows. So construed, impotence is not extraneous to anomie, as Dr. Cary-Lundberg contends, but its very essence. Impotence may derive from a dissociation from the conceptual system of the culture (or subculture) when the person is unable to respond to or understand the acts of others so that eventually his own actions become meaningless. Complete envelopment in the social structure may terminate in the same paralysis of the self, reducing the "actor" to a passive "re-actor." From both conditions there results emptiness, exhaustion, and spiritual defeat — the symptoms usually ascribed to anomie.

We assumed that the sense of meaninglessness was common to almost all suicides — in our culture. But, according to Dr. Cary-Lundberg, Durkheim maintains that there is no common ground behind all suicides but rather "three possible grounds – egoism, altruism and anomie – occasionally in combination." It seems to us that these three components are always intermixed. Clinically, it is impossible to distinguish these types of suicide.

Thus, there is no way to "distinguish the data for egoistic, altruistic, and anomic suicides," for these are not entities but phases of a single process. Durkheim's categories of egoism and anomie have come to be used interchangeably. MacIver, for instance, describes "anomy . . . as an extremer form of egoism . . . the fulfilment of the process of de-socialization, the retreat of the individual into his own ego. . . ."[15] This usage has been followed by Louis Wirth and several urban sociologists, by Sebastian de Grazia and many political theorists, by Elton Mayo and Peter Drucker in industrial sociology – all of whom have drawn liberally from Durkheim without troubling themselves with too strict adherence to his formal definitions. In the long, convoluted, always bewildering chain of causation which ends in self-murder it is impossible to differentiate Durkheim's egoism and anomie.

Similarly with altruism – the over-attachment of the self to the collectivity. Anthropological field studies substantiate Durkheim's observations on the altruistic suicide typical of primitive societies. But his interpretation of the military suicide as altruistic is dubious at best. More plausible is the thesis that an essentially anomic individual is inwardly driven to affiliate with a powerful organization – an army, a totalitarian political party, possibly a corporation – in a fruitless effort to find direction and purpose. Durkheim's own data could be used to verify this supposition: volunteers and re-enlistees have unusually high suicide rates, and the military rate increases more rapidly with age than does the civilian rate.[16] Both Parsons and Merton have recently come to regard compulsive conformity – the visible sign of Durkheim's altruism – as a form of deviance (anomie).[17] With insight and clarity that would do credit to Durkheim himself, Dr. Cary-Lundberg has examined the possibility that the suicide of the "organization man" is of the altruistic *type*. Certainly the elements of altruism are prominent here, but hardly more (or less) than in the case of the individualistic proprietor of the previous century. The bankrupt financier who kills himself because of "business reverses" exemplifies the altruistic dimension of suicide: over-committed to the norms of his subculture he cannot survive exclusion from it. Is this altruism or anomie? It is both. Both roads open on to the same abyss.

Therefore we submit that egoism and altruism are suicidogenic only when they eventuate in anomie, that is, meaninglessness. Dr. Cary-Lundberg's insistence on the separation of these three categories is a reification of the *word* of Durkheim which is quite alien to his spirit.

Elwin H. Powell
University of Buffalo

Notes

Chapter 1

1. Karl A. Menninger, *Man Against Himself* (New York: Harcourt, Brace, 1938).
2. Arthur Schopenhauer, "On Suicide" *Studies in Pessimism: A Series of Essays,* trans. T. Saunders (New York: Macmillan, 1903), 43-50.
3. James M. A. Weiss, "The Gamble with Death in Attempted Suicide," *Psychiatry,* XX (1957), 17-25.
4. Robert Burton, *The Anatomy of Melancholy* (East Lansing: Michigan State University Press, 1965), 141-5.
5. *Ibid.* 145.
6. *Ibid.* 186.
7. *Ibid.* 214-15.
8. *Ibid.* 103-4.
9. L. Crocker, "The Discussion of Suicide in the 18th Century," *Journal of the History of Ideas,* 13 (Jan. 1952), 47-72.
10. Robert Nisbet, "Sociology as Art" in M. Stein (ed.), *Sociology on Trial* (New York: Basic Books, 1961).
11. Emile Durkheim, *Suicide: A Study in Sociology,* trans. J. Spaulding and G. Simpson (Glencoe, Ill.: The Free Press, 1951), 288. See Barclay D. Johnson, "Durkheim's One Cause of Suicide," *American Sociological Review,* 30 (1965), 875-86.
12. *Ibid.* 248.

Chapter 2

1. Austin Porterfield, "Suicide and Crime in the Social Structure of an Urban Setting," *American Sociological Review,* 17 (June 1952), 341-9. On the exhaustively studied ecological variable, Calvin Schmid, *Suicide in Seattle, 1914-1925: An Ecological and Behavioristic Study* (Seattle: University of Washington Press, 1928); Ruth Cavan, *Suicide* (Chicago: University of Chicago Press, 1929); Peter Sainsbury, *Suicide in London: An Ecological Study* (London: Chapman and Hall, 1955), 50, *et passim.*

2. James M. Weiss, "Suicide: An Epidemiological Analysis," *Psychiatric Quarterly,* 28 (1954), 225-52.
3. H. D. Anderson and Percy E. Davidson, *Occupational Trends in the United States* (Palo Alto, Calif.: Stanford University Press, 1940), 1.
4. On the connection between the categories (space, time, causality) and social structure, see Stanley Taylor, *Conceptions of Institutions and the Theory of Knowledge* (New York: Bookman Associates, 1956); Emile Durkheim, *The Elementary Forms of the Religious Life,* trans. J. Swain (London: George Allen and Unwin, 1915), 440. For a valiant if doomed effort to move social science out of the positivist space-time of Newtonian mechanics see, P. A. Sorokin, *Sociocultural Causality, Space, Time: A Study of the Referential Principles of Sociology and Social Science* (New York: Russell and Russell, 1964). Peter S. McHugh, Order and Disorder in Social Time and Space (Evanston, Ill.: Unpublished Doctoral Dissertation, 1962).
5. Bohan Zawadski and Paul Larzarsfeld, "The Psychological Consequences of Unemployment," *Journal of Social Psychology,* VI (1935), 224-50.
6. Nancy C. Morse and Robert S. Weiss, "The Function and Meaning of Work," *American Sociological Review,* 20 (1955), 191-8.
7. Dan Wakefield, "Labor Shudders at Leisure: The Perilous Gift," *Nation,* 196 (April 20, 1963), 325-7. Wakefield says we need a new slogan, "Fun can be Fun."
8. Aaron Levenstein, *Why People Work: Changing Incentives in a Troubled World* (New York: Collier Books, 1964), 152. See Walter S. Neff, "Psychoanalytic Conceptions of the Meaning of Work," *Psychiatry,* 28 (1965), 324-33.
9. Betty Friedan, *The Feminine Mystique* (New York: W. W. Norton, 1963), 334, *et passim.*
10. Louis Wirth, "Preface" to Karl Mannheim's *Ideology and Utopia: An Introduction to the Sociology of Knowledge,* trans. Louis Wirth and E. A. Shils (New York: Harcourt, Brace, 1951), xxv; Sebastian de Grazia, *The Political Community: A Study of Anomie* (Chicago: University of Chicago Press, 1948), 47-76; Robert K. Merton, "Social Structure and Anomie" in *Social Theory and Social Structure* (New York: The Free Press of Glencoe, 1957).
11. George H. Mead, *Mind, Self and Society* (Chicago: University of Chicago Press, 1934), 140, *et passim.* For clarification, see William L. Kolb, "A Critical Evaluation of Mead's "I" and "Me" Concepts," *Social Forces,* 22 (1944), 291-6. For the development of self as seen

by Mead and Buber, see, Paul Pfuetz (New York: Bookman Associates, 1954). See also, Van Meter Ames, "Mead and Sartre on Man," *Journal of Philosophy*, LIII (1956), 205-19.

12. R. E. L. Faris and H. Warren Dunham, *Mental Disorders in Urban Areas* (Chicago: University of Chicago Press, 1939), 158-9. For a brilliant critique, see Mark Kennedy, "Is There an Ecology of Mental Disorders?" *International Journal of Social Psychiatry*, X (1964), 119-33.

13. Erich Fromm, *The Sane Society* (New York: Rinehart, 1956), 16, speaks of a "pathology of normalcy" where the person conforms to the expectations of the culture, is not insane or deviant but suffers a severe, sometimes lethal, deadening of effect."

14. Philip Piker, "Eighteen Hundred and Seventeen Cases of Suicidal Attempts: A Preliminary Statistical Survey," *American Journal of Psychiatry*, XCV (1938), 97-115; Margaret von Andics, *Suicide and the Meaning of Life* (London: William Hodge, 1947), 49-94; Louis I. Dublin and Bessie Bunzel, *To Be or Not To Be* (New York: Harrison Smith and Robert Hass, 1933), 399; Andrew F. Henry and James F. Short, Jr., *Suicide and Homicide* (Glencoe, Ill.: The Free Press, 1954).

15. Elwin H. Powell, "Occupation, Status and Suicide: Toward a Redefinition of Anomie," *American Sociological Review*, 23 (April 1958), 131-9; Warren Breed, "Occupational Mobility and Suicide Among White Males," *American Sociological Review*, 28 (April 1963), 179-88.

16. Austin L. Porterfield and Robert H. Talbert, *Crime, Suicide and Social Well Being* (Ft. Worth: Texas Christian University Press, 1948), 99. Alcoholism rates per 100,000 are 490 for Oklahoma City, 710 for Tulsa, Mark Keller and Vera Efron "Alcoholism in the Big Cities of the United States," *Quarterly Journal of Studies of Alcohol*, 17 (1956), 63-72.

17. Calvin F. Schmid and Maurice D. van Arsdol, Jr., "Completed and Attempted Suicides: A Comparative Analysis," *American Sociological Review*, II (1935), 273-83.

18. W. W. Schroeder and J. A. Beagle, "Suicide: An Instance of High Rural Rates," *Rural Sociology*, XVII (1953), 45-52.

19. Elizabeth Kilpatrick, "A Psychoanalytic Understanding of Suicide," *American Journal of Psychoanalysis*, VIII (1948), 13-23; Herbert Hendin, Psychodynamic Motivational Factors in Suicide," *Psychiatric Quarterly*, XXV (1951), 672-8.

20. Erich Fromm, *Man for Himself* (New York: Rinehart, 1947), 45. Fromm's work has been freely utilized in this discussion.
21. Eugene A. Friedman and Robert Havinghurst, *The Meaning of Work and Retirement* (Chicago: University of Chicago Press, 1950).
22. That there is a significant difference in the outlook and attitude of the occupational types is substantiated by Richard Centers, *The Psychology of Social Class* (Princeton: Princeton University Press, 1949), 57, 229.
23. Talcott Parsons, "The Motivations for Economic Activities," *Essays in Sociological Theory, Pure and Applied* (Glencoe, Ill.: The Free Press, 1949), 214.
24. Type V is roughly the "lower-lower" class. Lloyd Warner and Paul L. Lunt, *The Social Life of a Modern Community* (New Haven: Yale University Press, 1941), 178-95, 200.
25. The lower-class suicide is definitely more irrational than the middle-class suicide. It appears that flight reactions such as physical drifting, alcoholism, and schizophrenia are associated with low-prestige occupations. Robert E. Clark, "Psychoses, Income and Occupational Prestige,"*American Journal of Sociology,* LIV (1949), 433-40; A. B. Hollingshead and F. G. Redlich, "Social Stratification and Schizophrenia," *American Sociological Review,* XIX (1954), 302-3, 306.
26. Gladys L. Palmer, "Attitudes Toward Work in an Industrial Community," *American Journal of Sociology,* LXII (1957), 17-26.
27. R. W. Mack, "Occupational Ideology and the Determinate Role," *Social Forces,* XXXVI (1957), 34-44; Henri de Man, *Joy in Work,* trans. Eden and Cedar Paul (London: George Allen and Unwin, 1929), 59-63.
28. Martin L. Needleman, Anomie and the American Dream: A Study of the Thought Style of the White Collar Worker (Buffalo: Unpublished M.A. Thesis, State University of New York, 1965), 37-38.
29. Durkheim, *op. cit.* 258.
30. Melvin Tumin, "Some Unapplauded Consequences of Social Mobility in a Mass Society," *Social Forces,* 36 (1957), 32-37.
31. Max Scheler, *The Nature of Sympathy* (New Haven: Yale University Press, 1954), 42.

Chapter 3

1. Peter Putnam, *Cast Out the Darkness* (London: Peter Davies, 1959), 26.

2. A. Angyal, *Neurosis and Treatment: A Wholistic Approach* (New York: John Wiley, 1965), 76.
3. Jurgen Ruesch, "The Interpersonal Communication of Anxiety," *Symposium on Stress* (Washington, D.C.: Army Medical Service Graduate School, 1952).
4. Arthur Kobler and Ezra Stotland, *The End of Hope: A Social-Clinical Study of Suicide* (New York: The Free Press of Glencoe, 1964), 14-15. Clinicians have often observed that suicides occur when the depressed patient seems to be getting better, and begins to organize his behavior. Often in the extremes of depression the person does not even have energy enough to kill himself.
5. Bertram D. Lewin, *The Psychoanalysis of Elation* (London: Hogarth Press, 1951), 52. Lewin adds that "denial is called upon mainly to avoid anxiety," 53.
6. Jack P. Gibbs and Walter T. Martin, *Status Integration and Suicide: A Sociological Study* (Eugene: University of Oregon Press, 1964).
7. Willard Waller, "Insight and the Scientific Method," *American Journal of Sociology,* 40 (1934), 285-97. On the uses of suicide notes, Jerry Jacobs, "A Phenomenological Study of Suicide Notes," *Social Problems,* 15 (1967), 60-72.
8. L. Crocker, "The Discussion of Suicide in the 18th Century," *Journal of the History of Ideas,* XIII (Jan. 1952), 47-72.
9. C. W. Wahl, "Suicide as a Magical Act," *Bulletin of the Menninger Clinic,* 21 (1957), 91-99.
10. An almost identical case is presented as typical of the executive suicide by H. Levinson, "What Killed Bob Lyons? Executive's Emotional Problems," *Harvard Business Review,* 41 (1963), 127-42.
11. T. S. Eliot, "The Love Song of J. Alfred Prufrock," *Collected Poems 1909-1935* (London: Faber and Faber, 1936, New York: Harcourt, Brace), 12.
12. A. Pokorny, "A Follow-up Study of 617 Suicidal Patients," *American Journal of Psychiatry,* 122 (1966), 1109-16. E. Stengel and Nancy Cook, *Attempted Suicide, Its Social Significance and Effects* (London: Institute of Psychiatry, Maudsley Monographs, 1958), 27-32, *et passim.*
13. Rollo May, *The Meaning of Anxiety,* (New York: Ronald Press, 1950), 53.

Chapter 4

1. Paul Citrome, "Conclusions d'une enquête sur suicide dans les camps concentration," *Cahiers Internationaux de Sociologies,* XX (1952), 147-9; Elie A. Cohen, *Human Behavior in the Concentration Camp,* trans. M. H. Braaksma (New York: Grosset and Dunlap, 1953), 282-3.
2. Kurt Goldstein, *The Organism: A Holistic Approach to Biology Derived from Pathological Data in Man* (Boston: Beacon Press, 1939), 293-301.
3. Paul Tillich, "Anxiety Reducing Agencies in Our Culture," *Anxiety,* (eds.) Paul H. Hoch and Joseph Zubin (New York: Hafner Publishing Co., 1964), 19.
4. Edgar C. Trautman, "Fear and Panic in Nazi Concentration Camps: A Bio-Social Evaluation of the Chronic Anxiety Syndrome," *International Journal of Social Psychiatry,* X (Spring 1964), 134-41.
5. C. Prudhomme, "The Problem of Suicide in the American Negro," *Psychoanalytic Review,* XXV (1938), 187-204.
6. Ralph Ellison, *Invisible Man* (New York: Signet Books, 1947), 254.
7. Jean-Paul Sartre, *La République du silence* as quoted by Fritz Pappenheim, *The Alienation of Modern Man* (New York: Monthly Review Press, 1959), 29-30.
8. Quoted by Ralph Ginsburg, *100 Years of Lynchings* (New York: Lancer Books, 1962), 10-11. For similar cases, 144-5, *et passim.*
9. Raymond Aron, *The Century of Total War* (Boston: Beacon Press, 1955), 76.
10. Alfred B. Lindesmith and Anselm L. Strauss, *Social Psychology* (New York: Henry Holt, 1956), 16.
11. E. Franklin Frazier, *The Negro in the United States* (New York: Macmillan, 1957), 661-2.
12. E. Gartly Jaco, *The Social Epidemiology of Mental Disorder—A Psychiatric Survey of Texas* (New York: Russell Sage Foundation, 1960), 112-14. See Solomon Rosenthal, "Racial Difference in the Incidence of Mental Disease," *Journal of Negro Education* (July 1934), 484-93.
13. E. M. Jellinek and Mark Keller, "Rates of Alcoholism in the United States of America, 1940-48," *Quarterly Journal of Studies of Alcohol,* 13 (1952), 49-59.
14. Abram Kardiner and Lionel Oversey, *The Mark of Oppression* (New York: W. W. Norton, 1951), 338.

15. Louis Dublin, *Suicide: A Sociological and Statistical Study* (New York: Ronald Press, 1963), 33-34.
16. *Ibid.* 220-21.
17. Martin Gold, "Suicide, Homocide and the Socialization of Aggression," *American Journal of Sociology,* LXIII (1958), 651-61.
18. See Brian MacMahon, Samuel Johnson, and Thomas Pugh, "Relation of Suicide Rates to Social Conditions," *Public Health Reports,* 78 (April 1963), 285-93. The authors also note that the Negro rate in the northern cities is as high as the white rate up to the age of 35.
19. B. Balser and J. Masterson, "Suicide in Adolescents," *American Journal of Psychiatry,* 115 (1959), 400-4, note that official statistics between 1930 and 1945 reported no suicide deaths under the age of 5, between 39 and 59 per year in the age range 5-14. James M. Toolan, "Suicide in Childhood and Adolescence" in H. L. P. Resnik (ed.), *Suicidal Behaviors: Diagnosis and Management* (Boston: Little, Brown, 1968), 220-27, states that of 102 admissions to the children and adolescent services unit of Bellevue Hospital in New York City for suicide *threats* (my italics) and attempts, 18 were under 12, 84 from 12 to 17 years of age, and one was a 5-year-old boy who "repeatedly attempted suicide by burning himself with a gas heater and by pouring scalding water upon himself" (222). Toolan says suicidal acts steadily increase from the age of 8, but does not give any frequency distribution for his under-12 category. Whether the *body*-punishment of Toolan's 5-year-old is the equivalent of the *self*-punishment of the suicide is debatable. L. F. Leibermann, "Three Cases of Attempted Suicide in Children," *British Journal of Medical Psychology,* XXVI (1953), 110-14, reports as a suicide attempt a three-year-old who "developed mutism and failure to eat as a result of trauma caused by the mother." Leibermann's other two "child" suicides were aged 12 and 13. Charles R. Shaw and Ruth Schelkun, "Suicidal Behavior in Children," *Psychiatry,* 28 (May 1965), 157-68, note the extreme rarity of suicidal acts before the age of 10.
20. Hans Gerth and C. Wright Mills, *Character and Social Structure: The Psychology of Social Institutions* (New York: Harcourt, Brace, 1953), 142.
21. Similar to suicide in so many ways, alcoholism too seems connected with "the anxiety syndrome of adolescence," E. Y. William, "The Anxiety Syndrome in Alcoholism," *Psychiatry Quarterly,* XXIV (1950), 782-8.

22. Percy Mason, "Suicide in Adolescents," *Psychoanalytic Review,* XLI (1954), 48-54.
23. Ivan Belknap and Hiram Friedsam, "Age and Sex Categories as Sociological Variables in the Mental Disorders of Later Maturity," *American Sociological Review,* XIV (1949), 367-76. See Neville P. Lancaster, "Involutional Melancholia as a Disease of Adaptation," *Journal of Clinical and Experimental Psychopathology,* 18 (1957), 3598-666.
24. Frazier, *op. cit.* 102-27.
25. Kardiner and Oversey, *op. cit.* 73.
26. Osamu Dazai, *No Longer Human* (New York: New Directions, 1958), 22.
27. David Riesman, "Themes of Heroism and Weakness in Freud's Thought," *Individualism Reconsidered* (Glencoe, Ill: The Free Press, 1954), 365-86.
28. Helen V. McLean, "The Emotional Health of Negroes," *Journal of Negro Education,* VII (1949), 283-90; "Why Negroes Don't Commit Suicide," *Negro Digest* (February, 1947).
29. Robert Coles, *Children of Crisis: A Study of Courage and Fear* (New York: Delta Books, 1964), 329.
30. Emile Durkheim, *Suicide* (Glencoe, Ill.: The Free Press, 1951), 366.
31. E. Franklin Frazier, *Black Bourgeoisie* (Glencoe, Ill.: The Free Press, 1957), 213-32.
32. Arthur Schopenhauer, *Studies in Pessimism* (London: Swan Sonnenschein, 1903), 12.

Chapter 5

1. Fustel de Coulanges, *The Ancient City: A Study on the Religion, Laws and Institutions of Greece and Rome* (Garden City, N.Y.: Doubleday Anchor Books, 1956), 127-34. For a judicious appraisal of Coulanges' work, first published in 1864, see P. A. Sorokin, *Contemporary Sociological Theories* (New York: Harper, 1929).
2. Robert E. Park, "The City and Civilization," *Human Communities* (Glencoe, Ill.: The Free Press, 1952).
3. Alvin Gouldner, *Enter Plato: Classical Greece and the Origins of Social Theory* (New York: Basic Books, 1965), 166. See William S. Ferguson, " 'Polis' and 'Idia' in Periclean Athens: The Relation Between Public Service and Private Activities," *The American Historical Review,* XLV (1940), 269-78.

4. Josiah Strong, *The 20th Century City* (New York: Baker and Taylor, 1898), 181.
5. Lewis Mumford, *The Culture of Cities* (New York: Harcourt, Brace, 1938), 288-91.
6. Margie Stamberg, "Mailer: People's Hero He's Not," *The Guardian,* June 7, 1969.
7. Oswald Spengler, *The Decline of the West: Perspectives on World History,* trans. C. Atkinson (New York: Knopf, 1927).
8. V. C. Wynne-Edwards, *Animal Dispersion in Relation to Social Behavior* (New York: Hafner Publishing Co., 1962), 530-56.
9. Georg Simmel, "The Metropolis and Mental Life" in *Reader in Urban Sociology,* (eds.) Paul K. Hatt and Albert J. Reiss, Jr. (Glencoe, Ill.: The Free Press, 1951), 563-74; quote on 567.
10. Stamberg, *op. cit.*
11. Simmel, *op. cit.*
12. R. E. Park, "The City: Suggestions for the Investigation of Human Behavior in the Urban Environment" in *Reader in Urban Sociology,* 5. This Park article sounded the keynote of Chicago urban sociology and was first published in 1916.
13. Louis Wirth, "Urbanism as a Way of Life," in *Reader in Urban Sociology,* 32-49; esp. 40.
14. Julie Meyer, "The City and the Stranger," *American Journal of Sociology,* LVI (March 1951), 476-83; Robert C. Angell, *The Integration of American Society* (New York: McGraw-Hill, 1941), 203.
15. Kingsley Davis, *Human Society* (New York: Macmillan, 1949), 329-36.
16. Ruth Alihan, *Social Ecology* (New York: Columbia University Press, 1938).
17. Walter Firey, *Land Use in Central Boston* (Cambridge: Harvard University Press, 1947), 290-2, 323-40, *et passim.* "Value systems underlie all ecologically significant phenomena," says Sidney Willhelm, *Urban Zoning and Land Use Theory* (Glencoe, Ill.: The Free Press, 1961), 216.
18. Elwin H. Powell, The City and Communal Life: A Re-examination of Urban Sociological Theory (Unpublished Doctoral Dissertation, Tulane University, 1956) is an attempt at a comparative study of the medieval and modern city. For the basic idea behind this study and the general critique of the demographic-ecological school of urban sociology, I am deeply indebted to William L. Kolb.
19. Don Martindale, "Prefatory Remarks: The Theory of the City" to

Max Weber's *The City*, trans. and ed., Don Martindale and Gertrud Neuwirth (New York: Collier Books, 1958), 9-60, 31.

20. F. J. Teggart, *The Theory and Processes of History.* (Berkeley: University of California Press, 1941).

21. Gideon Sjoberg, *The Pre-Industrial City* (Glencoe, Ill.: The Free Press, 1960); Horace Miner, *The Primitive City of Timbuctoo* (Princeton: Princeton University Press, 1953).

22. Howard Becker, "Culture Case Study and Greek History," *American Sociological Review,* 23 (Oct. 1958), 489-504.

Chapter 6

1. Lewis Mumford, *Culture of Cities* (New York: Harcourt, Brace, 1938), 185.

2. For the urban impact on forms of thought, see Nicholas Spykman, "The Social Philosophy of the City," *The Urban Community,* ed. E. W. Burgess (Chicago: University of Chicago Press, 1926).

3. R. E. Park, *Human Communities* (Glencoe, Ill.: The Free Press, 1952), 91-95, *et passim.*; "Human Migration and the Marginal Man," in *Personality and the Social Group,* ed. E. W. Burgess (Chicago: University of Chicago Press, 1926), 57-66. For an astute analysis of Park's position, see William L. Kolb, "The Structure and Function of Cities," *Economic Development and Cultural Change,* III (1954), 30-50.

4. Ellicott Evans, "Reminiscences of Joseph Ellicott, *"Publications of the Buffalo Historical Society* (hereafter abbreviated *PBHS*), 11 (1880), 180-98.

5. George E. Probst (ed.), *The Happy Republic: A Reader in Tocqueville's America* (New York: Harper Torchbooks, 1962). The text from Tocqueville: "This people is one of the happiest in the world."

6. Harriet Martineau, *Retrospect of Western Travel* (New York: Harper & Bros., 1942), 91. (First edition 1838).

7. Capt. Marryat, *Diary in America, With Remarks on Its Institutions* (London: Longmans, Orme, Brown, Green and Longmans, 1839), 166-7.

8. *Ibid.,* 208.

9. Guy Salisbury, "The Speculative Craze of 1836," *PBHS,* IV (1896), 317-37. An address given in 1863.

10. Samuel M. Welch, *Recollections of Buffalo During the Decade 1830-40* (Buffalo: Peter Paul, 1891), 30.

11. Martha Fitch Poole, "The Social Life of Buffalo in the 1830s and

40s," *PBHS,* XVII, (1913), 67-90. Mrs. Poole lived in Buffalo through the 1830's and 1840's, wrote this paper in the 1860's, a masterful sociological analysis by a woman who had never heard of sociology.

12. *The Journal of Mary Peacock: Life a Century Ago as Seen in Buffalo and Chautauqua County by a Seventeen Year Old Girl* (Buffalo: Privately Printed, 1938).

13. See Carl Bridenbaugh, *The Colonial Carftsman* (New York: New York University Press, 1950), 65-124, for a similar situation in an earlier period.

14. John T. Horton, *History of Northwestern New York* (New York: Lewis Historical Publishing Co., 1947), 80-83. This remarkable book is an untapped mine of sociological data and has a significance far beyond the sphere of local history.

15. *Proceedings of the Board of Supervisors of Erie County* (Buffalo: C. E. Young, 1852), 10.

16. W. H. Glover and Frank W. Copley, "Spaulding as Mayor of Buffalo," *Niagara Frontier,* 7 (Spring 1960), 3-10, for a picture of the 1850's.

17. Poole, *op. cit.* 493.

18. Data from *The Mayor's Annual Message to the City Council: 1879.*

19. *Buffalo Express,* January 17; August 1, 1877.

20. Arthur Schlesinger, *The Rise of the City, 1878-98* (New York: Macmillan, 1933), 119. The author also notes a 50 per cent rise in the number of prison inmates from 1880 to 1890 and a growth in the murder rate from 24.7 (1880) to 68.5 (1890) to 107.2 (1898) per million of the population while the murder rate was declining in European countries such as Germany and England . . . Fundamental blame was attached to unhealthy urban growth. Essentially, Buffalo follows the national pattern.

21. *History of the United Trades and Labor Council of Erie County* (Buffalo: 1897), 505; see Richard Hofsteader, *The Age of Reform* (New York: Knopf, 1955), 62-70.

22. Mable Dodge Luhan, *Intimate Memories: Background* (New York: Harcourt, Brace, 1933), 3.

23. *Buffalo Poets* (Buffalo: Privately Printed, 1893).

24. *David Gray, Life, Letters, Poems,* ed. J. N. Larned (Buffalo: Courier Co., 1888), 93.

25. James Fraser Gluck, "David Gray: Some Reflections on His Work and Life (A Memorial)," *PBHS* (1889).

26. Luhan, *op. cit.* 153.
27. *Memorial of the City and County Hall Opening Ceremonies* (Buffalo: Courier Company, 1876), 137.
28. *The Mayor's Annual Message to the City Council:* 1875.
29. *Ibid.* 1882.
30. *Ibid.* 1895.
31. *Proceedings of the Common Council,* 1908 (Buffalo: Enquirer Press, 1909), 3-5, 23-4, indicates there were strong pressures for municipal ownership of gas, light, and street car companies as well as unsuccessful efforts to break the grip of the railroads, which had paralyzed harbor development for over forty years.
32. By the 1930's two-thirds of the work force was employed by outside controlled industry and only one-half of the downtown retail business was locally owned. Lewis Froman, *The Ownership and Control of Buffalo Business* (Buffalo: Whitney Graham, 1942), 44.
33. *Buffalo Express,* March 26, 1906; March 2, 1909.
34. Robert J. Donovan, *The Assassins* (New York: Harper, 1955), 82-107, points out that Leon Czologosz, McKinley's assassin, was not a member of any anarchist organization but a schizoid personality with the delusion he was an anarchist. The best account of the event and times is Emma Goldman's *Living My Life* (New York: Knopf, 1931). See Sidney Fine, "Anarchism and the Assassination of McKinley *American Historical Review,* LX (1955), 777-99.
35. Quoted in Horton, *History of Northwestern New York,* 256.
36. *Ibid.* 293.
37. Rev. Laurens P. Hicock, D.D., *A Wise Self Reliance Secures Success: An Address before the Young Man's Association of the City of Buffalo* (Buffalo: Jewett, Thomas, 1848).
38. George A. Dunlap, *The City in the American Novel* (Philadelphia: University of Pennsylvania, 1934), 11-41. See especially the analysis of the "economic chance world" in the novels of William Dean Howells.
39. Lewis Mumford, *City Development: Studies in Disintegration and Renewal* (New York: Harcourt, Brace, 1945), 14.
40. *United Trades and Labor Council of Erie County: Official Program and Journal* (Buffalo: William Grazer, 1913), 3.
41. Lincoln Steffens, *Shame of the Cities* (New York: Sagamore Press, 1957), 40.
42. For a savage account of Buffalo in the 1930's see Wyndham Lewis, *America I Presume* (New York: Howell Soskin, 1940), 107.

43. The most recent instance was in 1954, when a 1000-acre farm designated for park use was sold to Republic Steel. Thesis Alice Grailcourt, *The Buffalo Common Council at Work* (Buffalo: Unpublished M.A., University of Buffalo, 1956).

Chapter 7

1. Stanley Taylor, *Conceptions of Institutions and the Theory of Knowledge* (New York: Bookman Associates, 1956).
2. C. Wright Mills, *The Power Elite* (New York: Oxford University Press, 1959), 3-29.
3. M. Rostovtzeff, *The Social and Economic History of the Roman Empire* (Oxford: Clarendon Press, 1957), Vol. I., 495-7 is a classic interpretation of this transition from a consensual to an anomic-coercive order. See also, J. Huizinga, *The Waning of the Middle Ages* (New York: Doubleday Anchor Books, 1954); and P. A. Sorokin, *Social and Cultural Dynamics* (New York: American Book Co., 1937), Vol. III, 500-506, *et passim* for massive documentation of this thesis.
4. On the consolidation of capitalist power, see Charles A. and Mary Beard, *The Rise of American Civilization: The Industrial Era* (New York: Macmillan, 1927), 166-210, *et passim;* Matthew Josephson, *The Robber Barons: The Great American Capitalists, 1861-1901* (New York: Harcourt, Brace, 1934).
5. Louis Adamic, *Dynamite: The Story of Class Violence in America* (New York: Viking Press, 1931); Henry David, *The Haymarket Affair: A Study of Social Revolutionary Movements in America* (New York: Columbia University Press, 1936).
6. The first real impetus for industrial, as opposed to craft, unionism came from the use of federal troops in the railway strikes of 1877; see Robert V. Bruce, *1877: Year of Violence* (Indianapolis: Bobbs Merrill, 1959).
7. Richard Hofsteader, *The Age of Reform: From Bryan to FDR* (New York: Knopf, 1955); Walter Lippmann, *Drift and Mastery: An Attempt To Diagnose the Current Unrest* (Englewood Cliffs, N.J.: Prentice-Hall, 1961). Lippmann wrote in 1914 of the Bryan-Wilson reform ideology " . . . competitive business takes on a halo of life. . . . The pretty record of competition through the Nineteenth Century is forgotten. Suddenly all that is a glorious past which we have lost. You would think that competitive commercial-

ism was really a generous, chivalrous, high minded stage of human culture. . . . Wilson doesn't really fight the oppressions of property. He fights the evil done by large property holders to small ones."

8. "Trade Unionism is the conservative movement of our time," Frank Tannenbaum, *A Philosophy of Labor* (New York: Knopf, 1951), 3.

9. "The New Deal did not reverse the political and economic relations of the 1866-1920 era, but it did create within the political arena, as well as in the corporate world itself, competing centers of power that challenged those of the corporate directors." Mills, *op. cit.* 272.

10. For the earlier period, Elwin H. Powell, "The Evolution of the American City and the Emergence of Anomie: A Culture Case Study of Buffalo, New York, 1810-1910," *British Journal of Sociology,* XIII (June 1962), 156-68.

11. John T. Horton, *History of Northwestern New York* (New York: Lewis Historical Publishing Co., 1947), 232.

12. John J. Kager, A History of Socialism in Buffalo (Buffalo: Unpublished M.A. Thesis, Canisius College, 1951), 100. Apparently Rochester followed the same pattern, J. J. Dutko, Socialism in Rochester (Rochester: Unpublished M.A. Thesis, University of Rochester, 1954).

13. R. E. MacTeggart, A Labor History of Buffalo, 1846-1917 (Buffalo: Unpublished M.A. Thesis, Canisius College, 1940), 220.

14. *Ibid.* 222.

15. Kager, *op. cit.* 104.

16. MacTeggart, *op. cit.* 277.

17. Arthur E. Wood, "A Study of Arrests in Detroit, 1913-19," *Journal of Criminal Law and Criminology,* XXX (May 1930–Feb. 1931), 168-200.

18. Irma Dickman, A Comparative Study of Public Opinion in the United States and Buffalo During the Neutrality Years, 1914-17 (Buffalo: Unpublished M.A. Thesis, Canisius College, 1941), 136.

19. *Ibid.* 277.

20. Daniel Sweeny, *History of Buffalo and Erie County, 1914-19* (Buffalo: City of Buffalo, 1919), 21. The author was city-clerk and ex-editor of the *Buffalo Times.*

21. *Ibid.* 23.

22. *Ibid.* 27-28.

23. *Ibid.* 34.

24. H. S. Foster, "How America Became Belligerent: A Quantative

Study of War News, 1914-17," *American Journal of Sociology,* 40 (1934-5), 464-75.
25. Henry W. Hill, *Municipality of Buffalo, New York: 1720-1923,* Vol. III, (New York: Lewis Historical Publishing Co. 1923), 860-83.
26. Sweeny, *op. cit.* 56.
27. *Ibid.* 433.
28. *Ibid.* 340.
29. Robert K. Murray, *Red Scare: A Study in National Hysteria 1919-20* (Minneapolis: University of Minnesota Press, 1955), 135-52.
30. Gordon S. Watkins, "Revolutionary Communism in the United States" *American Political Science Review,* XIV (Feb. 1920), 14-34. On the split of the left-socialists to form the Communist party, Theodore Draper, *The Roots of American Communism* (New York: Viking Press, 1957), 148-64.
31. *Dau's Blue Book: Buffalo* (New York: Dau's Blue Book, 1920).
32. "Editorial," *The Nation,* 110 (Jan. 17, 1920).
33. William Preston, "The Ideology and Techniques of Repression, 1903-33" in *American Radicals,* ed. Harvey Goldberg (New York: Monthly Review Press, 1957), 239-64.
34. Eldridge F. Dowell, *A History of Criminal Syndicalism Legislation in the United States* (Baltimore: Johns Hopkins University Press, 1939).
35. See *infra,* Chapter 10.
36. S. Kirson Weinberg, *Social Problems in Our Time* (Englewood Cliffs, N.J.: Prentice-Hall, 1960), 418.
37. Ferdinand Lundberg, *America's 60 Families* (New York: Citidel Press, 1937), 100. "In 1900 there were 149 trusts of $4,000,000,000 capitalization; when the trust busting Roosevelt breezed out of the White House, there were 10,020, with $31,000,000,000 of capitalization."
38. Lewis Corey, *The Decline of American Capitalism* (New York: Covici-Friede, 1934), 35.
39. Walter Lippmann, *Drift and Mastery,* 17. On the desertion of the intellectuals see Henry F. May, *The End of American Innocence: A Study of the First Years of Our Own Time* (New York: Knopf, 1959), 302-29.
40. H. G. Peterson and Gilbert C. Fite, *Opponents of the War, 1917-18* (Madison: University of Wisconsin Press, 1957).
41. Arthur M. Schlesinger, Jr., *The Crises of the Old Order, 1919-33* (Boston: Houghton Mifflin, 1957), 39.

42. James Weinsteing, "The Socialist Party: Its Roots and Strengths, 1912-1919," *Studies on the Left,* I (Winter 1960), 5-27.

43. Jack London, *The Iron Heel* (New York: Review of Reviews, 1907) is an uncanny anticipation of the capitalist counterrevolution.

44. P. F. Bissenden, *The I. W. W.: A Study of American Syndicalism* (New York: Russell and Russell, 1956), x-xi. (First edition 1919.)

45. Murray, *Red Scare,* 269.

46. Schlesinger, *op. cit.* 44.

47. Irving Bernstein, *The Lean Years: A History of the American Worker, 1920-33* (Boston: Houghton Mifflin, 1960), observes: "In the mansion of the dominant business philosophy [of the 1920's] there was no room for trade unionism. Those shrewd managers who conceived the American Plan sold the idea that collective bargaining was worse than bad, it was un-American. The mood of the time stressed individualism; one got ahead by himself not by collective action. This notion permeated the outlook of the working class" (88). The results were noticeable in the decline of "union membership from 5,047,800 in 1920 . . . to 3,622,000 in 1923 . . . and 3,422,600 in 1929 . . . a bare 10.2% of the labor force . . . a marked drop from 19.4% in 1920" (84). Moreover, "no prior era in the history of the Supreme Court approached the twenties in the number of statutes invalidated, most of them labor laws" (242).

48. *Ibid.* 80.

49. Alan Valentine, *1913: America Between Two Worlds* (New York: Macmillan, 1962), v.

50. A. A. Berle, *Power without Property: A New Development in American Political Economy* (New York: Harcourt, Brace, 1959), 98.

51. *Ibid.* 111.

52. The New York State Lusk Committee, *Revolutionary Radicalism* (Albany: J. B. Lyon, 1920). This mammoth four-volume work devotes two volumes to the analysis of revolutionary movements and the remaining two to the presentation of constructive measures to counteract radicalism through Americanization. All four volumes are equally absurd but nevertheless revealing. The anti-radical campaign attempted to correct the thinking of the radical rather than the conditions that give rise to radicalism.

53. "Normative Reactions to Normlessness," *American Sociological Review,* 25 (Dec. 1960), 803-10.

Chapter 8

1. Clarence Jeffry, "Crime, Law and Social Structure," *Journal of Criminal Law, Criminology and Police Science* (hereafter abbreviated, *JCLCPS*), 47 (1956), 423-35.
2. A. M. Guhl, "The Social Order of Chickens," *Scientific American*, 194 (Feb. 1956), 43-46.
3. S. L. Washburn and Irven de Vore, "The Social Life of Baboons," *Primate Social Behavior*, ed. Charles Southwick (Princeton: D. Van Nostrand, 1963), 107-8.
4. A. J. Haddow, "Field Studies of the African Redtail Monkey: The Composition, Size and Behavior of Bands," *Primate Social Behavior*, 52-68; quote, 53.
5. C. R. Carpenter, "Societies of Monkeys and Apes," *Primate Social Behavior*, 24-52. On social disorganization as the cause of destructive fighting, see John P. Scott, "Hostility and Aggression in Animals," *Roots of Behavior: Genetics, Instinct and Socialization in Animals' Behavior*, ed. Eugene Bliss (New York: Harper and Brothers, 1962), 167-79; *Animal Behavior* (Chicago: University of Chicago Press, 1958), 229, *et passim*.
6. V. C. Wynne-Edwards, *Animal Dispersion in Relation to Social Behavior* (New York: Hafner Publishing Co., 1962), 142. See also, Ch. 19, "The Uses of Tradition," 449-65; Ch. 22, "Socially Induced Mortality," 530-56.
7. Emile Durkheim, *The Division of Labor in Society*, 70, defines crime as any "*act* which invokes against its author the characteristic reaction which we term punishment." But societies also officially punish deviants for their *being* as well as their action; the vagrant, defined as a person without visible means of support, can be imprisoned on grounds that he *might* commit an illegal action; see Forrest W. Lacey, "Vagrancy and Other Crimes of Personal Condition," *Harvard Law Review*, 66 (1952-3), 1203-26.
8. "The real explanation for crime . . . lies in Durkheim's [concept of] anomie," Walter Lunden, "Pioneers in Criminology—Emile Durkheim," *JCLCPS*, 49 (1958), 2-9. See Leon Radzinowicz, *Ideology and Crime* (New York: Columbia University Press, 1966), 86-100, *et passim*.
9. William I. Thomas and Florian Znaniecki, *The Polish Peasant in Europe and America* (New York: Dover, 1958), 773-4.
10. Jackson Toby, "Social Disorganization and Stake in Conformity:

Complementary Factors in the Predatory Behavior of Hoodlums," *JCLCPS*, 48 (1957), 12-17.

11. John Dollard, *Caste and Class in a Southern Town* (Garden City, N.Y.: Doubleday Anchor, 1957), 271-80, *et passim*.

12. E. P. Thompson, *The Making of the English Working Class* (New York: Vintage Books, 1966), 61.

13. George Rusche and Otto Kirchheimer, *Punishment and Social Structure* (New York: Columbia University Press, 1939), 19-20.

14. Thompson, *op. cit.* 61.

15. Julius Goebel and T. Raymond Naughton, *Law Enforcement in Colonial New York: A Study in Criminal Procedure (1664-1771)* (New York: Commonwealth Fund, 1944), 194.

16. Edwin Powers, *Crime and Punishment in Early Massachusetts 1620-1692: A Documentary History* (Boston: Beacon Press, 1966), 319.

17. Goebel and Naughton, *op. cit.* 704.

18. *Ibid.* 707.

19. Powers, *op. cit.* 388.

20. Thomas C. Cochran and William Miller, *The Age of Enterprise: A Social History of Industrial America* (New York: Harper Torchbooks, 1942), 27.

21. Carl Bridenbaugh, *Cities in Revolt: Urban Life in America 1743-1776* (New York: Knopf, 1955), 110.

22. Albert H. Hobbs, "Relationship between Criminality and Economic Conditions," *JCLCPS*, 34 (1943-4), 5-10.

23. Gustavus Myers, *History of Great American Fortunes* (New York: Modern Library, 1937), 68-69. (First edition 1907.) Gustave de Beaumont and Alexis de Tocqueville, *On the Penitentiary System in the United States and Its Application in France* (Carbondale, Ill.: Southern Illinois University Press, 1964), 41-42. (First edition 1830's.) Richard C. Wade, *The Urban Frontier: The Rise of Western Cities, 1790-1830* (Cambridge: Harvard University Press, 1959), 36-46. Paul Dolan, "The Rise of Crime in the Period of 1830-60," *JCLCPS*, 30 (1939-40), 857-64.

24. Mark S. Hubbell, *Our Police and Our City: The Official History of the Buffalo Police Department* (Buffalo: Bensler and Wesley, 1893), 60.

25. Roger Lane, *Policing the City: Boston 1822-1885* (Cambridge: Harvard University Press, 1967), 29.

26. Hubbell, *op. cit.* 63.

27. *Ibid.* 54-66.

28. Nathaniel Wilgus, "The Trial and Execution of the Three Thayers," *PBHS*, I (1879), 179-83.
29. Sidney Burr, *The Record of Crimes in the United States* (Buffalo: Sidney Burr, 1833).
30. Frank H. Severence, "A Builder of Buffalo," *PBHS*, 16 (1912), 71-103.
31. Miriam Beard, *A History of Business: From the Monopolists to the Organization Man* (Ann Arbor: The University of Michigan Press, 1963), II, 165.
32. Nineteenth-century jails were wretched places but more detention centers than torture chambers. Robert Reinders, *End of an Era: New Orleans, 1850-1860* (New Orleans: Pelican Publishing Company, 1964), 72, describes a New Orleans parish prison with 400 inmates: "Cells were seldom locked and prisoners walked about the corridors, sunned themselves on the galleries . . . conversed with friends through the fence. Prisoners were encouraged to decorate their cells with paintings which prison officials respected in their twice-weekly white washings . . . The monotony of prison life was broken occasionally by an escape or by the "edifying spectacle" of a public execution . . ."
33. Thomas L. Nichols, *Journal in Jail: Kept During a Four Months' Imprisonment for Libel in the Jail of Erie County* (Buffalo: A. Dinsmore, 1840), 220.
34. *Ibid.* 247.
35. Nichols was one of the most remarkable men ever to grace the Buffalo scene. At 23 he wrote: "I am conscious of a brilliant destiny. My life will be useful to mankind and that is my highest ambition" (*Buffalonian*, May 8, 1838). He left Buffalo for Rochester, followed the editor's trade a few years, then took an M.D.; later joined Josiah Warren's anarchist community, Modern Times, and became a fellow of the "Society of Individual Sovereigns." According to John Humprey Noyes, *History of American Socialisms* (New York: Hillary House Publishers, 1961), 93. (First edition 1870), when Nichols published his "Esoteric Anthropology" in 1853 . . . he inaugurated the system of "Free Love," or Individual Sovereignty in sexual intercourse . . . but afterwards he swung clear back to Roman Catholicism. Nichols developed a convincing theory of what would today be called psychosomatic illness, contending that 4/5 of the diseases of women were connected in some way with "derangements of the reproductive system." According to Nichols,

deprivation of exercise was also a cause of disease and he noted even in the 1850's that "gluttony kills a hundred where one dies of starvation," Thomas L. Nichols, M.D., *An Introduction to Water Cure: Founded in Nature and Adapted to the Wants of Men* (New York: Fowlers J. Wells, 1851), 12-14. Nichols went to England in 1860 to avoid involvement in the Civil War, remained to write a dozen books and end a happy life at the age of 85 calling himself a social scientist. His *Forty Years of American Life,* first published in 1864, remains today a classic on Tocquevillian America.

36. Patrick Pringle, *Hue and Cry: The Story of Henry and John Fielding and Their Bow Street Runners* (London: William Morrow, 1953), 52.

37. Lane, *op cit.* 10-12.

38. Raymond D. Fosdick, *American Police Systems* (New York: Century Company, 1920), 60.

39. Ernest J. Hopkins, *Our Lawless Police: A Study of the Unlawful Enforcement of the Law* (New York: Viking Press, 1931), 33.

40. Lane, *op. cit.* 187-8.

41. John T. Horton, *History of Northwestern New York,* 91-92.

42. Hubbell, *op. cit.* 109.

43. *Ibid.* 112.

44. Marvin A. Rapp, The Port of Buffalo: 1825-1880 (Durham, N.C.: Unpublished Ph.D. Dissertation, Duke University, 1945), 250.

45. *Annual Report of the Buffalo Police Department* (1876), 82.

46. See Otto Pollak, *The Criminality of Women* (Philadelphia: University of Pennsylvania Press, 1950).

47. Erik Eklund, "Criminal Statistics: The Volume of Crime," *JCLC,* 32 (1942), 540-47. That the pattern obtains throughout the United States and in cities other than Buffalo is shown by the following studies: Betty B. Rosenbaum, "The Relationship Between War and Crime," *JCLCPS,* 30 (1939-40); Marshall B. Clinard, The Process of Urbanization and Criminal Behavior (Chicago: Unpublished Doctoral Dissertation, 1938); Ellen E. Guillot, *Social Factors in Crime as Explained by American Writers of the Civil War and Post Civil War Period* (Philadelphia: University of Pennsylvania Press, 1943). Charles A. Ellwood, "Has Crime Increased in the United States Since 1880?" *JCLC,* I (1910), 378-85. Sam Bass Warner, *Crime and Criminal Statistics in Boston* (Cambridge: Harvard University Press, 1934), 136. Arthur E. Wood, "A Study of Arrests in Detroit, 1913-19," *JCLC,* 30 (1930-31), 168-200; Edith Abbott,

"Crime and War," *JCLC* (1918), 32-45; "Recent Statistics Relating to Crime in Chicago," *JCLC* (1922), 329-58, notes that arrests in Chicago increased from 81,269 in 1910 to 137,910 in 1917 and then dropped to 93,453 in 1920. William D. Miller, *Memphis During the Progressive Era, 1900-17* (Madison: American History Research Center, 1957) notes that murder cases rose from 43 in 1906 to 105 in 1910 to 124 and 134 for 1915 and 1916 respectively; the suicide rate rose from 6.4 per 100,000 in 1902 to 22.8 in 1910. Allegedly, Memphis had the highest suicide and homicide rate in the country during the progressive period. Harry Willbach, "Trend of Crime in New York City," *JCLC,* 29 (1938), 62-75; "Trend of Crime in Chicago," *JCLC,* 31 (1940-41), 720-27. George B. Vold, "The Amount and Nature of Crime," in William F. Ogburn (ed.), *Social Changes During the Depression and Recovery* (Chicago: University of Chicago Press, 1934), 801-10.

48. Dorothy S. Thomas, *Social Aspects of the Business Cycle* (London: George Routledge and Sons, 1925), 137.

49. Austin L. Porterfield, "A Decade of Serious Crime in the United States: Some Trends and Hypotheses," *American Sociological Review,* 13 (1948), 44-54.

50. H. Willbach, "Crime in New York City as Affected by the War," *JCLC,* XXXIV (1943-4), 371-6.

51. Lane, *op. cit.* 118-19.

52. Ferdinand Lundberg, *America's 60 Families* (New York: Citadel Press, 1937), 53.

53. Gustavus Myers, *History of Great American Fortunes* (New York: Modern Library, 1937), 549-50. Myers' work, published in 1907 and later updated, casts doubt on the idea that the Protestant ethic was the motive of the spirit of capitalism. The Robber Barons of the post-Civil War world represent an "adventurer's capitalism"; had they been saddled with the Protestant ethic, American capitalism would have never gotten off the ground.

54. *Ibid.* 444.

55. Miriam Beard, *A History of Business: From the Monopolists to the Organization Man,* II, 171-2.

56. Herbert Asbury, *The Gangs of New York: An Informal History of the Underworld* (New York: Macmillan, 1928), 174. Chicago followed a similar course, see Herbert Asbury, *Gem of the Prairie: An Informal History of the Chicago Underworld* (New York: Knopf, 1940).

57. Edward Crapsey, *The Nether Side of New York, Or Vice, Crime, and Poverty of a Great Metropolis* (New York: Sheldon, 1872). For other accounts of the time, Charles Brace, *The Dangerous Classes of New York* (New York: Wynkop Hallenbeck, 1872); Arthur Kember, *Mysteries and Miseries of the Great Metropolis* (New York: D. Appleton, 1874).
58. Quoted by Horton, *op. cit.* 238. See Allan Nevins, *Grover Cleveland: A Study in Courage* (New York: Dodd, Mead, 1934), 57-63, for a portrait of Buffalo.
59. Charles E. Knowles, compiler, *Edward H. Hutchinson* (Buffalo: Privately Printed, 1932), 98-99.
60. H. Willbach, "Trend of Crime in Chicago," *JCLC*, 31 (1941) 62-75.
61. *The Statistical History of the United States from Colonial Times to the Present* (Stamford, Conn.: Fairfield Publishers, 1960), 723.
62. President's Report, *The Challenge of Crime in a Free Society* (Washington, D.C.: U.S. Government Printing Office, 1967), 91.
63. Edward Engberg, *The Spy in the Corporate Structure and the Right to Privacy* (Cleveland: World Publishing Company, 1967), 31-32.
64. Edwin H. Sutherland, *Principles of Criminology* (Philadelphia: J. B. Lippincott, 1955), 330. This is the Fifth Edition of the Sutherland work, as revised by Donald R. Cressey.
65. Alexis de Tocqueville, *Democracy in America,* trans. Henry Reeve. (New York: Vintage Books, 1954), 300.
66. Martha Derthick, "Militia Lobby in the Missile Age—The Politics of the National Guard" in *Changing Patterns of Military Politics,* ed. S. P. Huntington (Glencoe: The Free Press, 1962), 190-234.
67. Herbert Spencer, "On Militant and Industrial Types of Society" in his *Principles of Sociology* (New York: D. Appleton, 1895), II, 568-642. (First published 1876); recently reprinted in C. Wright Mills, *Images of Man* (New York: George Braziller, 1962).

Chapter 9

1. B. Malinowski, "War—Past, Present and Future" in *War as a Social Institution,* eds. J. D. Clarkson and T. C. Cochran (New York: Columbia University Press, 1941).
2. L. T. Hobhouse, G. C. Wheeler, and Mr. Ginsberg, *The Material Culture and Social Institutions of the Simpler Peoples: An Essay in Correlation* (London: Chapman and Hall, 1930), 228-89.

3. J. B. Scott, *Animal Behavior* (Chicago: University of Chicago Press, 1958), 229.

4. Robert Ardrey, *African Genesis: A Personal Investigation into the Animal Origins and Nature of Man* (New York: Atheneum, 1962), 29.

5. Kenneth P. Oakley, "On Man's Use of Fire, with Comments on Tool Making and Hunting" in Sherwood L. Washburn ed., *Social Life of Early Man* (Chicago: Aldine Publishing Co., 1964), 189.

6. Raymond Dart, "The Predatory Implemental Technique of Australopithecus," *American Journal of Physical Anthropology*, 7 (1949), 1-38.

7. Luis Pericot, "The Social Life of Spanish Paleolithic Hunters as Shown by Levantine Art," in *Social Life of Early Man*, 194-213; quote 207-8.

8. R. F. Fortune, "Arapesh Warfare," *American Anthropologist*, 41 (1939), 22-41.

9. W. W. Newcomb, Jr., "A Re-examination of the Causes of Plains Warfare," *American Anthropologist*, 52 (1950), 317-30.

10. Robert F. Murphy, "Intergroup Hostility and Social Cohesion," *American Anthropologist*, 59 (1957), 1018-35.

11. Maurice Davie, *The Evolution of War: A Study of Its Role in Early Societies* (New Haven: Yale University Press, 1929), 37-38.

12. Other things being equal, war-cultures generate more suicide than peace-cultures. Ruth Benedict, in *Patterns of Culture* (New York: Mentor Books, 1934), 52, mentions that the "Apollonian" Zuñi Indians cannot even conceive of the idea of suicide—nor do they have a war-system. But the "Dionysian" Plains Indians, for whom war is a central activity, "could well understand the violent gesture of flinging away one's life" in suicide. Suicide in the ancient world was intimately connected with war, and the suicide traditions of Western society today probably date back to the tribal periods of medieval Europe, the sixth and tenth centuries A.D. The Goths, Visigoths, and Celts had a war-derived traditions of altruistic suicide. In nineteenth- and twentieth-century Europe the seemingly war-like Germanic peoples have had higher suicide rates than the seemingly peaceful English and Italians.

13. Leon J. Saul, *The Hostile Mind: The Sources and Consequences of Rage and Hate* (New York: Random House, 1956).

14. See D. O. Hebb and W. R. Thompson, "The Special Significance of Animal Studies," *Handbook of Social Psychology*, ed. Gardner Lind-

zey (Reading, Mass.; Addison-Wesley Publishing Co., 1954), 532-61, which confirms most of what Peter Kropotkin, *Mutual Aid: A Factor in Evolution* (Boston: Beacon Press, 1952), wrote in the 1880's. For the neo-Darwinianism of the 1960's, Konrad Lorenz, *On Aggression* (New York: Harcourt, Brace and World, 1963).

15. Davie, *op cit.*
16. Ralph Linton, *The Study of Man* (New York: D. Appleton-Century, 1936), 240-44.
17. *Ibid.* 243
18. *Ibid.* 244.
19. *Ibid.* 250.
20. Max Weber, "Politics as Vocation" in *Essays of Max Weber,* trans. and ed. Hans Gerth and C. Wright Mills (London: Routledge and Kegan Paul, 1948), 78.
21. R. E. Park, "The Social Functions of War," *American Journal of Sociology,* 46 (1940-41), 551-70.
22. Bertrand de Louvenal, *Power: The Natural History of Its Growth* (London: Hutchinson and Co., 1945).
23. Robert Nisbet, *The Quest for Community* (New York: Oxford University Press, 1953), 98-121.
24. Gaetano Mosca, *The Ruling Class,* trans. Hannah D. Kahn (New York: McGraw-Hill, 1939).
25. Harold D. Lasswell, *National Security and Individual Freedom* (New York: McGraw-Hill, 1950).
26. P. A. Sorokin, *Social and Cultural Dynamics: Fluctuation of Social Relationships, War and Revolution* (New York: American Book Co., 1937), 261.
27. Georges Lefebvre, "A Series of Class Revolts" in F. Kafker and J. Laux, eds., *The French Revolution: Conflicting Interpretations* (New York: Random House, 1968), 6.
28. Karl Liebknecht, *Militarism* (New York: B. W. Huebsch, 1917), 117. (First edition 1906.)

Chapter 10

1. Thorstein Veblen, *The Nature of the Peace and the Terms of Its Perpetuation* (New York: Viking Press, 1949), 21.
2. John U. Nef, *War and Human Progress: An Essay on the Rise of Industrial Civilization* (Cambridge: Harvard University Press, 1952), 369.

3. R. M. MacIver, "War and Civilization," *International Journal of Ethics* XX (1912), 127-45.
4. Michael Howard, *The Franco-Prussian War: The German Invasion of France, 1870-71* (New York: Macmillan, 1962), 8-9.
5. Quoted by Walter Goerlitz, *The History of the German General Staff: 1657-1945*, trans. Brian Battershaw (New York: Praeger, 1953), 66.
6. Frederick B. Artz, *Reaction and Revolution: 1814-1832* (New York: Harper 1934), 49.
7. Karl Marx, *The Eighteenth Brumaire of Louis Bonaparte*, ed. Samuel Beer (New York: Appleton-Century-Crofts, 1955), 47-52.
8. Howard C. Payne, *The Police State of Louis Napoleon Bonaparte, 1851-1860* (Seattle: University of Washington Press, 1966), 28. See Leo Loubere, *Louis Blanc: His Life and His Contribution to French Jacobin-Socialism* (Evanston, Ill.: Northwestern University Press, 1961), for a picture of the radicalism of the period.
9. Quoted by Priscilla Robertson, *Revolutions of 1848* (Princeton, N.J.: Princeton University Press, 1952), 193.
10. *Ibid.*, 413-15.
11. Jacob Burckhardt, *Force and Freedom: An Interpretation of History* (New York: Meridian Books, 1955).
12. Gordon A. Craig, *The Politics of the Prussian Army, 1640-1945* (New York: Oxford University Press, 1964), 91.
13. *Ibid.* 92.
14. *Ibid.* 94.
15. *Ibid.* 130.
16. *Ibid.* 179.
17. *Ibid.* 217.
18. Heinrich von Treitschke, *Politics*, ed. Hans Kohn (New York: Harcourt, Brace and World, 1963), 241-5.
19. Thorstein Veblen, *Imperial Germany and the Industrial Revolution* (New York: Viking Press, 1954), 81.
20. *Ibid.* 82.
21. *Ibid.* 247.
22. Gunther Roth, *The Social Democrats in Imperial Germany* (New York: Bedminster Press, 1963).
23. Alistair Horne, *The Fall of Paris: The Siege and the Commune 1870-71* (New York: St. Martin's Press, 1965), 15.
24. Pitirim A. Sorokin, *Social and Cultural Dynamics Vol. III: Fluctuation of Social Relationships, War and Revolution* (New York: Bedminster Press, 1962), 470-71.

25. William E. Livezey, *Mahan on Sea Power* (Norman: University of Oklahoma Press, 1947), 265-6.
26. Lewis F. Richardson, *Arms and Insecurity: A Mathematical Study of the Causes and Origins of War*, eds. Nicolas Rashevsky and Ernesto Trucco (Chicago: Quadrangle Books, 1960).
27. Francis W. Hirst, *Armaments: The Race and the Crisis* (London: Cobden-Sanderson, 1937), 19.
28. Munroe Smith, *Militarism and Statecraft* (New York: G. P. Putnam's Sons, 1918), 262.
29. Craig, *op. cit.* 291.
30. Caroline E. Playne, *The Neuroses of the Nations* (New York: Thomas Seltzer 1925), 455.
31. Edmund Taylor, *The Fall of the Dynasties: The Collapse of the Old Order, 1905-1922* (Garden City, N.Y.: Doubleday, 1963), 216.
32. *Ibid.* 206.
33. Barbara Tuchman, *Guns of August* (New York: Dell 1962), 91.
24. Taylor, *op. cit.* 206.
35. *Ibid.* 242-3.
36. *Ibid.*
37. On the war plan as a cause of war, see Tuchman, *op. cit.*
38. Edward Crankshaw, *The Fall of the House of Habsburg* (New York: Viking Press, 1963), 405-6.
39. Fritz Fischer, *German War Aims in the First World War* (New York: W. W. Norton, 1967), 92.
40. Craig, *op. cit.* 312.
41. Hans Peter Hanssen, *Diary of a Dying Empire*, trans. O. Winther (Bloomington: Indiana University Press, 1955), 149.
42. Craig, *op. cit.* 305.
43. William S. Woods, *Colossal Blunders of the War* (New York: Macmillan, 1930), 78.
44. Leon Wolff, *In Flanders Fields: The 1917 Campaign* (New York: Ballantine Books, 1958), 26.
45. *Ibid.* 236.
46. Karl Kautsky, *The Guilt of William Hohenzollern* (London: Skeffington and Sons, 1919), 255.
47. *Ibid.* 236.
48. Michael T. Florinsky, *The End of the Russian Empire* (New York: Collier Books, 1961) 222-3.
49. *Ibid.*
50. Richard Watt, *Dare Call It Treason* (New York: Simon and Schuster, 1963), 301.

51. B. H. Liddell-Hart, *The War in Outline: 1914-1918* (New York: Award Books, 1965), 206.

52. Goerlitz, *op. cit.* 193; for on-the-scene accounts of a neutral observer see Hanssen, *op. cit.* Hanssen was a Danish member of the German Reichstag.

53. Lawrence Wilson, *The Incredible Kaiser: A Portrait of William II* (New York: A. S. Barnes, 1963), 169.

54. Hanson Baldwin, *World War I: An Outline History* (New York: Grove Press, 1962), 160.

55. Winston Churchill as quoted by J. F. C. Fuller, *The Conduct of War, 1789-1961 A Study of the Impact of the French, Industrial and Russian Revolutions on War and Its Conduct* (New York: Minerva Press, 1961), 42.

Chapter 11

1. Michael Howard, *The Franco-Prussian War: The German Invasion of France 1870-71* (New York: Macmillan, 1962), 456.

2. Jerome Davis, *Peace, War and You* (New York: Henry Schuman, 1952), 20.

3. Ivan S. Block, *The Future of War: In Its Technical, Economic and Political Relations,* trans. R. C. Long (New York: Doubleday, McClure, 1899), xi.

4. Karl Menninger, *Man Against Himself* (New York: Harcourt, Brace, 1938), 464-5.

5. Hannah Arendt, "Imperialism: Road to Suicide. The Political Origins and Use of Racism," *Commentary,* I (February 1945-46), 27-35.

6. B. H. Liddel-Hart, *Deterrence or Defense: A Fresh Look at the West's Military Position* (New York: Frederick A. Prager, 1960), v.

7. Austin Porterfield, "Traffic Fatalities, Suicide and Homicide," *American Sociological Review,* 25 (1960), 897-901 found that areas with a high suicide-homicide incidence also had high rates of fatal automobile accidents, suggesting a common cause for these diverse "disorders."

8. Arnold Toynbee, *War and Civilization* (New York: Oxford University Press, 1950), 1.

9. Emile Durkheim, *Suicide,* 217-18; 228.

10. Helmuth Englebrecht, *Revolt Against War* (New York: Dodd, Mead, 1937), 60.

11. Block, *op. cit.* 33-34.

12. *Ibid.* 353 (italics mine).

13. George Stratton, "The Docility of the Fighter," *International Journal of Ethics,* 26 (April 1916), 368-77.

14. Gilbert Murray, *The Ordeal of This Generation* (New York: Harper, 1929, 11 (italics mine).

15. John U. Nef, *War and Human Progress: An Essay on The Rise of Industrial Civilization* (Cambridge: Harvard University Press, 1950), 401-9.

16. Quoted by Walter Goerlitz, *The History of the German General Staff, 1657-1945,* trans. E. Buttershaw (New York: Frederick A. Praeger, 1953), 100.

17. Heinrich von Treitschke, *Politics,* ed. Hans Kohn (New York: Harcourt, Brace, 1916), 241-5.

18. "The Soldiers Faith" in *The Mind and Faith of Justice Holmes: His Speeches, Essays, Letters and Judicial Opinions,* ed. Max Lerner (New York: Modern Library, 1943), 18-25; quote 20.

19. See Robert Adams, *Nil: Episodes in the Literary Conquest of the Void During the Nineteenth Century* (New York: Oxford University Press, 1966), 237.

20. Irving L. Horowitz, *Radicalism and the Revolt Against Reason: The Social Theories of Georges Sorel* (London: Routledge and Kegan Paul, 1961), 118.

21. Saul K. Padover, "Patterns of Assassination," *Public Opinion Quarterly,* 7 (Winter 1943), 680-93.

22. See Chapter IX *Infra.* Thorstein Sellin, "Is Murder Increasing in Europe?" *The Annals* (1926), 29-33.

23. Veli Verko, *Homicides and Suicides in Finland and Their Dependence on National Character* (Copenhagen: G. E. C. Gads, 1951), contains statistics on Nineteenth and Twentieth Century Europe. For Britain, see Douglas Swinscow, "Some Suicide Statistics, *British Medical Journal* (Jan. 23, 1951), 1417-23.

24. Gerhard Fuellkrug, *Der Selbsmord in der Kriegs und Nachkriegszeit* (Schwerin-in-Mecklenberg: Verlag Friedrich Bahn, 1927), 22.

25. Theodor Reik, *Masochism in Modern Man* trans. M. Beigel and G. M. Kurth (New York: Grove Press, 1962), 7. First published 1941.

26. From Weber's "Lebensbild" as quoted by Gerhard Masur, *Prophets of Yesterday: Studies in European Culture 1890-1914* (New York: Macmillan, 1961), 199.

27. Quoted by Henry R. Fedden, *Suicide: A Social and Historical Study* (London: Peter Davies, 1938), 294.

28. Quincy Wright, *A Study of War* (Chicago: University of Chicago Press, 1965), 208. First published 1942.

29. Oswald Spengler, *Decline of the West: Perspectives on World History,* trans. C. Atkinson (New York: Knopf, 1927), Vol. II, 103-4.

30. Edward Crankshaw, *The Fall of the House of Habsburg,* 401.

31. A. J. P. Taylor, *From Napoleon to Lenin: Historical Essays* (New York: Harper Torchbooks, 1952), 157.

32. Quoted by John R. Staude, *Max Scheler, 1874-1928: An Intellectual Portrait* (New York: The Free Press, 1967), 67.

33. Masur, *op. cit.* 198.

34. Quoted by Arthur Marwick, *The Deluge: British Society and the First World War* (Boston: Little, Brown, 1965), 47.

35. Crankshaw, *op. cit.* 401.

36. Caroline Playne, *The Neuroses of the Nations* (New York: Thomas Seltzer, 1925), 463.

37. *War, Mutiny and Revolution in the German Navy: The World War I Diary of Seamen Richard Stumpf,* ed. and trans. Daniel Horn (New Brunswick, N.J.: Rutgers University Press, 1967), 23 (italics mine).

38. Quoted by Marwick, *op. cit.* 49.

39. Reginald Pound, *The Lost Generation of 1914* (New York: Coward-McCann, 1964), 25-28.

40. Richard M. Watt, *Dare Call it Treason* (New York: Simon and Schuster, 1963), 55.

41. Stefan Zweig, *The World of Yesterday: An Autobiography* (New York: Viking Press, 1943), 223-4.

42. Leon Trotsky, *My Life: An Attempt at an Autobiography* (New York: Scribner, 1930), 226-7.

43. *Ibid.* 233.

44. Isaac Deutscher, *The Prophet Armed: Trotsky: 1879-1921* (New York: Vintage Books, 1965), 380. (First publisher.)

45. Bertrand Russell, "Autobiography, 1914-18," *Harpers,* 236 (Jan. 1968), 32-33.

46. Fredrich Nietzsche, *The Will to Power: An Attempted Transvaluation of All Values,* trans. Anthony M. Ludovici (New York: Russell and Russell, 1964), 54.

47. *Ibid.* 42-43.

48. *Ibid.* 51-52.

49. Quoted by Nef, *op. cit.* 409.

50. Quoted by Samuel J. Warner, *The Urge to Mass Destruction* (New York: Grune and Stratton, 1957), 112.

51. Conrad Knickerbacker, "One Night on a Kansas Farm," *New York Times Book Review*, Jan. 16, 1966, 1.
52. René Albrecht-Carrie, *The Meaning of the First World War* (Englewood Cliffs, N.J.: Prentice-Hall, Inc. 1965), 99.
53. By John MacCrae, "In Flanders Fields," as quoted by Leon Wolff, *In Flanders Fields: The 1917 Campaign* (New York: Ballantine Books, 1958), 1.
54. Erich M. Remarque, *All Quiet on the Western Front* (New York: E. P. Dutton, 1929).

Chapter 12

1. Raymond Aron, *The Century of Total War* (Boston: Beacon Press, 1955), 31.
2. Leo Alexander, "Destructive and Self-Destructive Trends in Criminalized Society: A Study of Totalitarianism," *Journal of Criminal Law and Criminology*, 39 (Jan.-Feb. 1949), 553-64.
3. Gregor Ziemer, *Education for Death: The Making of the Nazi* (New York: Oxford University Press, 1941), 121.
4. Ziemer, *op. cit.* 167.
5. Peter Nathan, *The Psychology of Fascism* (London: Faber and Faber, 1943), 55.
6. Ziemer *op. cit.* 28.
7. Edward Crankshaw, *Gestapo: Instrument of Tyranny* (New York: The Viking Press, 1956), 16-19.
8. *Ibid.* 27.
9. Elie A. Cohen, *Human Behavior in the Concentration Camp,* trans, M. Braaksma (New York: Grosset and Dunlap, 1953), 266.
10. Quoted Konrad Heiden, *Der Fuehrer: Hitler's Rise to Power,* trans. R. Manheim (Boston: Houghton Mifflin, 1944), 312.
11. Quoted by H. R. Trevor-Roper, "The Mind of Adolf Hitler" in *Hitler's Secret Conversations, 1941-1944* (New York: Farrar, Strauss and Young, 1953), xix.
12. William Jenks, *Vienna and the Young Hitler* (New York: Columbia University Press, 1960), 219.
13. Adolf Hitler, *Mein Kampf,* trans. R. Manheim (Boston: Houghton Mifflin, 1943), 23. (First edition 1925).
14. Jenks, *op. cit.* 38-39.
15. Hitler, *op. cit.* 28.
16. *Ibid.* 59-64.

17. *Hitler's Secret Conversations,* 12.

18. For details, see Eliot B. Wheaton, *Prelude to Calamity: The Nazi Revolution, 1933-35* (Garden City, N.Y.: Doubleday, 1968), 42-43; Heiden, *op. cit.* 77-86.

19. Heiden, *op. cit.* 81-82.

20. *Ibid.* 82. See Robert Jay Lifton, "On Death and Death Symbolism: The Hiroshima Disaster," *Psychiatry* (1965), 191-210.

21. James A. M. Weiss, "Attempted Suicide as a Gamble with Death," *Psychiatry,* XX (1957), 17-25.

22. *Mein Kampf,* 206.

23. Otto D. Tolischus, *They Wanted War* (New York: Reynal and Hitchcock, 1940).

24. Barry Pitt, *1918: The Last Act* (New York: Ballantine Books, 1962), 290-91.

25. *Mein Kampf,* 224.

26. Fritz Stern, *The Politics of Cultural Despair: A Study in the Germanic Ideology* (Garden City, N.Y.: Doubleday Anchor Books, 1965), 324-35, *et passim.*

27. Frederick L. Schuman, *The Nazi Dictatorship: A Study in Social Pathology and the Politics of Fascism* (New York: Knopf, 1935), 290.

28. William Shirer, *The Rise and Fall of the Third Reich: A History of Nazi Germany* (New York: Crest Book, 1959), 69-70.

29. Theodore Abel, *The Nazi Movement: Why Hitler Came to Power* (New York: Atherton Press, 1966), 142-6, *et passim.* (First published 1938.)

30. Werner T. Angress, *Stillborn Revolution: The Communist Bid for Power in Germany, 1921-1923* (Princeton: Princeton University Press, 1963) 475-8 *et passim.* See Richard A. Comfort, *Revolutionary Hamburg: Labor Politics in the Early Wiemer Republic* (Stanford, Cal.: Stanford University Press, 1966), 170-71.

31. Heiden, *op. cit.* 351-2.

32. Abel, *op. cit.* 69-70.

33. *Ibid.* 180.

34. Hans B. Gisevius, *To the Bitter End* (Boston: Houghton Mifflin, 1947), 103.

35. Eugen Kogon, *The Theory and Practice of Hell: The German Concentration Camps and the System Behind Them,* trans. Heinz Norden (New York: Farrar, Strauss, 1949), 33.

36. Gisevius, *op. cit.* 121-2.

37. Wheaton, *Prelude to Calamity*, 447, *et passim*.
38. Shirer, *op. cit.* 272.
39. Crankshaw, *Gestapo*, 16-19.
40. William S. Allen, *The Nazi Seizure of Power: The Experience of a Single German Town, 1930-35* (Chicago: Quadrangle Books, 1965), 179; 203-26.
41. Felix Kersten, *The Kersten Memoirs, 1940-45,* trans. C. Fitzgibbon and J. Oliver (London: Hutchinson, 1956), 294-8.
42. Kogon, *op. cit.* 31-2.
43. Robert J. O'Neill, *The German Army and the Nazi Party, 1933-39* (London: Cassell, 1966), 99-100, *et passim*.
44. Quoted by D. F. Fleming, *The Origins of the Cold War* (Garden City, N.Y.: Doubleday, 1961), Col. I, 96.
45. Allen, *op. cit.* 255.
46. Shirer, *op. cit.* 705-9.
47. *Ibid.* 1114.
48. *Ibid.* 1118.
49. *Ibid.* 1119-20.
50. Alexander Dallin, *German Rule in Russia, 1941-45: A Study in Occupation Politics* (London: Macmillan, 1957), 662.
51. *Ibid.* 669.
52. Shirer, *op cit.* 1218.
53. H. R. Trevor-Roper, *The Last Days of Hitler* (New York: Berkeley Publishing Corporation, 1947), 69.
54. Ibid. 72-73.
55. Terrence Prittie, *Germans Against Hitler* (Boston: Little, Brown, 1964), 266.
56. *The Kersten Memoirs,* 292.
57. Quoted by Roger Manvell and Heinrich Fraenkel, *Himmler* (New York: G. P. Putnam's Sons, 1965), 252.
58. *Ibid.* 136-7.
59. *Ibid.* 99.
60. Kersten, *op. cit.* 126.
61. Heiden, *op. cit.* 312.
62. *Ibid.*
63. Quoted by Reginald Pound, *The Lost Generation of 1914* (New York: Coward-McCann 1965), 25-28.
64. James W. Gerad, *My Four Years in Germany* (New York: George H. Doran, 1917), 308.
65. *Letters of Oswald Spengler, 1913-1918,* trans. A. Helps (New York: Knopf, 1966), 17.

66. Ernst Roehm, "A Soldier Believes in Plain Talk," in George L. Mosse ed., *Nazi Culture: Intellectual, Cultural and Social Life in the Third Reich* (New York: Grosset and Dunlap, 1966), 101-3.
67. Joost A. M. Meerloo, *Suicide and Mass Suicide* (New York: Grune and Stratton, 1962) 67-75.

Chapter 13

1. William G. Sumner, *War and Other Essays* (New Haven: Yale University Press, 1911).
2. As quoted by Quincy Wright in *A Study of War* (Chicago: University of Chicago Press, 1965), 72-73. (First edition 1942.)
3. *Ibid.*
4. *Ibid.* 140.
5. Elwin H. Powell, "Anomie and Force: The Case of Rome," *Catalyst* (Spring 1969), 79-103.
6. Randolph S. Bourne, *War and the Intellectuals, Essays, 1915-19* (New York: Harper Torch Books, 1964), 82.
7. Sebastian de Grazia, *The Political Community: A Study of Anomie* (Chicago: University of Chicago Press, 1949), 156-61; Elie A. Cohen, *Human Behavior in the Concentration Camp* (New York: Grosset and Dunlap, 1953), 283.
8. Jack Douglas, "Suicide: Social Aspects," *International Encyclopedia of the Social Sciences,* ed. David L. Sills (New York: Macmillan, 1968), Vol. 15, 375-85.
9. *Supra,* p. 11; Gerhard Fuellkrug, *Der Selbsmord in der Kriegs und Nachkriegszeit* (Schwerin-in-Mecklenberg: Verlag Fredrich Bahn, 1927).
10. Emile Durkheim, *Suicide* (Glencoe, Ill.: The Free Press, 1949), 208.
11. *The Living Thoughts of Clausewitz,* ed. Col. Joseph I. Greene (New York: Longman's, Green, 1943), 20-23.
12. Aristotle, "Politics," *Greek and Roman Classics in Translation* trans. C. Murphy, K. Guinagh, and W. Oates (New York: Longman's, Green, 1947), 606.
13. Data from Neal D. Houghton, "War Making and the Constitution" *Social Science,* 39 (April 1964), 67-78.
14. Charles Horton Cooley, *Human Nature and the Social Order* (New York: Schocken Books, 1964), 326-7. (First edition 1902.)
15. Joseph M. Jones, *The Fifteen Weeks* (New York: Viking Press, 1955), 259.

272   NOTES

16. William James, "The Moral Equivalent of War," *Essays and Memoirs* (London: Longman's, Green, 1911).

17. Willard Waller, "War and Social Institutions" in W. Waller, ed. *War in the Twentieth Century* (New York: Random House, 1940), 486.

18. C. Vann Woodward, *The Strange Career of Jim Crow* (New York: Oxford University Press, 1955), 54-55. Until the turn of the century Negroes voted in large numbers throughout the South. The suddenness of disfranchisement is shown by statistics from Louisiana, typical of the entire South. In 1896 there were 130,334 registered Negro voters in Louisiana, in 1904, 1,342. On "Anglo-Saxonism" see Richard Hofstadter, *Social Darwinism in American Thought* (Boston: Beacon Press, 1955), Ch. 9: "Racism and Imperialism," 170-200. See Sidney Willhelm, *Who Needs the Negro* (Cambridge: Schenkman Publishers, 1970).

19. Kenneth T. Jackson, *The Ku Klux Klan in the City 1915-1930* (New York: Oxford University Press, 1967), 173-4.

20. Allan R. Bosworth, *America's Concentration Camps* (New York: Bantam Books, 1967), vii.

21. Herbert Spencer, *Principles of Sociology* (New York: D. Appleton, 1895), 594-6. (First edition 1879.) See Pitirim A. Sorokin, "Variations on the Spencerian Theme of Militant and Industrial Types of Society," *Social Sciences* 36 (Spring 1961), 91-99.

22. Louis N. Robinson, "Crime Statistics in Germany, France and England," *Journal of Criminal Law and Criminology,* I (1910), 259-79.

23. Arthur A. Ekirch, Jr., *The Civilian and the Military* (New York: Oxford University Press, 1956), 155.

24. William G. Sumner, *The Conquest of the United States by Spain and Other Essays* (Chicago: Henry Regnery, no date), 139-73. (First published in 1899.)

25. E. H. Sutherland, *Principles of Criminology* (Philadelphia: J. B. Lippincott, 1955), 208.

26. Jerome H. Skolnick, *Justice without Trial: Law Enforcement in Democratic Society* (New York: John Wiley, 1967), 45.

27. Richard Flacks and Milton Mankoff, "Revolt in Santa Barbara: Why They Burned the Bank," *The Nation,* 210 (March 23, 1970), 337-40.

28. Thucydides, *The Peloponnesian War,* trans. B. Jowett (New York: Bantam Books, 1960), 62.

Chapter 14

1. Ole R. Holsti and Robert C. North, "History of Human Conflict" in *The Nature of Human Conflict*, ed. Elton B. McNeil (Englewood Cliffs, N.J., Prentice-Hall, 1965), p. 156.
2. C. Wright Mills, *The Sociological Imagination* (New York: Oxford University Press, 1959), p. 146.
3. F. R. Cowell, *The Revolutions of Ancient Rome* (New York: Frederick A. Praeger, 1963), pp. 116–31.
4. Cf. Bert Cochran, *The War System* (New York: Macmillan, 1965), p. 163, for explanation, not endorsement of the idea.
5. Tenney Frank, *Roman Imperialism* (New York: Macmillan, 1921), p. 238.
6. Samuel Dill, *Roman Society: From Nero to Marcus Aurelius* (New York: Meridian Library, 1956), p. 11. First published 1904.
7. Details of the founding of the city are still debated but the evidence "certainly suggests the existence of a creator of Rome—you may call him Romulus or otherwise," Arnold Momigiano, "An Interim Report on the Origins of Rome," *Journal of Roman Studies*, Vol. 53 (1963), p. 112.
8. Lewis H. Morgan, *Ancient Society or Researches in the Lines of Human Progress from Savagery through Barbarism to Civilization* (Chicago: Charles H. Kerr, 1877), pp. 318–19.
9. Fustel de Coulanges, *The Ancient City: A Study on the Religion, Laws and Institutions of Greece and Rome* (Garden City, N.Y.: Doubleday Anchor Books, 1956), pp. 285–6. First published 1864.
10. H. H. Saulland, *A History of the Roman World, 753–146 B.C.* (3rd ed.; London: Methuen, 1961), p. 41.
11. *Ibid.*, p. 349.
12. H. E. L. Mellersh, *The Roman Soldier* (New York: Taplinger Publishing Company, 1964), p. 36.
13. *Ibid.*, p. 36.
14. Quoted by Stringfellow Barr, *The Mask of Jove: A History of Graeco-Roman Civilization from the Death of Alexander to the Death of Constantine* (Philadelphia: J. B. Lippincott, 1966), p. 70.
15. Cowell, *op cit.*, pp. 65–76.
16. Mellersh, *op cit.*, pp. 26–27.
17. Lily Ross Taylor, *Party Politics in the Age of Caesar* (Berkeley and Los Angeles: University of California Press, 1961), p. 4.
18. George Willis Botsford, *The Roman Assemblies: From Their Origin to the End of the Republic* (New York: Macmillan, 1909, p. 476.
19. Frank, *op. cit.*, p. 60.
20. *Ibid.*, p. 33.

21. *Ibid.*, pp. 7–8.
22. *Ibid.*, pp. 113–14.
23. *Ibid.*, pp. 120–1.
24. *Ibid.*, p. 126.
25. Arnold J. Toynbee, *Hannibal's Legacy: The Hannibalic War's Effects on Roman Life* (London: Oxford University Press, 1965), Vol. II, p. 9.
26. *Ibid.*, p. 19.
27. *Ibid.*, p. 19.
28. *Ibid.*, p. 24.
29. *Ibid.*, p. 19.
30. *Ibid.*, p. 19.
31. *Ibid.*, pp. 99–100.
32. *Ibid.*, p. 105.
33. *Ibid.*, p. 317.
34. *Ibid.*, p. 322.
35. *Ibid.*, p. 324–31.
36. Cowell, *op. cit.*, p. 81.
37. *Ibid.*, pp. 95–105.
38. Frank, *op. cit.*, p. 270.
39. Ronald Syme, *The Roman Revolution* (London: Oxford University Press, 1939), p. 515.
40. Cowell, *op. cit.*, p. 147.
41. See J. W. Heaton, "Mob Violence in the Late Roman Republic," *Illinois University Studies in the Social Sciences*, Vol. 23 (1938–39), pp. 90–110.
42. Syme, *op. cit.*, p. 513.
43. R. W. MacIver, *The Modern State* (London: Oxford University Press, 1929), pp. 245–6.
44. Ramsey MacMullen, *Soldier and Civilian in the Later Roman Empire* (Cambridge: Harvard University Press, 1963), p. 65, *et passim*.
45. W. G. Sinnigen, "The Roman Secret Service," *Classical Journal*, Vol. 57 (1961), p. 68.
46. M. Rostovzeff, *The Social and Economic History of the Roman Empire* (Oxford, Clarendon Press, 1957), p. 449.
47. Botsford, *op. cit.*, p. 477.
48. Frederick H. Cramer, "Bookburning and Censorship in Ancient Rome: A Chapter in the History of Freedom of Speech," *Journal of the History of Ideas*, Vol. 6 (1945), p. 165.
49. D. McAlindon, "Senatorial Opposition to Claudius and Nero, *American Journal of Philology*, Vol. 77 (1956), pp. 113–32.
50. F. R. Cowell, *Everyday Life in Ancient Rome* (London: B. T. Batsford, 1961), p. 149.

51. *Ibid.*, p. 150.
52. *Ibid.*, p. 140.
53. Harold Mattingly, *Roman Imperial Civilization* (London: Edward Arnold Publishers, 1957), p. 165.
54. Dill, *op. cit.* p. 173.
55. *Ibid.*, p. 12.
56. Emile Durkheim, *Suicide* (Glencoe, Ill.: Free Press, 1951), p. 256. First published 1899.
57. Dill, *op. cit.*, pp. 293; 320–26, *et passim*.
58. *Ibid.*, p. 326.
59. *Ibid.*, p. 328.
60. *Ibid.*, p. 322.
61. Durkheim, *op. cit.*, pp. 217–240; 329–32.
62. Dill, *op. cit.*, p. 12.
63. Barr, *op. cit.*, p. 290.
64. Cowell, *Everyday Life in Ancient Rome, op. cit.*, p. 106.
65. William L. Wetermann, *The Slave Systems of Greek and Roman Antiquity* (Philadelphia American Philosophic Society, 1955), pp. 75–82.
66. Cowell, *op. cit.*, p. 106.
67. W. Warde Fowler, *Social Life at Rome in the Age of Cicero* (London: Macmillan, 1922), p. 231.
68. *Ibid.*, p. 232.
69. For a brilliant analysis of the link between anomia and slavery in Greek thought, see Alvin Gouldner, *Enter Plato: Classical Greece and the Origins of Social Theory* (New York: Basic Books, 1965).
70. Fowler, *op. cit.*, p. 235.
71. Dill, *op. cit.*, p. 12.
72. Barr, *op. cit.*, p. 309.
73. *Ibid.*, p. 309.
74. Fowler, *op. cit.*, p. 66.
75. *Ibid.*, p. 29.
76. *Ibid.*, p. 29.
77. Cowell, *op. cit.*, p. 142. Cf. Ludwig Friedlander, *Roman Life and Manners Under the Early Empire* (New York: E. P. Dutton, n.d.), Vol. II, pp. 1–130.
78. *Ibid.*, p. 171.
79. Dill, *op. cit.*, p. 234.
80. Mattingly, *op. cit.*, p. 165.
81. *Ibid.*, p. 177.
82. Simone Weil, "The Great Beast," in *Selected Essays 1934–43* ed. and tr. Richard Rees (London: 1962), p. 102, quoted by Barr, *op. cit.*, p. 530.
83. J. Pokrovsky, *History of the Roman Law*, quoted by P. A. Sorokin, *Social*

and Cultural Dynamics: Fluctuations of Systems of Truth, Ethics and Law (New York: American Book Company, 1937), Vol. II, p. 610.

84. Jacob Burckhardt, *The Age of Constantine the Great*, tr. Moses Hadas (Garden City, N.Y.: Doubleday Anchor, 1956). First published 1852.

85. M. Rostovzeff, *op. cit.*, pp. 491–2.

86. *Ibid.*, p. 491.

87. *Ibid.*, p. 492.

88. *Ibid.*, p. 505.

89. G. E. F. Chilver, "The Army in Politics, A.D. 68–70," *Journal of Roman Studies*, Vol. 47 (1957), pp. 29–35. "Was the soldier championing the class he originally belonged to? No element of the Rostovzeff's [thesis] has stood examination." (p. 31).

90. Burckhardt, *op. cit.*, pp. 208–9.

91. *Ibid.*, pp. 208–9.

92. *Ibid.*, p. 349.

93. Bar, *op. cit.*, p. 510. Cf. G. E. M. Ste. Croix, "Why Were The Early Christians Persecuted?" *Past and Present*, Vol. 26 (1963), pp. 6–38. The earliest persecutions were in A.D. 64 when Nero made the Christians scapegoats for the burning of Rome. Generally provincial governors played a more significant role in persecutions than did the emperors. But the provincial governors were pragmatists and were not likely to instigate persecutions, except on popular demand.

94. Bar, *op. cit.*, p. 451.

95. Ramsey MacMullen, *Enemies of the Roman Order: Treason Unrest and Alienation in the Empire* (Cambridge: Harvard University Press, 1966), p. 196.

96. *Ibid.*, p. 192.

97. *Ibid.*, p. 193.

98. *Ibid.*, p. 193.

99. Bar, *op. cit.*, p. 458.

100. MacMullen, *op. cit.*, p. 194.

101. Samuel Dill, *Roman Society in the Last Century of the Western Empire* (London, Macmillan, 1905), pp. 227–29.

102. *Ibid.* pp. 227–29.

103. Ramsey MacMullen, "Social Mobility and the Theodosian Code," *Journal of Roman Studies*, Vol. 54 (1964), pp. 49–53.

104. Dill, *Roman Society in the Last Century, op. cit.*, pp. 234–5.

105. MacMullen, *Enemies of the Roman Order, op. cit.*, p. 197.

106. Dill, *op. cit.*, pp. 227–9.

107. MacMullen, *op. cit.*, p. 199.

108. Richard Manfield Haywood, *The Myth of Rome's Fall* (New York: Thomas Y. Crowell, 1958), p. 5.

109. John C. Russell, "Medieval Population," *Social Forces*, Vol. 15 (1937), pp. 503–511.
110. Dill, *op. cit.*, p. 281.
111. Quoted by Barr, *op. cit.*, p. 300.

Appendix

1. Emile Durkheim, *Le Suicide*, Paris: Félix Alcan (Presses Universitaires), 1897, 1930; *Suicide*, translated by John A. Spaulding and George Simpson, Glencoe, Ill.: Free Press, 1951. References to this work will be given as *Ibid.*, p. (French): p. (English).
2. *Ibid.*, pp. 445–451: pp. 386–391.
3. *Ibid.*, p. 281: p. 253. Innumerable alternatives suggest themselves: a state of "lawlessness," of "deregulation," of "unregulatedness," of "unruliness," of "uncontrollability," etc. It is worth noting that Durkheim typically expresses his own feeling about the term he created by using "state of" in connection with it, as *etat de desagregation,* or *de perturbation*, or *d'anomie conjugale,* etc.
4. *Ibid.*, pp. 321, 332, 408–410: pp. 285, 293, 357–359. Powell finds a correlation between homicide-suicides and blue- and white-collar occupations (*op. cit.*, pp. 134, 135, 137).
5. *Ibid.*, p. 283: p. 254.
6. *Ibid.*, pp. 289, 307, 442–444: pp. 259, 273, 384–386. Powell's data on marital instability show up also as blue- and white-collar differences.
7. *Ibid.*, p. 336: pp. 299–300.
8. *Ibid.*, p. 288: p. 258. The type Durkheim found "most widespread" was egoistic suicide, which he claimed is never an auxiliary to crime. "It is characterized by a state of depression and apathy produced by exaggerated individuation." (p. 406: p. 356) Durkheim devotes two consecutive chapters to Egoistic Suicide. This category does not figure in Powell's study. Nevertheless, because a feeling of "emptiness" is so frequently associated with it, and because "thought thrown back upon itself" can produce it, egoistic suicide might readily account for the voluntary deaths of some persons in involuntary retirement.
9. *Ibid.*, p. 321: p. 284. Durkheim says that anomic suicides differ from the first two types in that "their act is essentially passionate." Also, the attributed assigned to "Anomic suicide" in the Etiological and Morphological Classification Table," are: "Irritation, disgust; Violent recriminations against life in general; Violent recriminations against one person in particular (homicide-suicide)." (p. 332: p. 293)
10. Powell is not unaware of this, for he observes that "This corresponds to Durkheim's altruism in several ways." (p. 138, footnote 38)
11. *Ibid.*, p. 287: p. 257. Compared with agriculture, the contrast would be sharper,

"if, among suicides of industry, employers were distinguished from workmen, for the former are probably most stricken by the state of anomy. . . ." In Powell's study this is borne out: "self-employed proprietors" have the highest rates. (p. 135)

12. *Ibid.*, p. 247–261: p. 228–239.
13. *Ibid.*, pp. 233: pp. 217.
14. The reader is cautioned against construing the "corporations" which figure in Durkheim (p. 284 and pp. 434–442 in French, pp. 387–384 in English) as being the same as, or counterparts of, modern corporations. Durkheim's reference is to the integrating action of the monopolistic and medieval *corporations des arts et des métiers*, which required the Revolution's force to bring them to an end.
15. R. M. MacIver, *The Ramparts We Guard*, New York: Macmillan, 1950. pp. 76–77.
16. *Suicide*, translated by John A. Spaulding and George Simpson, Glencoe, Ill.: Free Press, 1951. pp. 232–233.
17. R. K. Merton, *Social Theory and Social Structure*, Glencoe, Ill.: Free Press, 1957. pp. 163–4.

Index